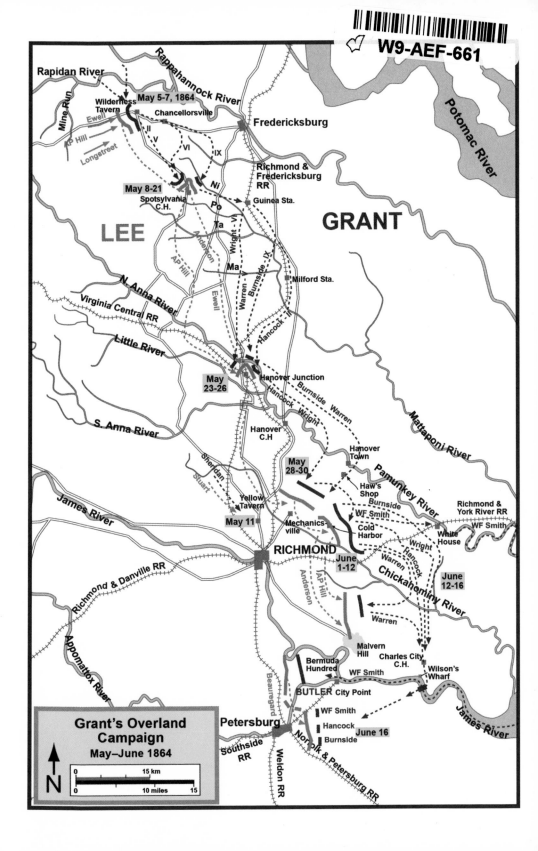

Rapidan River

Rappahannock River

May 5-7, 1864

Wilderness Tavern

Chancellorsville

Fredericksburg

Ewell

Mine Run

AP Hill

Longstreet

II

V

VI

IX

Ni

Richmond & Fredericksburg RR

May 8-21

Spotsylvania C.H.

Guinea Sta.

Po

Ta

Anderson

AP Hill

Wright - V

Ma

Warren

Burnside - IX

Ewell

Milford Sta.

LEE

GRANT

N. Anna River

Virginia Central RR

Little River

Hancock - II

May 23-26

Hanover Junction

Burnside

Warren

Hancock

Wright

S. Anna River

Hanover C.H

Hanover Town

Pamunkey River

Mattaponi River

Sheridan

Stuart

Yellow Tavern

May 11

May 28-30

Haw's Shop

Burnside

WF Smith

Cold Harbor

Richmond & York River RR

WF Smith

White House

Mechanicsville

RICHMOND

June 1-12

Wright

Warren

Hancock

June 12-16

James River

Richmond & Danville RR

AP Hill

Anderson

Chickahominy River

Warren

Appomattox River

Malvern Hill

Charles City C.H.

Wilson's Wharf

Bermuda Hundred

WF Smith

BUTLER

City Point

James River

Beauregard

Petersburg

Southside RR

Weldon RR

Norfolk & Petersburg RR

WF Smith

Hancock

Burnside

June 16

Grant's Overland Campaign
May–June 1864

N

0   15 km
0   10 miles   15

BATTLE OF WILLS

ALSO BY DAVID ALAN JOHNSON

Yanks in the RAF

Decided on the Battlefield

BATTLE OF WILLS

ULYSSES S. GRANT, ROBERT E. LEE, AND THE LAST YEAR OF THE CIVIL WAR

DAVID ALAN JOHNSON

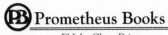 Prometheus Books

59 John Glenn Drive
Amherst, New York 14228

Inquiries should be addressed to
Prometheus Books
59 John Glenn Drive
Amherst, New York 14228
VOICE: 716–691–0133
FAX: 716–691–0137
WWW.PROMETHEUSBOOKS.COM

20 19 18 17 16   5 4 3 2 1

Library of Congress Cataloging-in-Publication Data

Names: Johnson, David Alan, 1950- author.
Title: Battle of wills : Ulysses S. Grant, Robert E. Lee, and the last year of the Civil
    War / by David Alan Johnson.
Description: Amherst, New York : Prometheus Books, 2016. |
    Includes bibliographical references and index.
Identifiers: LCCN 2016021593 (print) | LCCN 2016029001 (ebook) |
    ISBN 9781633882454 (hardback) | ISBN 9781633882461 (ebook)
Subjects: LCSH: Grant, Ulysses S. (Ulysses Simpson), 1822-1885—Psychology. |
    Grant, Ulysses S. (Ulysses Simpson), 1822-1885—Military leadership. | Lee,
    Robert E. (Robert Edward), 1807-1870—Psychology. | Lee, Robert E. (Robert
    Edward), 1807-1870—Military leadership. | Generals—Biography. | United
    States—History—Civil War, 1861-1865—Campaigns. | BISAC: HISTORY /
    United States / Civil War Period (1850-1877). | HISTORY / United States /
    19th Century. | HISTORY / Military / United States.
Classification: LCC E470 .J715 2016 (print) | LCC E470 (ebook) |
    DDC 973.8/2092—dc23
LC record available at https://lccn.loc.gov/2016021593

Printed in the United States of America

To Laura, with sincere thanks for everything.

CONTENTS

INTRODUCTION

The rivalry between General Ulysses S. Grant and General Robert E. Lee during the Virginia campaign of 1864 and 1865 is one of the pivotal events of American history. The relationship between the two began during the Mexican War, between 1846 and 1848, when they were both officers in the "old army," as Grant would call it. Lee and Grant were from two completely different backgrounds—Grant was a working-class boy from Ohio, while Lee was a Virginia aristocrat. They did not oppose each other until the spring of 1864, when Grant was appointed general-in-chief of all Union forces. Lee never got the measure of Grant during the brutal campaign of 1864 and 1865, at the Battle of the Wilderness, at Spotsylvania, at North Anna, at Cold Harbor, or at Petersburg. Their individual characters and outlooks finally brought them both to the village of Appomattox in April 1865, where Lee surrendered to Grant and changed the history of the United States and, ultimately, the world.

President Abraham Lincoln appointed General U. S. Grant as his general-in-chief to command all Union armies in March 1864 because he was so impressed with Grant's war record. The general was renowned as the victor of Shiloh, Vicksburg, Fort Donelson, and Chattanooga, and for winning battles in the West when his counterparts in the East were being routinely routed by Confederate general Robert E. Lee and his fabled Army of Northern Virginia. Although President Lincoln expected great things from his new commanding general, a good many officers and men of the Army of the Potomac refused to be impressed. The veterans of Antietam and Fredericksburg and Gettysburg considered the Western campaign nothing but a glorified sideshow compared with the war they had been fighting in Virginia. Grant may have been a hero in the West, in Tennessee and Mississippi, but he had not yet met Bobby Lee.

But Grant *had* met Robert E. Lee. The two had served in the Mexican War. Lee was a captain in the elite Corps of Engineers, and Lieutenant "Sam" Grant was an infantry officer. According to one story, Captain Lee met Grant's unit one day, and Lee gave the young lieutenant a severe dressing down for having a scruffy and unbuttoned uniform. In Mexico, Grant saw enough of his future opponent to know that Lee was anything but invincible, even though the Confederate general had acquired a reputation of a superman by the spring of 1864. "I had known him personally," Grant would write, "and knew that he was mortal."[1] Grant was not intimidated by Bobby Lee, or by his reputation.

Lee did not remember Grant, which was understandable. Robert E. Lee belonged to one of the first families of Virginia. His father was General Henry "Light Horse Harry" Lee, one of George Washington's cavalry commanders, and two of his relatives had signed the Declaration of Independence. He married the great-granddaughter of Martha Washington, George Washington's wife. U. S. Grant was a nobody from the wilds of Ohio, a short, stumpy little man and the son of a tanner. When Grant was appointed general-in-chief by President Abraham Lincoln in March 1864—the job that Lee had been offered in 1861, but declined in order to join the Confederate army when Virginia seceded from the Union—Lee had the feeling that Grant would be a different general than all of his predecessors. No fewer than six Union generals had opposed Lee since 1862; all six had been outfought and outgeneraled by him. President Lincoln hoped that he had finally found a general who would be able to both outfight and outthink Lee when he appointed Grant his general-in-chief.

Robert E. Lee and his army "carried the rebellion on its bayonets," as Winston Churchill somewhat romantically put it, for four years.[2] The statement is true enough, even though it might be on the romantic side. Lee and the Confederate armies certainly had held the Confederacy together since Fort Sumter. By the early part of April 1865, General Lee was finally convinced that no miracle would take place that would save him and his army from U. S. Grant. At the town of Appomattox Court House, Virginia, Lee surrendered to General Grant on April 9, 1865. The Confederate States of America, which had been kept alive by its armies in the field, effectively ceased to exist.

At Appomattox, Lee and Grant met face to face for the first time since the Mexican War. Lee was dressed in his best uniform, just as his mentor from the Mexican War, Winfield Scott, would have been dressed. Grant showed up at the meeting dressed in his dirty and unkempt field uniform, as Zachery Taylor, his own mentor from the Mexican War, would have done. Grant told Lee that he remembered him from the "old army" days. Lee admitted that he did not remember Grant at all.

Grant was able to keep Lee from using his tactics of maneuver that he had employed so ably—sometimes brilliantly—against other Union generals, and he had employed his own war of attrition against Lee. Grant outfought Lee with determination and superior numbers. He was also not intimidated by Robert E. Lee, which most of his predecessors had been. This turned out to be as great an advantage for Grant as any other factor.

Chapter One

ROADS BEGINNING

CURING A HEADACHE

General Grant could not help smiling at Colonel Horace Porter's words of encouragement. The general had been tormented by what he described as a sick headache all day long, the kind of blinding, throbbing pain that made him hold his head and pace back and forth in agony. Grant spent the night soaking his feet in a mixture of mustard and hot water and also applied mustard plasters to his wrists and to the back of his neck, which were the traditional, and colorful, ways of curing a headache. But nothing seemed to help. The headache stubbornly refused to go away.

This was not the first time that Colonel Porter had seen Grant in such pain—he was prone to these migraines. In a feeble but well-meant attempt to cheer up the general and offer some small comfort, Porter tried to convince Grant that the headache was probably a good omen.

"I never knew you to be ill that you did not receive some good news before the day passed," Colonel Porter reminded Grant on the subject of his migraines. "I have become a little superstitious regarding coincidences," Porter continued, "and I should not be surprised if some good fortune were to overtake you before night."[1]

Grant appreciated Colonel Porter's words of encouragement but said that he was not all that interested in good fortune just then, or in Porter's superstitions. All he really wanted was for his headache to go away. A few staff officers dropped by and persuaded Grant to visit General George Gordon Meade's headquarters, where he could get a cup of coffee. A dose of good, strong army coffee should help cure his headache, the general was told. Army coffee had the reputation for either curing the ailment or killing the patient. Coffee from the Army of the Potomac's commanding general should come with some added authority and might persuade the headache to surrender without further resistance.

After he had his coffee, Grant actually did feel a little better. Although the headache was still there, at least it had dissipated slightly. But he also had another kind of headache to deal with. For the past two days, since April 7, 1865, Grant had been corresponding with General Robert E. Lee on the subject of Lee's surrendering the Army of Northern Virginia. Today was Palm Sunday, April 9, and Lee had still not given any indication that he was willing to give up.

In his communications with Lee, Grant bore no resemblance to the "Unconditional Surrender Grant" of the Northern newspapers, or at least the pro-Lincoln and pro-Union Northern newspapers.[2] Far from demanding unconditional surrender, Grant was prepared to offer Lee and his army the most generous terms possible. Grant would accept Lee's surrender on just about any reasonable terms, and he was willing to meet with General Lee anywhere he liked to discuss the details. All he wanted was for the Army of Northern Virginia to surrender.

Grant had hoped that Lee would accept at least some sort of armistice. His army was surrounded. His men were half-starved and were deserting by the hundreds each day. According to one account, the southerners were living on corn that had been meant for the horses. But only the night before, Lee had sent a note to Grant refusing to surrender. Instead, he suggested a meeting to discuss "the Confederate States forces under my command, and tend to the restoration of peace," which did not really mean anything in particular.[3]

Grant was disappointed and more than just a little annoyed by Lee's response. What made the message all the more exasperating was a mention by Lee that "the restoration of peace" should be the subject of any discussion, which sounded like Lee wanted to talk about general peace terms.[4] Grant did not have the authority to talk about any subject but the surrender of the Army of Northern Virginia. President Abraham Lincoln had expressly forbidden Grant from discussing any sort of peace terms or any political issues at all. It looked as though Lee intended to drag his heels when it came to surrendering. As Grant put it, "It looks as if Lee meant to fight."[5] This did not help Grant to get rid of his headache.

Headache or not, Grant had to reply to Lee's latest communiqué. He sat down and wrote:

> Headquarters Armies of the U.S.
> April 9, 1865
>
> General R. E. Lee,
> Commanding C.S.A.
>   Your note of yesterday is received. As I have no authority to treat on the subject of peace, the meeting proposed for ten a.m. today could lead to no good. I will state, however, General, that I am equally anxious for peace with yourself, and the whole North entertains the same feeling. The terms upon which peace can be had are well understood. By the South laying down their arms they will hasten that most desirable event, save thousands of human lives, and hundreds of millions of property not yet destroyed. Seriously hoping that all our difficulties may be settled without the loss of another life. I subscribe myself, etc.
>   U. S. Grant,
>   Lieutenant General[6]

Lee and his army had been trying to escape westward for the past week, ever since his men had been driven out of their trenches outside Petersburg, Virginia, at bayonet point. Petersburg had been under siege for nearly ten months, since June 1864, but Grant finally forced Lee to abandon his lines on April 2. Federal troops entered Richmond on the following day, after President Jefferson Davis and the remnants of the Confederate government evacuated the city. But Grant's objective had never been the capture of Richmond. For the past year, he had only one goal in mind—the surrender of Robert E. Lee and his army. Now, the realization of that goal seemed to be at hand. But Lee would not agree to discuss the surrender of his army, at least not yet.

Ever since Lee abandoned Petersburg, he had been trying desperately to get away from Grant and General George Meade. Lee planned to make his way to North Carolina and join forces with what was left of General Joseph E. Johnston's Army of Tennessee. If everything went according to plan, Lee and Johnston would combine their diminished forces and destroy the army of Grant's old friend General William Tecumseh Sherman, which was moving through North Carolina to link up with Grant in Virginia. This meant that the Confederacy would still have life. If Lee's army was still in the field, the war would go on indefinitely. The famished and exhausted men of the Army of Northern Virginia staggered westward over bad roads, rambling along the north bank of the Appomattox River as quickly as they could drag themselves.

The Army of the Potomac was right behind them, filled with enthusiasm and looking for a fight. "They began to see the end of what they had been fighting four years for," Grant reflected. "Nothing seemed to fatigue them."[7] At least part of their enthusiasm was based on the rumor that they were heading for breakfast. They had not eaten in what seemed like ages, and the word was that a trainload of rations was waiting for them at Appomattox Station, just a short walk away.

After he had written his response to Lee's letter of April 8, Grant and several staff officers, including Colonel Horace Porter, rode off to meet General Philip Sheridan, the commander of the Army of the Shenandoah. Grant mounted his horse, Cincinnati, and galloped along a road leading to a village called Appomattox Court House, a few miles from Appomattox Station. He was the best horseman of the group, with the best horse, and he led the way. Grant guessed that he was only two or three miles from Appomattox, but he swung southward to avoid making contact with Lee's army. He knew that the Confederates were somewhere up ahead, and it would not do for the commander-in-chief of all Union forces to be taken prisoner by Southern pickets. Especially not on what might be the last day of the war.

Grant had not ridden very far, his head still pounding, when he and his party were overtaken by an officer from General Meade's staff. The officer handed Grant a new communication from General Lee. Sensing that this could very well be the letter he was waiting for, Grant immediately dismounted and read it.

April 9, 1865

General: I received your note of this morning on the picket line, whither I had come to meet you and ascertain definitely what terms were embraced in your proposal of yesterday with reference to the surrender of this army. I now request an interview in accordance with the offer contained in your letter of yesterday for that purpose.
R. E. Lee, General[8]

Lee would surrender. The strategy Grant had worked out with President Abraham Lincoln over a year before, to make Lee's army his main objective and to destroy it, had finally been brought to a successful conclusion. Grant had more than justified all the faith and confidence that Lincoln had placed in him. Ever since Lincoln had appointed Grant as his general-in-chief thirteen months before, which seemed like several centuries now, he had defended Grant and stood by him. He told all of the general's critics that Grant was a fighter and that he would keep on pounding Lee until he won. Now Grant had won. But the victory was Lincoln's as much as Grant's.

The terms proposed by Grant were simple and straightforward enough—he had insisted on nothing more than the complete disbanding of Lee's army. Any other conditions could be discussed during the course of the meeting that Lee was now almost miraculously requesting. The main thing was that Robert E. Lee had agreed to give up, finally and at long last, and that the war would soon be over.

Even though this was the moment he had been waiting for since the spring of 1864, when he had been appointed general-in-chief of all Union armies, Grant effectively managed to hide his feelings. He did not even blink. Everyone around him was astonished that Grant showed no emotion at all. But as soon as he read the communiqué, his headache instantly disappeared. "The pain in my head seemed to leave me the moment I read Lee's letter," he told Colonel Porter.[9]

Grant immediately scribbled a reply:

Headquarters Army of the U.S.
April 9, 1865

General R. E. Lee,
Commanding C.S.A.
     Your note of this date is but this moment (11:30 a.m.) received,
in consequence of my having passed from the Richmond and Lynchburg roads to the Farmville and Lynchburg road. I am writing this
about four miles west of Walker's Church, and will push forward to
the front for the purpose of meeting you. Notice sent to me on this
road where you wish the interview to take place will meet me.
     U. S. Grant,
     Lieutenant General[10]

Colonel Porter had been right about the headache, after all.
Grant certainly had received good news, the best news he ever could
have hoped for, the news he had been hoping and praying for since
last spring.

As soon as the general finished writing his response, he gave it
to Colonel Orville Babcock with instructions to deliver it to General
Lee. Babcock changed horses and, accompanied by another staff
officer, went galloping off toward the Confederate lines. Grant followed along behind Colonel Babcock with a few other officers, at a
much slower pace.

Now that his headache was gone, Grant could think more clearly
about the significance of what was about to take place. Before the
morning was over, he would be meeting Robert E. Lee, face-to-face,
to accept the surrender of the fabled Army of Northern Virginia. Lee
and his army had bedeviled Union generals for the past three years,
ever since he had forced General George B. McClellan to withdraw
the Army of the Potomac from the approaches to Richmond in 1862.
Now, Lee had been brought to bay.

In scores of pitched battles and skirmishes during the past eleven
months, and throughout the nine-month siege of Petersburg, Grant
had outfought his opponent, and sometimes outguessed him, as well.
During this time, he had come to understand Lee a lot better than
most people would give him credit for. He was not intimidated by

either Lee or his reputation, which had given him an overwhelming advantage over all of his predecessors. His understanding of Lee had also given him the ability to outfight Lee, which he did, relentlessly, for nearly a year. But now the fighting was finally over.

Grant was not the only man who realized that the meeting would effectively mean the end of the war. Every soldier in every regiment under Grant's command, from Maine to Michigan, had been hoping and praying for this day. When a messenger on horseback shouted the news of Lee's surrender to William Tecumseh Sherman's Twentieth Corps in North Carolina, a soldier shouted back, "You're the sonofabitch we've been looking for all these four years."[11]

As he rode off toward Appomattox Court House to meet with General Lee, it is more than likely that Grant recalled his first meeting with the general. That meeting had taken place many years before, in another time and place, when both Grant and Lee were junior officers in another war.

HE WAS MORTAL

Ulysses S. Grant's road to Appomattox began in Mexico, nineteen years earlier. Grant had served with Lee in the "old army," as Grant called it, during the Mexican War from 1846 to 1848. He would always remember that time with fond nostalgia and liked to reminisce with his fellow veterans about the days when he was a very young junior officer and war was an adventure.

He enjoyed talking about the things he had done and the people he had met in Mexico, and he frequently told the same stories over and over again. One favorite story was about the time when General Zachary Taylor, Grant's commanding general, mistakenly put several spoonfuls of mustard in his coffee instead of sugar and became livid with anger and embarrassment. Grant probably had hundreds of anecdotes from the time he spent in Mexico. But the war also gave him his first look at combat, as well as practical lessons in leading men in battle. It also introduced him to some young men who would leave a lasting impression on the impressionable lieutenant from Ohio.[12]

The two most influential factors in Ulysses Grant's military career were the Mexican War and his father, Jesse Root Grant. His experiences in Mexico—especially his acquaintances with other junior officers who would become famous in another war a decade and a half later—would all have a central effect on how General Grant conducted operations during the Civil War. Lessons Grant learned from Winfield Scott, who believed in staying on the offensive until the enemy was worn down and beaten, would be applied against Robert E. Lee in Virginia. Grant would also benefit from the aggressiveness of General Zachery Taylor and would also copy General Taylor's decidedly unmilitary appearance. Generals Scott and Taylor were largely responsible for Grant's tactics of attrition and relentless hammering, which he used so effectively against Lee in 1864 and 1865.

The personality of Grant's father would also have a great bearing on the way General Grant directed his forces against Lee but in a more indirect way. Jesse Root Grant could be a very difficult man, but he was also driven and determined. He became a successful businessman, working his way up from tanner's assistant to prosperous and well-to-do leather goods dealer in spite of economic hardships. Grant inherited his father's determination and refusal to give up and would use these traits the same way he used his infantry and cavalry against the Army of Northern Virginia in 1864 and 1865.

A good many officers who fought in Mexico with Grant, not just Robert E. Lee, would become Grant's enemies in the Civil War. When that war began in 1861, hundreds of officers resigned their commissions in the United States Army and joined the Confederate States Army. Many of them were Mexican War veterans.

Lieutenant James Longstreet fought alongside Grant at the Battle of Chapultepec (near Mexico City) in September 1847. He was also the best man at Grant's wedding to Julia Dent a year later; Julia was Longstreet's cousin. Seventeen years later, Confederate General Longstreet would be the commander of the renowned First Corps in Lee's Army of Northern Virginia. He and Grant would face each other in the Battle of the Wilderness, in Spotsylvania County, Virginia, in May 1864, the first battle in the brutal Overland Campaign.

Longstreet, Lee, and Grant were all graduates of the US Military Academy at West Point. Grant's real name was Hiram Ulysses Grant, but it was accidentally changed to Ulysses Simpson Grant when he applied for admission to the academy. A fellow cadet, future major general William Tecumseh Sherman, spotted Grant's name on a bulletin board: "U. S. Grant." Sherman and a few other cadets began to make up names to go along with the initials. One came up with "United States Grant." Another managed "Uncle Sam Grant." This seemed a little formal, so a third said, "Sam Grant." The name stuck. U. S. Grant became Sam Grant.

Grant was five feet seven or eight inches tall, depending upon which source is consulted, which was average height for the time. He was always untidy in his appearance, but his future sister-in-law, Emmy Dent, thought that the young lieutenant was very handsome. She even went on to say that he was pretty, and she compared him with one of her dolls. One of the reasons that Grant grew a beard was to make him look more like his idea of what a soldier should look like. He certainly did not like the idea of being "pretty."

Along with Longstreet and other junior officers who would go on to become generals, as well as household names, in another time and place, Grant learned what it felt like to be shot at by enemy troops while he was in Mexico. His first time under fire turned out to be more dramatic than terrifying.

During the Battle of Monterrey in September 1846, Lieutenant Grant volunteered to ride through the Mexican lines and bring back desperately needed ammunition. He had the reputation for being one of the best horsemen in the army, and he was about to justify that reputation.

He swung himself onto his horse, a grey mare named Nellie, put his foot over the back of the saddle and one arm around the horse's neck. While clinging to one side of the horse—"the side of the horse furthest from the enemy," Grant later pointed out—he set off on his rescue mission.[13]

"He rode through the streets of Monterrey like a trick rider in the circus," according to one biographer.[14] With a determination that would serve him well at places like Shiloh and Vicksburg and Petersburg, Grant pressed forward with his dash through the enemy-held town. "It was only at street crossings that my horse was under fire," he wrote, "but these I crossed at such a flying rate that generally I was past and under cover of the next block before the enemy fired."[15]

Unfortunately, his nerve-jangling ride did not accomplish anything except to enhance Grant's already formidable reputation as fabulous rider. Before any ammunition could be sent forward, his regiment had been ordered to withdraw from their position. Grant's only consolation was that he had not been wounded during his ride.

The Mexican War was all about acquiring territory. "Although the United States gave many reasons for fighting the Mexican War," an American writer was moved to comment, "the main purpose was to acquire the territories of California and New Mexico after Mexico had refused to sell them."[16] Actually, a lot more than that was acquired. The Mexican War secured what would become the states of Utah, Nevada, and California, along with sizeable parts of New Mexico and Arizona, smaller portions of Colorado and Wyoming, and about half of Texas. About one-quarter of the continental United States, the "lower forty-eight," was gained as a result of the war with Mexico.

The leading players in the Mexican War, at least as far as U. S. Grant's future army career was concerned, were General Winfield Scott and General Zachary Taylor. General Winfield Scott commanded an army that landed at the Gulf of Mexico city of Veracruz in March 1847 and forced the city to surrender after an eight-day siege. From Veracruz, Scott moved toward Mexico City and won decisive battles at Cerro Gordo, Molino del Rey, and Chapultepec. His army reached Mexico City in September 1847 and fought their way into the Mexican capital. The city surrendered to Scott, and the Mexican government agreed to American demands regarding the transferring of Mexican territory to the United States. For the second time in his life, Winfield Scott became a national hero. He had already made his reputation during the War of 1812, fighting British troops in the vicinity of Ontario, Canada, and being promoted to brigadier general at the age of twenty-seven.

General Taylor also became a household name and ended up becoming an even bigger hero than Winfield Scott. Taylor commanded American forces at the Battle of Monterrey in September 1846 and, five months later, at the Battle of Buena Vista. Both battles were overwhelming American victories and made Zachary Taylor the Dwight D. Eisenhower of his day. His war record in Mexico would carry him straight into the White House in 1848.

Because of his aggressiveness and his appearance, which can be diplomatically described as "casual," Zach Taylor was known as "Old Rough and Ready." He had very little in the way of formal education, was anything but an intellectual, and knew almost nothing of strategy or what would become known as "military science." But in spite of his lack of training, he fought with distinction as an officer in the War of 1812, in the Black Hawk War of 1832, and in the Second Seminole War between 1837 and 1840. "Everything Taylor did from a military point of view was wrong," a writer remarked, "expect win battles."[17]

Old Rough and Ready could not have cared less about the way he looked or about what other people saw when they looked at him. He usually wore what might be described as his old clothes—a weather-beaten shirt, a pair of old, faded trousers, a straw hat, and no indication of rank at all—and looked more like a farmer or an orderly than a general. A story circulated about a smart lieutenant who had just arrived from the east and happened to come across the general during a particularly casual moment. Seeing nothing but an old man wearing worn out clothes, the snotty young officer said, "I've just come and I want to meet General Taylor. Do you know him?"

The general was polishing his sword at the time. "Well, I guess I know the old hoss," he replied, carrying on with his sword polishing.

"Can't you say 'sir?'" the lieutenant responded, with some annoyance.

"I guess I can. Yes, sir."

"How about pointing out the general to me."

"I *am* General Taylor."[18]

A second variation of the story has it that the lieutenant mistook General Taylor for some sort of regimental servant. The young lieutenant offered to pay the scruffy-looking old man a quarter to polish his sword. Taylor shrugged his shoulders and agreed. He polished the sword to a high gloss, collected his twenty-five cents, and let the officer go on his way. On the following day, the lieutenant presented himself at General Taylor's headquarters tent, complete with his newly polished sword. When he was introduced to the general, the poor young lad nearly keeled over from shock and embarrassment.

The young officer's confusion was understandable. The person he encountered sitting on a log in his shirtsleeves did not look like anyone's idea of a general. But in Zach Taylor's mind, generals were not made of gold braid and engraved swords. A general was made of grit and iron and determination. Maybe that is why General Taylor had such a high opinion of Lt. Sam Grant.

Sam Grant was Zach Taylor's kind of officer. One day, Taylor happened to be riding past a detail of soldiers clearing underwater obstacles. Lieutenant Grant was in charge of the detail and decided to wade into the water to give the men a hand. Another version states that he went into the water so that he could direct the crew at closer proximity. At any rate, other officers ridiculed Grant for getting himself wet and dirty—this was certainly nothing they would have done themselves. But Zach Taylor was quite impressed by Grant's willingness to use his initiative. "I wish I had more officers like Grant, who would stand ready to set a personal example when needed," he admonished the other officers.[19] Taylor was so impressed, in fact, that he appointed Sam Grant to be the new regimental supply clerk. He thought that initiative should be rewarded, especially when shown by a young officer.

Even though his job with the Quartermaster Department represented a promotion, which came with an increase in pay, Grant was not happy about it. As far as he was concerned, he was an infantry officer, not some damned clerk keeping track of how many shoes and bedrolls and tent poles the regiment had on hand. Grant tried to get out of his quartermaster assignment and even wrote a letter of protest to his regimental commander, Colonel John Garland, regarding his new duties. But Colonel Garland did not want to hear any of Grant's complaints and rejected his objection out of hand. Lieutenant Grant was a member of the Quartermaster Department, whether he liked it or not.

General Taylor's disheveled appearance and plainspoken manner would have a profound influence on the young Lieutenant Grant's personality and character. Grant would copy these traits and carry them over into his later years. "General Taylor never made any great show or parade, either of uniform or retinue," Grant would recall many years later.[20] His fellow officers would make the same sort of comments about Grant, although these remarks would not always be complimentary.

In September 1846, Old Rough and Ready was determined to win the Battle of Monterrey and to capture the city. Lt. Sam Grant was equally determined to take part in the battle. His opportunity came sooner than he expected.

On the first day of the three-day battle, September 21, 1846, Grant heard artillery fire several miles up ahead. He knew that he was not supposed to take part in combat—in fact, he had been ordered to stay in camp. Technically, Grant was not even in the infantry at the time, due to his reassignment to the Quartermaster Department. But the young lieutenant simply could not ignore the sound of the guns, and the temptation was just too much to resist. Grant casually decided to disregard his orders and join the attack anyway. "My curiosity got the better of my judgement, and I mounted a horse and rode to the front to see what was going on," he said.[21] He did not think of the danger, just the excitement. It was an instance of valor getting the better part of discretion.

Grant arrived at the front just as his former regiment, the Fourth Infantry, was ordered to advance on the lower batteries defending Monterrey. Also making the charge along with the Fourth Infantry were the Mississippi Rifles, commanded by Colonel Jefferson Davis. The advance was "ill-conceived and badly executed," as noted by Grant. As the troops moved forward, "they got under fire from batteries guarding the east, or lower end of the city, and musketry. About one-third of the men engaged in the charge were killed or wounded in the space of a few minutes."[22] The charge was not a success, and the battle for Monterrey would go on until September 24. The attack is notable mainly for the fact that the future president of the Confederacy and the future general-in-chief of all Union forces had taken part in it. Nobody could possibly have known that Grant would be the cause of President Davis's undoing just under eighteen and a half years later.

This would not be the last time that Sam Grant would take part in a battle. Although he disliked the Quartermaster Department, he soon discovered that "being a quartermaster in war did not have to be the dull blanket-counting business it was in peace."[23] Delivering

supplies to the troops meant constant trips to the front lines, which
sometimes meant making contact with the Mexican army.

Grant had at least one confrontation with Mexican troops during
these supply excursions, a sudden and furious firefight that Grant
seems to have relished. He gave his own account of the fight to his
commander, Colonel Garland. "I lost one man, and had a horse
wounded," Grant reported. "We captured three of the enemy, three
horses and a flag, and we had a handsome fight."[24] This way of
thinking, that a handsome fight was not something that should be
avoided, would carry over to Fort Donelson and Vicksburg and the
Wilderness and Appomattox during the Civil War.

Lieutenant Grant also took part in the war's final campaign,
which resulted in the capture of Mexico City. This operation was commanded by General Winfield Scott, Old Fuss and Feathers himself,
and would give Grant another encounter with Mexican troops. The
main attack was made from the west, along a road called the San
Cosme Causeway. American troops had already overrun Chapultepec,
the fortress that defended the city's western approaches. But Mexican
troops had built a barricade in front of a gateway that Grant identified as the Garita San Cosme, which was effectively blocking the
American advance into the city. Before any US troops could capture
their objective, the Mexican units would have to be dislodged from
behind their barricade.

Grant discovered a way to neutralize the Mexican strongpoint.
"I found a church off to the south of the road, which looked to me
as if the belfry would command the ground back of the Garita San
Cosme," he recalled.[25] If he could get a gun up into that belfry, he
would be in a position to shell the barricade, along with any troops
near the gatehouse. He located an artillery officer, who had a mountain howitzer and the crew to operate it, and talked the artilleryman
into going along with his scheme. The crew dismantled the small
cannon and lugged the parts through several ditches filled with
water and around a group of Mexican soldiers, keeping moving until
they arrived at their destination.

When Grant and his gun crew finally reached the church, the
priest who opened the door took one look at the Americans and
refused to let them in. But the future victor of Fort Donelson and

Vicksburg was not about to be put off by some Mexican parish priest. With his limited Spanish, Grant told the priest that he was coming in, whether anybody liked it or not. "I explained to him that he might save property by opening the door, and he certainly would save himself from becoming a prisoner, for a time, at least."[26] The priest could see by the expression on Grant's face that he was not joking, and "began to see his duty in the same light that I did and opened the door, though he did not look as if it gave him any special pleasure to do so."

Once inside the church, the gun crew manhandled the howitzer up a ladder into the belfry, piece by piece, put the gun back together, and started firing at the San Cosme barricade. "We were not more than two or three hundred yards from San Cosme," Grant said. "The shots from our little gun dropped upon the enemy and created great confusion."[27]

The officer commanding Grant's division, General William Jenkins Worth, watched the effects of Grant's exertions on the Mexican troops and was highly impressed. He sent one of his staff officers to bring Grant to him so that he could congratulate the young lieutenant in person. The staff officer General Worth sent was another young lieutenant, by the name of John Pemberton. Sixteen years later, the same John Pemberton, by that time a lieutenant general in the Confederate States Army, would surrender the city of Vicksburg, Mississippi, to Major General U. S. Grant, in one of the turning points of the Civil War.

The fire from Grant's howitzer was instrumental in allowing General Worth's men to fight their way past the San Cosme barricade and into Mexico City. On the following day, September 14, 1847, Mexican general Antonio Lopez de Santa Anna evacuated the city with his army. American troops marched into the city and raised the Stars and Stripes over the National Palace, which was romantically known as the "Halls of the Montezumas."

One of Grant's many, many biographers was moved to remark that "Grant had a remarkable war," which is a remarkable piece of understatement.[28] Grant himself wrote that in his sixteen months in Mexico he had been "in all the engagements possible for one man."[29] He had earned two brevet promotions for gallantry, including for his circus ride through Monterrey, but did not receive any promotion for hauling the field howitzer into the church belfry at San Cosme. And he managed to come through it all without a scratch.

"My experience in the Mexican War was a great advantage for me," Grant would write many years after the war ended.[30] One of the most significant lessons he absorbed during his time in Mexico was that only an offensive campaign could win a war, something that he learned from General Winfield Scott. "The Mexicans had fought mostly on the defensive," a writer noted, "while Scott, always outnumbered, had taken the war to the enemy and won."[31] Even though Scott had been outnumbered by a margin of more than two to one, he kept up his offensive against Mexico City until he reached his objective and won the war.

Grant would apply this lesson to the fighting in Virginia in 1864 and 1865: the only way to destroy an enemy force was for an army to stay on the offensive. Grant would never be outnumbered—Union forces would always have superior numbers throughout the fighting in Virginia—but he always took the war to Lee and kept applying the pressure by attacking Lee and his army until Lee was forced to give up the fight.

During his time in Mexico, Lieutenant Grant served with a good many able soldiers who would become high-ranking Confederate officers: Joseph E. Johnston, who would fight Grant's old friend William Tecumseh Sherman north of Atlanta in 1864; A. P. Hill, who would rescue Lee's Army of Northern Virginia at the Battle of Antietam/ Sharpsburg in September 1862 and would be killed by Grant's men only a week before Appomattox; George E. Pickett, who would become legendary because of his failed charge at Gettysburg; as well as James Longstreet and John Pemberton. "The acquaintance thus formed was of immense service to me in the war of the rebellion—I mean what I learned of the characters of those to whom I was afterwards opposed," Grant later reflected.[32] Unquestionably, the most advantageous and valuable of these acquaintances was his "appreciation" of Robert E. Lee, as Grant would later call it—"my appreciation of my enemies" is the way he described these associations in his memoirs.[33]

Lee was certainly the most famous of all the officers Grant knew during his "old army" days in Mexico, if anyone can say that they actually knew Lee. During the Mexican War, Lee was the chosen engineer of General Winfield Scott, the general-in-chief of the United States Army. Captain Lee had the reputation for being one of the best engineers in the army, as well as one of its most able officers. Grant had seen the renowned captain of engineers on several occasions, usually accompanied by other junior officers. One morning, Lieutenant Grant "rode up and joined Captain Robert E. Lee and several other officers," according to one story, "including lieutenants George B. McClellan and PGT Beauregard, as they prepared to observe the fire of a new battery that had just been brought into the fight."[34] In April 1861, Confederate General Beauregard would begin the war between the North and South by bombarding Fort Sumter, in Charleston Harbor. General Grant would come to grips with General Beauregard a year afterward, when they fought each other at the Battle of Shiloh.

Lieutenant Grant and Captain Lee met face-to-face when Lee paid a visit to Colonel John Garland's brigade one day. It was not a happy meeting.

One of Grant's jobs with the Quartermaster Department was to acquire provisions for the troops. He had just returned from one of these foraging expeditions, buying vegetables and other supplies from local farmers, when Captain Lee dropped by. Grant was never much for spit-and-polish to begin with. Whenever he returned from one of his forays, he was usually covered with dust, which made him even more unkempt and scruffy looking than usual. On this particular occasion, he also had his uniform unbuttoned for comfort.

Lee, on the other hand, was very much for spit-and-polish. He believed that an officer should always look the part, which meant being as neat and tidy and well-groomed as possible at all times. When he came across what a biographer called "an untidy young captain"—he was actually an untidy young lieutenant—the imperious Captain Lee was appalled by Grant's extremely unmilitary bearing, to put it mildly.[35] The six-foot-tall Lee looked down his nose at the scruffy little subaltern from Ohio and gave Grant what was apparently a severe dressing down. According to one writer's account, "the wording was harsh enough that Grant would remember it for the rest of his life."[36]

Even though Grant would always remember Robert E. Lee, he would never be intimidated by him. By 1864, when U. S. Grant was appointed general-in-chief of all Union forces, he was probably the only man in the Union army who was not intimidated. Since the beginning of the war, Lee had acquired an almost supernatural reputation with the Army of the Potomac and with much of the Northern press. He had out-generaled several Union commanders by that time and had given the Army of the Potomac humiliating defeats at the Second Battle of Bull Run/Manassas, Fredericksburg, and Chancellorsville. As far as the Union army was concerned, Lee could do anything he wanted, short of walking on water. And he could probably do that if he needed to, if there was no other way of outflanking the enemy. Bobby Lee, as the Army of the Potomac called him, was a terrifying combination of god, devil, bogeyman, and magician.

But Grant was not easily frightened. He clearly remembered Captain Lee from Mexico, and he knew that the former Captain of Engineers was anything but superhuman. Lee had a much-deserved reputation for being a first-rate soldier and officer, but he was no magician and he was certainly no god. For one thing, he spent too much time worrying about unimportant details, including whether or not an officer's uniform was buttoned. "I had known him personally," Grant would recall, "and knew that he was mortal."[37] That knowledge, and Grant's total lacking of fear of Lee and his reputation, would have a profound effect upon the fighting in Virginia sixteen years later, as well as upon the outcome of the war.

CAPTAIN OF ENGINEERS

Of all the things that occupied Robert E. Lee's anxious mind on the morning of April 9, 1865, stories about the Mexican War would certainly not have been among them. U. S. Grant definitely would have been very much in his thoughts that morning, just as he had been for the past eleven months. But he would have been thinking about the "Unconditional Surrender" Grant of the Northern newspapers, the relentless adversary who had been pounding his army since the previous May, not Lieutenant Sam Grant of Mexican War days.

By April 1865, General Lee had finally been forced to admit the shattering truth: his attempts to stop General Grant, and to force the Army of the Potomac out of Virginia at gunpoint, had failed. At that point, continuing to fight on could only mean postponing the inevitable. Richmond, the Confederate capital, had been captured by Union troops the week before. His men had been forced out of their lines at Petersburg after withstanding a nine-month siege, and they were now desperately trying to escape from Grant and his pursuing army. A week before, on April 2, Lee had written that he could see "no prospect if doing more than holding our position here till night," just before the army left Petersburg, and "I am not certain that I can do that."[38] The remains of his once-storied Army of Northern Virginia were half-starved skeletons, and more men kept deserting every day. There was no hope at all of breaking through the enemy's lines. The glory days of the Mexican War, when he had first been called a military genius, seemed like something that had happened to someone else a thousand years ago.

The war in Mexico had certainly influenced Robert E. Lee's life and military career as much as it had affected U. S. Grant's. Like Grant, Lee also had an extremely lively war. He fought at the battles of Cerro Gordo and Mexico City, in addition to several others, and won three brevet promotions for gallantry. Captain Lee of the Engineers was also one of General Winfield Scott's favorite officers. Scott called Lee "the very best soldier I ever saw in the field." A biographer pointed out that Scott had "an almost idolatrous fancy for Lee, whose military genius he estimated far above that of any other officer of the army."[39]

If imitation really is the sincerest form of flattery, Captain Lee more than returned the compliment. He observed how Winfield Scott employed troop movements and noted that outmaneuvering the enemy was a lot more effective than trying to outfight him. Many years after the Mexican War ended, General Lee would apply the lessons he learned from Scott in Mexico at other battlefields, including Chancellorsville and Manassas.

Besides being influenced by Winfield Scott, another item that Robert E. Lee had in common with U. S. Grant was that they were both greatly influenced by their fathers. Only young Robert was influenced in a negative way—his father was definitely not someone he wanted to use as a role model. Jesse Root Grant started at the bottom and worked his way to the top through determination and hard work. Henry Lee the third, better known as "Light-Horse Harry Lee," started at the top and, because of a disastrous sense of business and a skewed sense of morality, worked his way down into debtor's prison.

Harry Lee began life with all the advantages his family's name and wealth and connections could give him. He attended the College of New Jersey (now Princeton University) along with future president James Madison. When the War of Independence began, he was commissioned as a captain in the Virginia Light Dragoons. In the cavalry, Harry Lee soon acquired a reputation as a daring leader of hit-and-run raids, along with his colorful nickname. His commanding officer, General Nathaniel Greene, had nothing but praise for Harry Lee, claiming that he was one of the most admired officers in either America or Europe. After the war, Lee entered politics and had a successful career in both the Virginia Assembly and the US Congress. He also served as a Gentleman Justice in Westmoreland County, Virginia, and was elected Governor of Virginia in 1791.

His war record was a great help in Harry Lee's postwar career—the nickname "Light-Horse Harry" was probably worth a sizeable block of votes all by itself. But besides being bold and dashing, he was also a cheat and an embezzler. He speculated in land—buying large tracts of land and hoping to resell those tracts at a much higher price—but most of his investments turned out to be catastrophic. The price of land did not go up, as he had expected, but fell sharply. As the result of his total lack of talent and luck in the field of land speculation, he ran up an astonishing number of debts that he was unable to repay. Because he had no money and could not raise any through his unfortunate land deals, Harry Lee turned to fraud and deception.

In a bogus attempt to settle his debts and finance his bad land-speculating deals, Harry Lee paid his creditors with bad checks—including a bad check to George Washington. He also used other less than honest means of trying to raise money. There were instances of land buyers discovering that Harry Lee had already sold the same property to another customer. A story circulated that he had sold a farm without the owner's permission. His blatant dishonesty went against every aspect of a southern gentleman's code of honor—a gentleman simply *did not* resort to double-dealing to pay his debts, and he did not try to defraud another gentleman by paying him with underfunded checks.

To make matters even worse, he also began selling off subdivisions of his family's plantation, Stratford. Just before she died in 1790, his wife, Matilda, did her best to keep her husband from taking control of Stratford, but the trustees of the estate allowed Harry to go on selling units of the Lee plantation in spite of Matilda's wishes. By this time, Harry Lee had such a disgraceful reputation that his sister-in-law wrote him out of her will—she made a special point of insisting that Lee should have no control at all over her estate. No one trusted him, especially his relatives—the people who knew him best trusted him least.

In April 1809, when Robert E. Lee was only two years old, Light-Horse Harry Lee was put in the Westmoreland County Jail because of his inability to pay his debts. Just a few years earlier, he had sat as a Gentleman Justice in the courthouse there. Now he was a prisoner in that same courthouse. He stayed there for a little less than a year, until he declared bankruptcy and was released. But declaring bankruptcy—which was something else that a gentleman never did—and serving time in debtor's prison did nothing to improve his already ravaged reputation.

During the summer of 1810, Harry, his second wife, Ann, and their children left Stratford and moved to a small rented house in Alexandria, Virginia. When young Robert took his leave of Stratford for the last time, he returned to the nursery to kiss the angels on the room's iron fireplace goodbye. Or at least that is the myth, another of the many myths in the Lee legend.

Light-Horse Harry sailed off to Barbados when Robert was six, never to see Virginia or his son again. He tried desperately to raise money, but he was no more successful in the Caribbean than he had been in Virginia. He returned to the United States and ran into political trouble when he became involved with fiercely partisan Federalists who opposed the War of 1812. In Baltimore, Maryland, a mob of locals, just as fiercely partisan in favor of the war, attacked Harry Lee and a few of his friends with clubs, killing at least one man and leaving Harry for dead. His health was never the same after this. He died in March 1818, on Cumberland Island, off the coast of Georgia, at the home of his commander from the War of Independence, General Nathaniel Greene.

Not only had Harry Lee disgraced his own name and reputation, as well as the Lee family name, but he had also let down his wife and children. Before Harry Lee began his career as an embezzler, the Lees lived an aristocratic existence in a great plantation house that had been the family home for several generations. The rented house in Alexandria they lived in following his ruin was several giant steps down the social ladder, which would have been especially galling for a family as prominent as the Lees of Stratford.

Robert E. Lee never really knew his father, but Light-Horse Harry Lee's reputation influenced his son all throughout his life. This influence was almost completely negative—Robert went out of his way to be as dissimilar to Light-Horse Harry as possible. His mother, Ann Carter Lee, knew all about her husband's failings long before Robert was born and raised her son to be dutiful and honorable—in other words, to be nothing like his father. Robert did his best to live the sort of life his mother had in mind for him.

Two writers who investigated Lee's life and background made a point of mentioning the shame Lee felt regarding his father. One described Light-Horse Harry as "the man he [Robert] never knew and whose life he had spent much of his own trying to live down." The second noted that by the time he was ready for West Point, "Robert knew that as far as the honor of the Lees was concerned he had his work cut out for him."[40]

At West Point, Cadet Lee became known as the "Marble Model" because of his lofty academic standing and for the fact that he famously did not receive a single demerit during his four years at the academy. He obeyed all the rules and regulations and worked hard at his studies and at succeeding as a cadet—he did his best to be dutiful and honorable and nothing like his father.

During the Virginia campaign against U. S. Grant, General Lee refused to abandon Richmond, even though many of his officers advised him to fight Grant in the open country away from the capital. When an aide, Colonel Charles Venable, asked General Lee why he would not even consider abandoning Richmond, Lee was annoyed by the question. He explained that if he abandoned the Confederate capital, he would be guilty of treason against the Confederate government. Lee was convinced that it was his duty to defend Richmond. It never occurred to him that if he continued to chain his army to Richmond, there would be no Confederate government to let down or betray.

The reason behind Lee's refusal to cut loose from Richmond and meet the Army of the Potomac on open ground has been written about and talked about since 1864. A central motive behind Lee's decision, which has been frequently either overlooked or completely ignored, was the influence of his father. Abandoning Richmond might have been a sound strategic move, but in Lee's eyes it also would have been dishonorable, something that Light-Horse Harry Lee might have done. Robert E. Lee was all too aware of his father's well-deserved reputation for dishonesty and disloyalty. He did not want to follow in his father's footsteps.

Harry Lee had run off to the Caribbean when Robert was only a child, leaving his family in a desperate financial situation. He had also resigned his commission in the Continental Army in 1782, when the war was still being fought, for reasons that are still not all that clear. It might have been because some of his fellow officers, or superiors, snubbed him or insulted him—he reached the conclusion that he was underappreciated. The vague reasons he gave to his commanding general, Nathaniel Greene, were "disquietude of mind & infirmity of body."[41] For whatever reason, Harry Lee had run away from his family, and had also left the army in the middle of a war. These were not activities to be proud of, and young Robert was not proud of what his father had done.

The stigma of his father's reprehensible life stayed with Lee throughout all of his days, and he did his best to be the polar opposite. By defending Richmond, Lee was not only defending his family name and honor, but was also protecting his own name—he did not want to be remembered as the general who abandoned Virginia's capital city, or as another Lee who had ran out on his duties and obligations. As far as Robert E. Lee was concerned, leaving Richmond to the enemy would have been dishonest, and much worse than anything his father had ever done.

After the war, Robert E. Lee edited his father's *Memoirs*, which Harry Lee had written during his time in debtor's prison. As he edited them, Lee also totally reinvented his father. There is no mention of Harry Lee's bad debts, bad checks, bankruptcy, or the year he spent in debtor's prison. In his *Memoirs of Robert E. Lee*, A. L. Long also does not say anything about these unpleasantries, concentrating instead of Light-Horse Harry's war record. Lee—and A. L. Long—knew all about Harry Lee's unsavory past; they just chose to ignore it.

But Robert E. Lee was not just trying to make his father's past go away. He was trying to overcome it. Living down his father's life and reputation would not only affect Robert E. Lee's own life but would also influence the way in which he would conduct the war. He would not only be fighting U. S. Grant in 1864 and 1865 but also the memory of his own father. A biographer made this pointed observation: "Lee suffered all his life from a birth defect: he was the son of Light-Horse Harry Lee."[42]

Sam Grant may have been mentioned in the reports of General Zachery Taylor, but Captain Robert E. Lee of the elite Corps of Engineers was chosen by General Winfield Scott as his most able and reliable officer. When Scott named officers for his personal staff—he called it his "little cabinet"—he made certain that Captain Lee was first among its members. Lee's close association with General Scott would teach the young captain many things about leading an army in battle, including taking calculated risks and waging a war of movement and maneuver to outflank an enemy. These lessons would be put to very practical use by General Lee in Virginia in a future that no one could have imagined at the time.

General Winfield Scott's army landed at Veracruz on March 9, 1847, in one of the first major amphibious landings ever attempted by an American force. Among the officers who came ashore with Captain Lee were Lieutenant Joseph E. Johnston and Lieutenant P. G. T. Beauregard, along with Lieutenant George Gordon Meade. Lieutenant Meade was attached to the Topographical Corps and had been given the job of drawing detailed maps of the Mexican countryside for the advancing American troops. Sixteen years later, at the end of June 1863, Major General Meade would be appointed commander of the Army of the Potomac. Only a matter of days later, Meade would face General Robert E. Lee and his Army of Northern Virginia in one of the climactic battles of the Civil War. At the time of their landing on the Mexican coast, neither Captain Lee nor Lieutenant Meade had probably ever even heard of a small town in southern Pennsylvania called Gettysburg.

One of Captain Lee's first assignments in Mexico was to advise General Scott concerning the fortifications at Veracruz. After examining the condition of the city's walls, Lee reported that the defenses were in excellent condition and that new barricades and fortifications were being built at that very moment.

After listening to what his chief engineer had to say, General Scott came to the conclusion that a siege would be the most effective and least costly method of capturing the city. A direct assault would end in a slaughter and would probably fail. Artillery was brought up from the beach and hauled into position, and the siege began. Captain Lee was ordered to direct a battery of naval guns against the city's formidable defenses.

The artillery barrage literally pulverized the city walls. In two days, the big guns fired nearly 7,000 rounds into the fortifications that protected the approaches to Veracruz from the land. Lee's battery alone fired 1,800 rounds. Besides demolishing the walls, the pounding also smashed the morale of the defenders. The city leaders could see no chance at all of saving themselves from the terrible Yankee guns and sent a message that they would surrender. After two days of negotiating—some would call it haggling—the surrender of Veracruz was finally carried out on the morning of March 29, 1847.

Now that Veracruz was in his possession, General Winfield Scott began moving inland toward Mexico City. General Antonio Lopez de Santa Anna determined to stop Scott's advance at the village of Cerro Gordo, which was situated near two hills, called La Atalaya and El Telegrafo. Santa Anna occupied the village and both hills and waited for the Americans with 12,000 men. "Santa Anna harbored no doubt about his ability to stop the invaders at this very location," a writer commented.[43]

General Scott sent several junior officers to scout the approaches to Cerro Gordo. When they reported that the only feasible attack route was through an all but impassable ravine, which would take the Americans around the Mexican left flank, General Scott sent Captain Lee and another officer, John Fitzwalter, to make a closer examination of the area.

The two left camp early on the morning of April 15 and, after making their inspection, agreed that the ravine would be the only possible avenue of attack. Any other route would bring the Americans directly under Santa Anna's artillery. Even though the terrain was anything but hospitable, for either man or mule, Lee came to the conclusion that it would be possible for the army to cut a trail through the ravine and work their way around the Mexican line.

Before Lee and Fitzwalter could make their way back to camp, a group of Mexican soldiers came along to fill their canteens in a nearby stream. Lee and his companion had no choice but to hide behind a log—some versions of the story insist that it was a fallen tree—where they spent several hours bothered by crawling insects and fearful that the enemy soldiers would spot him. The Mexicans did not leave until the sun went down, giving the two Americans a very long and uncomfortable day. After the Mexicans finally went away, Lee and Fitzwalter slowly made their way back to their own camp in total darkness.

On the following day, after General Scott had read Lee's report, he sent Lee back to the ravine. This time, Lee took a construction crew and a detachment of soldiers with him. Under Lee's supervision, the men hacked out a roadway around the enemy's position. Even though it was fairly primitive and roughhewn, this roadway gave the American troops an advantage over the Mexicans, in spite of their prepared defenses.

Lee's job was not finished yet, though. On April 17, General Scott sent him back to guide General David Twiggs's division through the trail he had just created—Lee was certainly the best man for this particular job. Under Lee's guidance, General Twiggs's troops wound their way around the Mexican left flank and drove the Mexican troops off the hill known as La Atalaya, which was just to the northeast of Cerro Gordo.

During the night, American soldiers hauled cannon to the top of La Atalaya by rope, grunting and cursing and pulling until the guns were in place. A weary Captain Robert E. Lee supervised all this activity, which he managed to accomplish without arousing the suspicions of the enemy.

When morning came, General Santa Anna found himself confronted with a very nasty surprise when the artillery on La Atalaya began firing at his troops at Cerro Gordo and the neighboring hill, El Telegrafo. His secure, well-guarded base had been turned into a dangerously exposed position.

It had been a very busy day for Captain Lee, and it was not over yet. General Twiggs, with Lee nearby, kept pushing the demoralized Mexicans and succeeded in forcing them to retreat. "All of their cannon, arms, ammunition, and most of their men fell into our hands," Lee wrote to his family in Virginia.[44] He was right. About three thousand troops had been captured, along with most of the Mexican artillery and thousands of muskets.[45]

The Battle of Cerro Gordo turned out to be an absolute disaster for General Santa Anna. But even though he lost the battle, he still managed to get away from the advancing Americans. He made his escape by mule, abandoning all of his personal baggage, including all of his uniforms and a chest full of money. He also left behind his wooden (actually cork) leg—Santa Anna had a leg amputated after the French bombardment of Veracruz in 1838—which has to be one of the US Army's more unique war trophies.

Captain Lee and several other officers, including Lieutenant P. G. T. Beauregard, rode off to investigate Santa Anna's private estate on the following day. Among the more useful items they found in the general's rather grand and imposing house were maps of the Mexican countryside. These would be put to excellent use by American troops in the course of the next year's campaigning.

If Cerro Gordo was a humiliation for General Santa Anna—he was being referred to as "the Immortal Three-Fourths" throughout Mexico, because of his lost wooden leg—the battle was a triumph for Captain Lee of the Engineers.[46]

Lee's superior officers outdid themselves in praising the young engineer's gallantry. General Twiggs commented, "Captain Lee, of the engineer corps" for "the invaluable services which he rendered me . . . I consulted him with confidence, and adopted his suggestions with entire assurance."[47] Twiggs ended his report with, "His gallantry and good conduct on both days deserve the highest praise."

General Winfield Scott also commended Captain Lee. "I am compelled to make special mention of Captain R. E. Lee, Engineer," the general wrote in his report of the battle. "This officer was again indefatigable during these operations in reconnoissances [*sic*] as daring, as laborious, and of the utmost value. Nor was he less conspicuous in planting batteries and in conducting columns to their stations under the heavy fire of the enemy."[48]

Another officer who had been greatly impressed by Captain Lee's conduct was Lieutenant Sam Grant of the Quartermaster Department. While Grant was out scouting the countryside for supplies and provisions, the gallant Captain Lee was becoming something of a celebrity among the American troops in Mexico. Grant noted that the "reconnoissances" ordered by General Scott "were made under the supervision of Captain Robert E. Lee."[49]

Grant was also impressed by the fact that "the labor of cutting and making roads" had been carried out by Lee.[50] The most remarkable thing about all this activity, at least as far as Lieutenant Grant was concerned, was that Lee managed to carry out his road building and scouting "without the knowledge of Santa Anna or his army, and over ground where he supposed it impossible."

Sam Grant made these observations with pride, and maybe a touch of envy. He could see that the elegant Captain Lee of Virginia was clearly an officer with a brilliant career in front of him. Grant himself hoped that he would be able to leave the Quartermaster Department for what he considered to be a more suitable, and prestigious, assignment. That would be the only way by which a rumpled little lieutenant from the backwoods of Ohio would be able to get anywhere in the army.

As for Captain Lee, "Opportunity had come in his very first battle," a historian wrote, and "he had made the most of it."[51] He certainly had, and there would be more opportunities to come.

After his setback at Cerro Gordo, General Santa Anna decided to withdraw behind the walls of Mexico City. His army was not only exhausted but was also in very poor spirits. His best strategy, Santa Anna decided, would be to march his army westward to Mexico City, dig in behind the city walls, and wait for the Americans. He knew that they would have to capture the Mexican capital if they intended to win the war. And when they came, Santa Anna would be waiting for them.

General Scott began his march toward Mexico City after Cerro Gordo, just as Santa Anna anticipated. But when he reached the town of Puebla, about seventy-five miles or so from his objective, he stopped to wait for reinforcements. The enlistments of most of his volunteers were about to expire, and Scott did not intend to attack the walls of Mexico City with an army that was understrength.

While General Scott waited at Puebla, Captain Lee made a thorough study of the maps that he and Lieutenant Beauregard had removed from Santa Anna's estate. He could see that storming Mexico City was out of the question—all approaches were heavily defended by both artillery and infantry. General Scott agreed with Lee, his resident military genius. The only feasible route around Santa Anna's defenses would be to attack from the south. But this route had its own barrier—a supposedly impassable stretch of volcanic rock called the Pedregal.

A soldier who took part in the campaign described the Pedregal as "a field of volcanic rock like boiling scoria suddenly solidified," and went on to say that "a fall upon this sharp material would have seriously cut and injured one."[52] Crossing the Pedregal was like walking across the surface of the moon—it was like a lunar landscape covered with broken bottles. The sharp edges on the protruding lava shards could cut right through shoe leather. Santa Anna did not think that anyone would have the nerve even to try crossing it.

By early August, General Scott had his reinforcements. Brigadier General Franklin Pierce, who would become fourteenth president of the United States in 1852, arrived at Puebla with the First Brigade, which brought Scott's total force to 10,738 men. Scott finally had enough men to resume his advance on Mexico City.[53]

Because his supply lines stretched all the way back to Veracruz, about 150 miles, General Scott made the decision not to depend upon wagon trains to bring supplies and provisions from the coast. The wagons were too vulnerable, to Mexican army units operating behind Scott's army and to bandits out to steal anything they could find. Instead, Scott would send supply details out to the countryside to buy food from local farmers. This was how Grant happened to encounter Captain Robert E. Lee and how he would receive a dressing down that he would never forget.

Scott also made the decision that his best route to Mexico City, the route that would result in the fewest casualties, would be across the Pedregal. Crossing the Pedregal looked like a good idea on paper—it would allow his troops to outflank the Mexicans—but Scott had to find out if it was practical. Once again, Scott sent for his favorite engineer, Captain Robert E. Lee.

General Scott gave Lee the disagreeable job of finding a path through the lava field. It was another difficult assignment, but luck was with him. Along with Lieutenant P. G. T. Beauregard and an escort, Lee picked his way across the hostile landscape and came across a sort of primitive trail, the kind of pathway that might have been used by bandits or smugglers as a getaway route from soldiers. After following the trail for a few miles, Lee and his party were surprised by a Mexican patrol. But the Mexicans were more afraid of the Americans than Lee and Beauregard were afraid of them and, after a brief but harmless skirmish, the patrol ran off toward the north.

Instead of being frightened by the Mexican patrol, Lee was encouraged—if the Mexicans could cross the Pedregal on foot, then Lee and his party should be able to cross it as well. After the Mexicans ran off, Lee and his detachment resumed their slow walk until they came to the edge of the lava field. Captain Lee could see the six thousand Mexican soldiers that stood between General Scott's army and Mexico City.

General Scott was very glad to hear that the resourceful Captain Lee had found a pathway through the wilderness—if anyone could have done it, it was Captain Lee of the Engineers. That night, August 18, Scott decided to send Lee back to the Pedregal. This time, he would take a construction crew with him, along with five hundred soldiers and two batteries of horse-drawn "flying artillery." His instructions were to build a roadway across the Pedregal, just as he had done at Cerro Gordo—if he did it in April, he should be able to do it again in August. One of the artillery officers that would accompany Lee was Lieutenant Thomas J. Jackson, from the backwoods of Virginia, "a rawboned, all thumbs young lieutenant of artillery."[54] Fifteen years later, at the Battle of First Bull Run/Manassas, Jackson would acquire the nickname "Stonewall."

Lee and his detachment started across the lava field and found a place where the artillery could effectively be brought to bear on the enemy's positions. But by that time, the Mexicans had brought up their own artillery. Advancing across the Pedregal would have brought his men within range of the enemy's cannon fire, so Lee wisely decided to withdraw his detachment.

But that night, General Scott sent Lee back to the Pedregal for the third time. His instructions were to escort two infantry brigades through the lava field, toward the enemy's lines and the six thousand Mexican troops he had seen that morning. Lee had not slept in about thirty-six hours by this time, and it had begun to rain heavily. Going back out in the middle of the night to guide two brigades through a lava field in a rainstorm was not what he had in mind for an evening's relaxation. But an order was an order, and Lee soon found himself heading north toward Santa Anna's army.

The march began at three o'clock in the morning. By daybreak, Lee had taken the two brigades to within sight of "a large mass of infantry," as he described the Mexican force.[55] The enemy had dug themselves a deep trench just north of the town of Churubusco, but one of the American brigades managed to make their way around the entrenchments and attack the Mexicans from the rear. The fighting went on for three hours. "Our troops being now hotly engaged and somewhat pressed," Lee recalled later, "I urged forward the howitzer battery under Lt. Reno, who very promptly brought the pieces to bear upon the head of their column with good effect."[56]

As soon as the artillery fire was lifted, the infantry began moving forward. "An assault was at once made," a biographer commented, "the entrenchments of the enemy stormed, and in seventeen minutes after the charge was ordered the surprised Mexicans were in full flight and the American flag floating proudly over their works."[57] Lee joined in the pursuit of the fleeing Mexicans. But the effects of not having slept for nearly two days began to take their toll. That night, he slept the sleep of the totally exhausted.

Once again, Lee received the highest praise for his conduct. The commanders of the two brigades Lee had guided across the

Pedregal, General David Twiggs and General Gideon Pillow, were more than lavish in their admiration for Captain Lee of the Engineers. In his report of the battle, General Pillow wrote, "I cannot in justice omit to notice the valuable services of Captain Lee of the engineer corps, whose distinguished merit and gallantry deserves the highest praise."[58] General Twiggs also had nothing but compliments for the officer who had escorted his brigade through the hostile Pedregal: "To Captain Lee of the engineers, I have again the pleasure of tendering my thanks for the exceedingly valuable service rendered throughout the whole of these operations."[59]

For his own part, Lee did not seem to let all the excitement—either on the field of battle or off—break his stride. He was awarded a brevet promotion from captain to major after Cerro Gordo and was breveted to lieutenant colonel for his conduct at the Pedregal. But in spite of the two brevets and all the praise, Lee seemed anything but impressed with himself. In his written account of the fighting, he made no mention at all of his own role in it. Captain Lee was either so confident of his abilities that he did not feel the need to mention them or else he was so modest that he would have been embarrassed to say anything about them.

On the day after Lee's adventures on the Pedregal, Winfield Scott contacted the Mexican government to suggest negotiating a joint armistice. Mexico had obviously gotten the worse of the fighting so far, and General Scott wanted to bring an end to the war as quickly as arrangements could be made. Mexican authorities were only too willing to enter into negotiations, as Scott thought they would be, and an armistice was signed on August 24, 1847.

But General Santa Anna used the ceasefire to strengthen Mexico City's fortifications, which was not what Scott had in mind when he proposed an armistice. As soon as he learned what his opponent was up to, an angry Scott called off the truce. On September 6, just thirteen days after the ceasefire had been signed, General Scott called Lee and several other officers to discuss the details of a final assault on Mexico City. Scott decided to attack via the fortress of Chapultepec, which would be the most direct, or at least the least costly, route into the Mexican capital.

Once again, Captain Lee was put in charge of the artillery. His job was to bring guns to bear on Chapultepec in support of the advancing infantry. By the afternoon of September 12, he had three batteries of artillery in position, all pounding away at Chapultepec's defenses. Lieutenant Thomas Jackson and his "flying artillery" wheeled his guns around to the north, to support two infantry regiments that would be attacking from that direction.

Lee spent the night at General Scott's headquarters, preparing for the morning's attack. When the troops began their advance toward Chapultepec, Lee took part in the assault as a member of General Pillow's division. General Pillow was wounded during the advance, but Lee continued on toward Chapultepec after he had seen that Pillow's wound had been taken care of.

"The assault upon Chapultepec succeeded brilliantly," as understated by an American writer.[60] The defending Mexicans made a brave stand, firing down at the attackers with muskets and artillery. The clubbing and stabbing and shooting and killing continued even after the Americans climbed over the fortress ramparts. But by 9:30 a.m., the Stars and Stripes had been raised over what was left of the fort's ruined defenses. The flag had been hoisted by Lieutenant George E. Pickett and was visible to everyone on the battlefield, an exploit that made Pickett the hero of the hour. But Pickett's claim to fame would come as the result of another action on another battlefield.

With Chapultepec in the hands of the Americans, the way into Mexico City was wide open. Once again, General Scott sent Captain Lee on another reconnaissance errand. This time, his assignment was to scout the approaches to the Garita San Cosme in preparation for the coming all-out attack. A detachment of Mexican soldiers had manned a barricade that effectively blocked any advance through San Cosme. But Lieutenant Sam Grant and his crew of artillerymen were about to manhandle their mountain howitzer into a nearby church belfry, which would instantly change the situation in favor of the advancing Americans.

Lee had been pushing himself for the past several days, going without any sleep at all for over forty-eight hours. He had also been wounded—not a major wound, but serious enough to cause some loss of blood. The combination of lack of sleep and loss of blood were too much, even for the seemingly untiring Captain Lee, and he fell from his horse in a dead faint. As General Scott put it, "Captain Lee, so constantly distinguished, also bore important letters from me (September 13th) until he fainted from a wound and the loss of two night's sleep at the batteries."[61]

Sometime afterward, when he regained consciousness, Captain Lee was duly informed that General Santa Anna had evacuated Mexico City and that the Stars and Stripes were flying prominently over the National Palace. A division under General John Quitman occupied the city on the following day. The war was over. The Mexicans had given up. It had been a long six months of fighting for Lee, from Veracruz to Mexico City.

General Scott decided to make a show of occupying the Mexican capital. He rode into the city's Grand Plaza at the head of his army, decked out in full-dress uniform—fore-and-aft hat, gold-trimmed uniform, gold sash, dress sword. His staff officers rode right behind him—Lee watched from somewhere near the Plaza—along with an escort of dragoons. All in all, it was quite a parade.

Lieutenant Sam Grant was there as well, although he did not ride into town with the dragoons. He seemed to be as bemused by the spectacle as he was impressed by it. In his memoirs, Grant said that he was surprised that some Mexican in the crowd of onlookers did not take a potshot at the general. Scott certainly made an inviting target, up there on his horse with all that gold braid and all those shiny brass buttons—they did not call him "Old Fuss and Feathers" for nothing.

Even though the fighting had ended, the war was not yet at an end, at least not officially. The peace treaty between the United States and Mexico would not be signed until February 1848, in the town of Guadalupe Hidalgo. But for Robert E. Lee, the war ended at Mexico City. The next time he took the field against an enemy, he would be wearing the uniform of another country. And he would be fighting against his former countrymen.

During his tour of duty with General Winfield Scott's army, Lee learned a great many things from his mentor. The most obvious trait that Lee picked up was Scott's penchant for spit-and-polish. Lee also had a fondness for gold braid and brass buttons—on a distant Palm Sunday, he would make every effort to look his very best when presenting himself to General Grant at Appomattox Court House. But he learned a lot more from Scott than just the finer points of wearing a dress uniform.

Probably the most significant thing that Robert E. Lee learned from General Scott was the importance of going on the offensive, of taking the war to the enemy. Because of his dazzling push inland to Mexico City, the Duke of Wellington declared General Scott to be the greatest living general. This was the same lesson that Sam Grant learned. "Scott had taken six thousand men into uncharted terrain and humiliated a much larger army on its own ground," a commentator wrote about Scott's Mexican campaign.[62] General Lee and his most famous subordinate, General Thomas "Stonewall" Jackson, would do the same thing to several Union generals in Virginia in 1862 and 1863.

From serving on General Scott's staff and observing his tactics, Lee also learned something about how movement and maneuver can affect the outcome of a battle. If Scott had not sent his army around the Mexican flank at Cerro Gordo, the battle might have turned out to be a disaster for him instead of Santa Anna. Lee saw this and would put the lesson to use in another time and place. One of Lee's biographers pointed out that the march across the Pedregal and around the Mexican flank "found a more famous counterpart in Jackson's movement to the rear of Hooker's army at Chancellorsville."[63] The same writer called Second Manassas "Cerro Gordo on a larger terrain."

Like Sam Grant, Lee also became acquainted with many of his future opponents during his time in Mexico, notably Joseph Hooker and George B. McClellan. (Lee never got to know George Gordon Meade, who was ordered back to the United States shortly after coming ashore at Veracruz.) He acquired what might be called a "working knowledge" of them and their temperaments. "He may have been close enough to Captain Joseph Hooker of Pillow's staff to learn something of his qualities," was one observation.[64] In 1863, Lee and Stonewall Jackson famously humiliated General "Fighting Joe" Hooker at the Battle of Chancellorsville. (Lee sarcastically referred to his opponent as "Mr. F. J. Hooker.")

As for McClellan, Captain Lee often worked with him in setting up artillery positions and in carrying out other engineering duties. In such a small engineering corps, Lee "could not fail to see both the strong qualities and the weaknesses of the officer he was to face at a time when his understandings of the man helped to compensate for the many shortcomings of the Confederate staff."[65]

Lee would outthink and outgeneral McClellan during the Seven Days' Battles in 1862. Later on, much would be made of General Lee's ability for putting himself in his adversary's shoes and of his ability to read his opponents' minds. In the case of McClellan, Lee did not read his mind. He remembered the cautious, methodical officer he had worked with in Mexico, and he knew that the Union general would never resort to any tactic that was even remotely audacious or unconventional. This had nothing to do with mindreading, just with remembering his opponent.

Remembering McClellan's glaring weakness, Lee was able to push the Union army right down the entire length of the York/James peninsula in a single week. Lee was appointed commanding general of the army, which he named the Army of Northern Virginia in June 1862, and immediately went on the offensive. McClellan recoiled from Lee's constant attacks, retreating from his goal of Richmond and to within the safety of the Union gunboats at Harrison's Landing. He had been completely flummoxed by Lee's tactics, being too cautious to do anything but retreat in the face of the Confederate attacks—as Lee, who did not have to read his opponent's mind because he already knew his mind, knew McClellan would.

"Lee's study in human nature," as it has been called, included making the acquaintance of every commanding general of the future Army of the Potomac except John Pope, who actually commanded the short-lived Army of Virginia.[66] Pope would be roundly defeated by Lee at Second Bull Run/Manassas, where he "lost the field, his reputation, and about 16,000 men."[67] But, for whatever reason, Lee never got to know Lieutenant Sam Grant. Maybe Captain Lee of Virginia and the elite Corps of Engineers thought the untidy lieutenant with the scruffy beard was not worth knowing. Maybe he just never got around to meeting Grant socially—which is highly unlikely, since Lee knew just about every other future Union commander who served in Scott's army.

A few weeks after General Scott made his triumphal procession into Mexico City, some of his officers formed a social group they called the "Aztec Club," which was established "for the purpose of forming a resort for officers, as a promoter of good fellowship, and of furnishing a home where they could pass their leisure hours."[68] Any officer stationed in Mexico City could belong to the club, and most of them did. It gave the men some place to go and somebody to talk to, while they were waiting for the peace treaty to be signed—if they could not go home, this was the next best thing to it. The Aztec Club was very popular with the officers. Some of them continued to meet even after the armistice was signed and they had gone on to other duties and assignments.

Both Robert E. Lee and U. S. Grant belonged to the Aztec Club and would have spent many hours there when they were off duty. But there is no evidence that they ever met. No one can say if this was because of snobbism on Captain Lee's part or was just the result of a series of very odd coincidences, but Captain Lee never set eyes on Lieutenant Grant inside the Aztec Club. Later on, Lee would admit that he could not even remember what Grant looked like when they were both junior officers in Mexico—unlike Grant, who remembered Lee vividly.

A British writer and military historian went on record to declare that "Lee never fathomed Grant."[69] This failure to know Grant—or even to remember him—would be a factor during the last bitter, brutal year of the war.

As General Lee rode toward his appointment with General Grant on that Palm Sunday morning in 1865, maybe he tried to recall Grant's face from eighteen years earlier. Maybe he wished that he had paid more attention to the dust-covered lieutenant from the Quartermaster's Department, who would one day fight him to a standstill until he had no options except surrender or annihilation. No other Union general had been able to outfight him the way Grant had done, not John Pope, not Ambrose Burnside, who presided over the disastrous Battle of Fredericksburg in December 1862, not "Fighting Joe" Hooker, and certainly not George B. McClellan, the "Virginia Creeper." Even George Gordon Meade, who had stopped

Lee at Gettysburg, allowed his army to escape across the Potomac to Virginia.

Before U. S. Grant had taken command of all Union forces in March 1864, Lee had faced a total of six Union generals in northern Virginia, if George B. McClellan's two terms are counted separately. George B. McClellan was fired for his mishandling of the army, and everything else, during the Seven Days' Battles. After McClellan came John Pope, and then McClellan again—President Lincoln thought McClellan might have learned something from his experiences during the Seven Days, but he was wrong. Lincoln fired McClellan for the second time and replaced him with Ambrose Burnside. After losing the Battle of Fredericksburg, Burnside was replaced by Joseph Hooker. Hooker was replaced by George Gordon Meade when he was outgeneraled by Robert E. Lee at Chancellorsville. Meade would remain commander of the Army of the Potomac throughout the war. Grant would be general-in-chief, and would travel with Meade's army.

"I'm afraid they're going to keep making these changes until they get someone I don't understand," Lee said.[70] Which is exactly what happened—"they" finally got U. S. Grant. If he had been a more reflective soul, Lee might have considered that if he had taken the time to get acquainted with Sam Grant back in Mexico, he might not be riding off, in his best uniform, to surrender his Army of Northern Virginia to the unkempt man from Ohio he could not even remember.

Chapter Two

PREPARATIONS

TAKING ALL RESPONSIBILITY

The stress and tension of the war was taking its toll on General Robert E. Lee, as much as it was on General Grant. He did not have a migraine headache on the morning of April 9, 1865, but his staff officers could not help noticing how dejected and depressed he had been during the past several days.

General Lee had good reason to feel dejected. He had heard nothing but bad news for the past week, ever since Colonel Charles Venable excitedly told him that the enemy had broken his lines at Petersburg the previous Sunday. Since then, both Petersburg and the Confederate capital of Richmond had been evacuated. Just three days before, on April 6, 1865, he had lost nearly eight thousand men, killed, wounded, or captured at the Battle of Sayler's Creek, and had been forced to retreat westward along the north bank of the Appomattox River, with the Union forces right behind him.

For the past eleven months, he had been doing his best to outthink and outlast his unrelenting opponent, General U. S. Grant. All during this time, Lee's army had retreated southward, from the Rapidan to Petersburg. Now the Confederacy was on the verge of collapse. He had sent General John B. Gordon's corps to break through the enemy's position that morning, Sunday, April 9, hoping against hope that Gordon would be able to find a weak point in the enemy's defenses. By the end of the day, maybe General Gordon would send him the news he was hoping for—that he had managed to force his way through the Union lines.

Lee's objective—and General Gordon's—was to escape from Grant's pursuing army and link up with General Joseph E. Johnston's Army of Tennessee in North Carolina. If he could accomplish this, he would be able to keep his army in the field. He would also be able to keep the Confederacy from becoming extinct—as long as his army stayed in the field, he knew that the Confederacy would also survive. But in order to get away from Grant, he would have to reach the watershed between the Appomattox and James Rivers before Grant blocked his way.

There was also the problem of feeding his army. Several trains filled with food and provisions were to stop at Appomattox Station, a mile or so from the little courthouse town of Appomattox. Lee hoped to meet the trains, feed his men, and turn south before Grant could catch up with him. If he could do that, there was still hope that he could escape from Grant and link up with Joe Johnston.

General Grant had been trying to convince Lee to surrender for the past two days. Only the day before, Grant had sent a note requesting that General Lee meet him "at any point agreeable to you, for the purpose of arranging definitely the terms upon which the surrender of the Army of Northern Virginia will be received."[1] Grant did not demand Lee's "unconditional surrender." In fact, the tone of Grant's note was congenial, almost pleasant, which was quite unexpected.

But Lee was not ready to give up. In his reply, he agreed to meet with General Grant, but not to discuss surrender. He was only willing to discuss Grant's proposal in general terms, including how it "may affect the Confederate States forces under my command, and tend to the restoration of peace."[2] Lee had no intention of talking about surrender, at least not until he received word from General Gordon.

General Lee was not the only one who had the surrender of the Army of Northern Virginia on his mind. Several of Lee's own officers had also arrived at the conclusion that the army would never be able to fight its way through the Union lines and had appointed General J. C. Pendleton to bring up the subject of surrender to Lee. General Lee was not exactly overjoyed to hear what General Pendleton had to say, but no one is exactly sure of what he actually said in response. One version has him telling Pendleton, "Surrender? I have too many good fighting men for that!" In another account, he says, "I trust it has not come to that! We certainly have too many brave men to think of laying down our arms. They still fight on, and with great spirit, whereas the enemy does not."[3] Whichever version is believed, the meaning is the same: Lee was not ready to give up the fight.

By the end of the day on Saturday, that attitude had undergone a complete change. During the course of a staff meeting that night, which was attended by General Lee, General Gordon, General James Longstreet, and General Fitz Lee, Robert E. Lee's nephew, the word "surrender" was seriously mentioned for the first time. The four generals were forced to consider what might happen if Grant's army outmarched the Army of Northern Virginia and cut off their line of escape. If the Union troops blocking the way were cavalry, it was decided that Fitz Lee's men would charge them, with Gordon supporting, and clear the way for the advance. But if the Union troops turned out to be infantry instead of cavalry, this would mean that the army was virtually surrounded. Which would leave only one viable option—surrender. "The word could not be evaded now."[4]

Even though General Lee was hoping for good news from General Gordon, he was also preparing for the worst. During the early hours of April 9, General Pendleton visited Lee at his camp and was surprised to find him wearing his full-dress uniform, complete with red sash and engraved sword. When Pendleton asked the reason behind the brass buttons and finery, Lee had a very simple answer, one that would have made Winfield Scott smile. "I have probably to be General Grant's prisoner," he explained, "and thought I must make my best appearance."[5]

The Confederate attack began at about five o'clock in the morning, with artillery volleys booming across the countryside. Early morning fog covered the landscape, mixing with the cannon smoke and making it difficult to see anything. General Lee did his best to watch General Gordon's advance from nearby high ground, but through all the noise he could not tell if Gordon's troops were advancing or falling back. After about three hours of listening to the sounds of the battle, and not being able to tell which way the fighting was going, and also not receiving any word from General Gordon, Lee sent Colonel Venable to investigate. As Venable put it, he was to ask General Gordon "if he could break through the enemy."[6] Lee realized that the future of the war, and of the Confederacy, depended upon Gordon's answer.

When Colonel Venable located General Gordon, he found out that the advancing Confederate divisions had gone through the village of Appomattox Court House and found Union troops blocking the road on the other side of the village. Not knowing if the troops were cavalry or infantry, Gordon attacked with cavalry on the right and infantry on the center and left. The attack dislodged the enemy, clearing the road. But as the cavalry continued along the road, past the now abandoned Federal line, they ran into a mass of Union infantry, a blue line about two miles long, walking steadily toward them. "Slowly, this ominous procession rolled forward, picking up strength like a hurricane on the open sea," according to one description, "as a second division and parts of a third arrived and fell in alongside."[7] The enemy kept on coming and coming, as if there was no end to them.

If the Confederates were demoralized by the sheer number of the advancing Federal troops, Northerners found it hard to believe how few Southern troops were facing them across the lines. The Confederate regiments were so small, and their red battle dusters were so clustered together, that it seemed as if there were more rebel flags than soldiers. To one of the advancing Northern soldiers, "there were so many standards crimsoning each body of troops" that the advancing regiments "looked like marching gardens blooming with cockscomb, red roses, and poppies."[8] The once fabled Army of Northern Virginia had become nothing more intimidating than row after row of red flowers.

To make a desperate situation even worse, two other Union corps were closing in on the Confederate rear. As a Confederate private aptly remarked, "Lee couldn't go forward, he couldn't go backward, and he couldn't go sideways."[9] Gordon informed Colonel Venable, "Tell General Lee I have fought my corps to a frazzle, and I fear I can do nothing unless I am heavily supported by Longstreet's corps."[10]

This was the news that General Lee had been dreading but had also been expecting. He knew that Longstreet could not be brought up. His famous First Corps was holding off a Union attack in another sector, and there could be no possibility of withdrawing these troops to support General Gordon.

When Lee heard Gordon's reply, he realized that he had finally arrived at the end of the road. It had been a long, trying road that had run through Manassas, Sharpsburg, Fredericksburg, Chancellorsville, Gettysburg, the Wilderness, and Spotsylvania. It would now end at Appomattox. "Then there is nothing left me to do but go and see General Grant," he said, "and I would rather die a thousand deaths."[11]

His staff officers heard Lee's remark and knew exactly what it meant. Colonel Venable recalled that the overall reaction was anguish and that many of the officers were almost stunned with grief. One of them wondered what history would have to say about giving up the fight, after four years of struggle and sacrifice, and about surrendering the army. Lee had a quick response to this: "Yes, I know they will say hard things of us: they will not understand how we were overwhelmed by numbers." He went on, "But that is not the question, colonel: the question is, Is it right to surrender this army? If it is right, then *I* will take *all* the responsibility."[12]

Lee gave the impression of being calm and detached, the impression he always seemed to give, even under the pressures and anxieties of battle. But he was actually a good deal more upset by the prospect of having to surrender his army than he let on. A short time after listening to Colonel Venable's message from General Gordon, Lee let his mask slip. "How easily I could be rid of this, and be at rest!" he said. "I have only to ride along the line and all will be over!"[13] If he rode out there in full view of the enemy, General Lee knew that he could count on some Union sharpshooter putting a minie ball into him. This would spare him the humiliation of surrendering his army to a general who had been his subordinate during the Mexican War, a man that he could not even remember.

After a moment, Lee's renowned stoicism took hold once again. "But it is our duty to live," he said with conviction. "What will become of the women and children of the South if we are not here to protect them?"[14]

General James Longstreet soon joined the subdued meeting. As he put it, "General Lee called to have me ride forward to him."[15] Longstreet seemed surprised to see the general all dressed up in his best uniform, right down to a pair of gold spurs, but "the handsome appearance and brave bearing failed to conceal his profound depression."[16]

Lee explained the overall situation to Longstreet, that his forward columns could not break through the enemy lines and that General Meade was closing in on his rearguard, and asked for his views on surrendering the army. He had asked the same question two days earlier. At that time, Longstreet replied, "Not yet."[17] But that was two days ago. Since then, the situation for the Army of Northern Virginia had changed significantly, and very much for the worse.

Longstreet answered Lee's question with a question: would the sacrifice of his army help the cause in any way? In other words, would an all-out battle with the enemy's vastly superior numbers, which was sure to result in horrible losses, help to extend the life of the Confederacy itself? Lee said that he did not think so. Longstreet told Lee that he had just answered his own question—"Your situation speaks for itself."[18] The only choice open to Lee was surrender or annihilation.

When General Lee's twenty-nine-year-old commander of artillery, Brigadier General E. Porter Alexander, learned what Lee intended to do, he urged Lee to continue fighting. Let the men disappear into the countryside with their muskets, Alexander suggested, and resort to unrestricted guerilla warfare. "We would be like rabbits and partridges in the bushes and they could not scatter to follow us."[19] His idea was to terrorize the Union army with hit and run attacks, to inflict as much damage to the Yankee army, and to the Yankee cause, as possible. This would not win the war for the Confederacy—Alexander realized that—but it would keep General Grant from gloating over a defeated Army of Northern Virginia. Anything to keep the Yankees from declaring victory over the South would be well worth the effort.

Lee made it very clear that he wanted no part of General Alexander's suggestion. "If I took your advice the men would be without rations and under no control of officers," he explained. "They would be compelled to rob and steal in order to live." This armed band of marauders, Lee went on, would bring the enemy's cavalry down on them with a vengeance, as well as on "many sections they never have occasion to visit." It would take the country years to recover from such a protracted campaign of guerilla warfare. As far as Lee was concerned, "the only dignified course for me would be to go to General Grant and surrender myself, and take the consequences of my acts."[20]

Along with his reproach, Lee also offered General Alexander a few words of encouragement: "But I can tell you one thing for your comfort. Grant will not demand unconditional surrender." Lee thought Grant would offer "as good terms as this army has the right to demand," and he would be meeting him that very morning to discuss those terms. Alexander seemed satisfied with what Lee had to say. He later admitted that he was ashamed at having made his suggestion to General Lee, and that "I did not have a single word to say in reply."[21]

His conversations with Longstreet and Alexander seemed to have raised Lee's spirits slightly, but he was still "manifestly sick at heart," according to one of his biographers.[22] He mounted his horse, Traveller, to ride off for his meeting with General Grant at about 8:30, along with his adjutant, Lieutenant Colonel Walter H. Taylor, his military secretary, Colonel Charles Marshall, and Sergeant G. W. Tucker, chief courier of the Third Corps.

Sergeant Tucker led the way, riding ahead of the others and carrying a white flag. After about half a mile, they encountered a group of Union soldiers. Colonel Marshall rode forward, expecting to meet General Grant and his staff. Instead, a Union officer, Lieutenant Colonel Charles A. Whittier, and his flagbearer came out to meet Colonel Marshall. Colonel Whittier had a letter from General Grant, which he handed to Marshall. Marshall took the letter and galloped back to General Lee, who read it:

> Headquarters Army of the United States
> April 9, 1865
>
> General R. E. Lee,
> Commanding C.S. Armies
>   General: Your note of yesterday is received. As I have no authority to treat on the subject of peace the meeting proposed for 10 a.m. today could lead to no good. I will state, however, General, that I am equally anxious for peace with yourself, and the whole North entertain the same feeling. The terms upon which peace can

be had are well understood. By the South laying down their arms they will hasten that most desirable event, save thousands of human lives, and hundreds of millions of property not yet destroyed. Sincerely hoping that all our difficulties may be settled without the loss of another life, I subscribe myself,

Very respectfully, your obedient servant,

U. S. Grant,

Lieutenant-General U.S. Army[23]

General Lee was not happy that Grant would not even consider a discussion of peace on all fronts. He was also unhappy that Grant had not come out to meet him, and he feared that this might be a sign that harsher conditions might be imposed. When artillery fire began booming from the direction of the front, Lee took this to be another bad sign—it sounded like Grant was making another attack. The way things were beginning to take shape, it seemed to Lee that Grant might demand unconditional surrender after all.

The best thing to do, Lee thought, would be to reply to Grant's note as soon as possible. Colonel Marshall took his pencil and paper and wrote down what General Lee dictated as the firing from the front continued:

April 9th, 1865

General,

I received your note of this morning on the picket line whither I had come to meet you and ascertain definitely what terms were embraced in your proposal of yesterday with reference to the surrender of this army. I now request an interview in accordance with the offer contained in your letter of yesterday for that purpose.

Very respectfully,

Your obt. Servt,

R. E. Lee

Lt. Gen U. S. Grant,

Comdg U.S. Armies[24]

As soon as Marshall finished, he handed the letter to Lee for his signature. The general signed his name in very large letters, much larger than usual, either because he was not wearing his glasses or because he was so upset. Without waiting for Marshall to make a copy, Lee sent him off to give the letter to Colonel Whittier. He also instructed Marshall to send his regrets to General Grant via Colonel Whittier that they had not been able to meet.

Marshall took the letter and went galloping off toward Colonel Whittier, who was waiting nearby. Along the way, he could see Federal troops advancing. When he reached Whittier, Marshall divulged the contents of the letter and said that he hoped that another battle could be avoided until Lee's communiqué reached Grant. Colonel Whittier said that he had no authority and that he could only pass along the message, promising to bring a reply from Grant. General Lee waited in the road.

. . . AND THE WAR

Throughout the Army of Northern Virginia, everyone was waiting—waiting for orders, waiting to see what the day would bring. The leading topics of conversation of every soldier in every regiment were hunger and surrender: how soon would they be getting something to eat and when would General Lee be giving up the fight. The men had been talking about surrender for the past several days (and about hunger for a lot longer than that). Only two days before, General Lee had instructed his son, General William Henry Fitzhugh "Rooney" Lee, not to let his troops think about surrender, but that did not stop them; they kept thinking about it and talking about it.

One of the units that was waiting and talking was the "Stonewall Brigade," or at least what was left of it. There was a time, when the unit was led by General Thomas J. "Stonewall" Jackson himself, that the Stonewall Brigade was the scourge of the Union army. Because he marched his men with almost superhuman speed—the brigade was known as Jackson's "foot cavalry"—Northern soldiers joked that Jackson had the power to be in two places at the same time. During the Shenandoah Valley campaign in 1862, the Stonewall Brigade walked over six hundred miles in seven weeks. During that time, they also won five battles, defeated three generals, killed or wounded about 3,500 men, captured another 3,500, and kept 40,000 Union soldiers away from Richmond. His activities in the Valley cemented his reputation as a brilliant tactician.

Jackson and his brigade also fought alongside Lee at Antietam/ Sharpsburg, at Fredericksburg, and at Chancellorsville. His presence and his undisguised love for combat contributed to Lee's success in each battle. But after Jackson was accidentally shot and killed by his own men during the Battle of Chancellorsville in 1863, the brigade was never the same. Lee said that he lost his right arm when Stonewall Jackson died, and he was right. He never even came close to finding anyone who could replace Jackson. His successor as commander of the Stonewall Brigade, Richard S. "Baldy" Ewell, did his best, but Ewell was no Stonewall Jackson. Neither was anyone else in the Confederate army.

Lee was certainly not the same general after Jackson died. He realized that winning at Chancellorsville had cost him much more than he could ever afford to pay. Officers and men throughout all the Confederate armies knew that Jackson's death could not bring anything but bad fortune for the South. As General James Longstreet took his leave from Jackson after his funeral, he reflected, "we seemed to face a future bereft of much of its hopefulness."[25]

By the spring of 1865, the Stonewall Brigade had gone the way of its namesake.

Grant's campaign from the Rapidan River to Petersburg had taken its toll on Jackson's old unit, just as it had on the entire Army of Northern Virginia. At Spotsylvania in May 1864, the brigade was all but wiped out. Out of the six thousand men who were part of the Stonewall Brigade throughout the war, just over two hundred were left by April 1865.[26]

Robert E. Lee often thought about his most trusted, and most valued, officer, and the effect his death had upon his army and upon the war. Several years after the war ended, when Lee was president of Washington College, he opened his mind to a friend on the subject of the war and its outcome. It was an extremely rare incident—the war was a very painful subject, and Lee hardly ever spoke about it. He was out riding with James J. White, a professor at Washington College and someone Lee had come to know and respect, when the subject of Stonewall Jackson came up. Lee said emphatically that Jackson's death cost him the Battle of Gettysburg. "If I had had Stonewall Jackson with me, so far as man can see," he said, "I should have won the battle of Gettysburg."[27] As far as Lee was concerned, the Battle of Gettysburg was lost at Chancellorsville, when Jackson was fatally wounded by his own men.

There are other versions of what Lee said during this conversation: "If I had had Stonewall Jackson at Gettysburg, I should have won there a great victory, and if we had reaped the fruits within our reach, we should have established the independence of the Confederacy."[28] There is at least one other variation, as well, which is only slightly different. But even though these are almost certainly exaggerations of what Lee actually said, they say exactly what Lee meant: Jackson's death cost Lee the battle, which also cost the Confederacy any real chance of independence. After the third day of fighting at Gettysburg, Lee managed to get the remnants of his army safely across the Potomac, but the South had lost more than just a battle. "He carried with him his wounded and his prisoners," Winston Churchill would write. "He had lost only two guns, and the war."[29]

THE NEW LIEUTENANT GENERAL

"Grant is not taller than I am, round shoulders and a gross figure," is how Major Peter Vredenburgh described the new lieutenant general in a letter to his mother. "If he is a very capable man, his appearance libels him."[30]

Not very many people were impressed with Lieutenant General Ulysses S. Grant when they first set eyes on him. Which did not upset him in the slightest—he knew that he was not very impressive looking. He was five foot eight, but looked shorter because he usually slouched over. As far as his uniform was concerned, his model was General Zachery Taylor from his Mexican War days. Old Zach Taylor seemed to go out of his way to look as unmilitary as possible at all times, and Grant dressed just like him. Most of the time, Grant wore a private soldier's uniform, with his general's stars sewn on the shoulders.

Since March 1864, when President Lincoln made him commander of all the armies of the United States, Grant had three stars on his shoulders. He had more than 500,000 men under his command, but his appearance gave the impression that he was just an ordinary private. Like Taylor, Grant did not look like anybody's idea of a general.

He certainly did not look like any of his predecessors. He was not bombastic like Joe Hooker or dapper like Ambrose Burnside or conceited like George B. McClellan. He was not even very much like the current commander of the Army of the Potomac, the short-tempered Major General George Gordon Meade, who was called a goddamn goggle-eyed snapping turtle by his men. Even though Meade was at least the titular commander of the army, everyone called it Grant's army. Meade did not particularly like playing second fiddle to the new boy from the West, even if he was the hero of Vicksburg. But there was not very much he could do about it.

Ulysses S. Grant may have had three stars, but he was still "an unmistakable rural Middle Westerner, bearing somehow the air of the little farm and the empty dusty road and the small-town harness shop, plunked down here in an army predominantly officered by polished Easterners."[31] In spite of his three stars, and in spite of being the hero of Vicksburg and Fort Donelson, underneath it all he was still Sam Grant. The years and the numerous battles had taken their toll, and his sister-in-law Emily would not have thought of him as being as pretty as a doll anymore, but he was still basically the same lad who had grown up in Point Pleasant, Ohio, all those years ago.

Some of Grant's men were clearly disappointed by his rough and unpolished appearance, and they probably wished that he would at least make some sort of effort to look the part of a three-star general. When Grant reviewed the Sixth Corps in April 1864, Lieutenant Elisha Hunt Rhodes noted, "General Grant is a short thick set man and rode his horse like a bag of meal."[32] He went on to say, "I was a little disappointed in his appearance, but I like the look in his eye. He was more plainly dressed than any other General on the field." The look in Grant's eye that Rhodes mentioned—not a cold look, but an expression of quiet determination—turned out to be a lot more revealing of who Grant really was than the way he dressed or the way he sat his horse. It would not take very long before the rest of the army found this out for themselves.

But there were a good many people, especially in Congress, who worried about another issue, a subject they considered a lot more vital than Grant's appearance. Many congressmen wondered whether or not Grant would be able to stay sober long enough to exercise the authority that his new third star had given him. Rumors of Grant's drunkenness—or, as some more diplomatic souls put it, his "inordinate desire for stimulants"—had spread throughout the army and beyond.[33] Every soldier in every regiment knew at least two things about U. S. Grant—that he was the hero of Vicksburg and that he drank too much. Everyone in both houses of the US Congress knew the same two things.

There were certainly enough stories—many of which were unfounded—to give Congress cause for anxiety. During the Vicksburg campaign in 1863, a report began to circulate that General Grant had been "drinking heavily" and had become "stupid in speech and staggering in gait" as a result.[34] Another story got out about a fellow officer who had found several bottles of whisky in Grant's room and threw them out the window—much to Grant's considerable annoyance. Whether these tales of the bottle were true or not, there were enough of them to make senators and representatives wonder if Grant should be trusted with three stars.

Actually, the rumor mills and the tale-tellers were making the problem a lot worse than it really was. Although U. S. Grant was anything but a teetotaler, he was no falling-down drunk, either. Grant only drank to excess when he was bored. Life on an army post, or during the siege of Vicksburg, became tedious beyond endurance— beyond Grant's endurance anyway. Drinking gave him something to do besides think about when General John C. Pemberton, the Confederate commander, was finally going to surrender.

In spite of all the stories and all the gossip, Congress decided to award Grant his third star in March 1864, eight months after General Pemberton surrendered Vicksburg to him. President Lincoln heard all the stories about Grant's drinking as well, but he just laughed them off. Lincoln's reaction to all the gossip resulted in an anecdote that has gone down as one of the best-known legends in the

Lincoln mythology. When one of Grant's detractors—as a bona fide war hero, Grant had more than his share of critics and detractors—complained that he had a drinking problem, Lincoln allegedly told the complainer to find out exactly what brand of whisky Grant drank and to send all his other generals a barrel of it.[35]

The men of the Army of the Potomac were not all that interested in how much whisky the new lieutenant general drank, let alone what brand. But they were terribly concerned about something else—what would Grant do when he met Robert E. Lee?

Veterans of Antietam/Sharpsburg, Chancellorsville, Fredericksburg, and Gettysburg did not have a very high opinion of the war in the West, or of the men who were fighting it. As far as most of the Army of the Potomac were concerned, Shiloh and Fort Donelson, and even Vicksburg, were only glorified sideshows compared with the battles they had been fighting in Virginia. Easterners refused to be impressed by Grant's success in these battles. The real war was in the East, in Virginia.

The men were curious about Grant, and did not hold anything against him, but they had their doubts. "Who is this Grant that's made a lieutenant general?" a soldier of one regiment asked.

"He's the hero of Vicksburg," his companion answered.

"Well, Vicksburg wasn't much of a fight. The rebels were out of rations and they had to surrender or starve."

Another soldier piped up that Grant never would have trapped Lee the way he cornered General Pemberton. Lee would have sent Longstreet and Jeb Stuart out to find supplies somewhere, and he would have fought his way out of Vicksburg somehow. Old Bobby Lee was too damn smart to get himself trapped the way Pemberton did.[36]

This attitude was not surprising. Robert E. Lee had totally dominated the Army of the Potomac, from its commanding general down to every private in the ranks, ever since he took command of the Army of Northern Virginia. Whenever the two armies met, the Union forces had only one plan: "hold on if we can, wait and see what Lee is going to do, and then try to stop him."[37] There was rarely any thought of taking the initiative against Lee. Just holding on against Lee the magician was triumph enough all by itself.

Grant was about to change this way of thinking. But nobody knew that, at least not yet. Whenever anyone mentioned Grant's war record in the West, the men from Maine and Ohio and New Jersey refused to be convinced. "Well," a wary veteran said to one of Grant's men, "you never met Bobby Lee and his boys; it would be quite different if you had."[38]

But Grant *had* met Lee. He met him in Mexico, eighteen years before, and remembered him well. Even though Grant had been in Tennessee and Mississippi in 1862 and 1863, when Lee was acquiring his reputation as the bogey man of the Army of the Potomac, Grant was fully aware of what was taking place in Virginia at the time. Lee had used the tactics of movement and maneuver to get the better of several Union commanders, which were tactics he had learned from General Winfield Scott in Mexico. Under Scott's command, the American army had gone around General Santa Anna's flank at Cerro Gordo, forcing the Mexican forces to retreat. Lee had applied these same tactics against Joe Hooker's army at Chancellorsville sixteen years later, with the same result.

Grant had been at Cerro Gordo, as well, spotting artillery fire for Lieutenant George B. McClellan. Winfield Scott's tactics were as familiar to him as they were to Lee. He planned to use these tactics against Lee in Virginia, to take the war to Lee and his army and to stay on the offensive, just as Winfield Scott had done in his drive against Mexico City. He was also determined that he would not give Lee the chance to outmaneuver *him*, or to execute another Chancellorsville against him. Even though he had not faced Lee in battle yet, he had met Bobby Lee and knew what to expect from him.

THAT MAN WILL FIGHT US

Robert E. Lee was fully aware that General Grant was now general-in-chief of all US forces. His spies in the North had told him; so had the Northern press. Every newspaper between Maine and Michigan let the entire country know that Grant was now a three-star general. The *New York Times* was straightforward about the appointment: "GEN. GRANT IN COMMAND: Gen. GRANT formally assumed the command of the armies of the United States to-day."[39] Copies of the *New York Times* and dozens of other Northern newspapers found their way south to Richmond and points beyond. Northern papers were one of the best sources of information for Confederate intelligence agents; papers like the *New York Times* and the *World* gave information that was up-to-date and usually accurate. General Lee himself was known to devour every Northern newspaper he could get his hands on. He would have known all about General Grant and his new appointment, and only a day or two after readers in New York scanned the same headlines over their morning coffee.

General Lee may not have remembered U. S. Grant at all, not even what he looked like, but he did know Grant by reputation. He knew all about Vicksburg and Fort Donelson and Shiloh. In a conversation with his adjutant, Walter H. Taylor, he tried not to seem overly concerned about his new adversary: "Colonel, we have got to whip them; we must whip them, and it has already made me feel better to think of it."[40]

Colonel Taylor was in full agreement with the general. In Taylor's considered opinion, U. S. Grant was nothing but a shabby little man with an overblown reputation who did not belong on the same field of battle with Robert E. Lee. Taylor sarcastically referred to Grant as "the present idol of the North" and left no doubt that "Grant's Army" would be demolished by Lee—"we will defeat their last great effort & make this the last year of *serious* fighting."[41]

Colonel Taylor's opinion of the hero of Vicksburg sounds very much like that of the cynical Army of the Potomac: "He has been much overrated and in my opinion, I am sorry to say, owes much of his reputation to Gen'l Pemberton's bad management than to his own sagacity & ability," Taylor said.[42] He also reflected the Army of the Potomac's feelings of Grant's future against General Lee: "He will find, I trust, that General Lee is a very different man to deal with & if I mistake not will shortly come to grief if he attempts to repeat the tactics in Virginia which proved so successful in Mississippi."

But Colonel Taylor's opinions were frequently anything but unbiased and reliable. He also thought that Pickett's charge at Gettysburg was "the handsomest of the war as far as my experience goes," that the Confederate army was "not much affected by this repulse," and that the Union forces under General Meade "retired from Gettys-burg before we did and only claimed a victory after they had discov-ered our departure."[43]

A good many soldiers in the Army of Northern Virginia besides Colonel Taylor had a low opinion of U. S. Grant in the spring of 1864. Shortly after Grant had been appointed general-in-chief, General James Longstreet overheard an officer predicting that the "western general" would be easily routed when he came up against Robert E. Lee. Longstreet emphatically did not agree.[44]

"Do you know Grant?" Longstreet asked.

"No," came the reply.

"Well, I do," the General continued. "I was in the corps of cadets with him for three years, I was present at his wedding, I served in the same army with him in Mexico, I have observed his methods of warfare in the West, and I believe I know him through and through; and I tell you that we cannot afford to underrate him and the army he commands."

Having said this, Longstreet went on to make his point. "We must make up our minds to get into line of battle and to stay there; for that man will fight us every day and every hour till the end of the war. In order to whip him we must outmaneuver him and husband our strength as best we can."

General Lee had his own share of anxieties concerning the new three-star general. In a letter to Confederate president Jefferson Davis in March 1864, Lee confided his thoughts on the fighting that was to come. He wrote, "The indications that operations in Virginia will be vigorously prosecuted by the enemy are stronger than they were."[45] Lee then went on to say exactly why the indications were stronger: "General Grant has returned from the army in the West. He is, at present, with the Army of the Potomac, which is being orga-nized and recruited." President Davis was well aware that Grant was in Virginia—he read the Northern newspapers as well—but Lee wanted to make sure that Davis was aware of his own thoughts on the new general.

During the spring of 1864, Lee's thoughts certainly were cen-tered upon the fact that Grant had taken command. "I think we can assume that if General Grant is to direct operations in this frontier, he will concentrate a large force on one or more lines, and prudence dictates that we shall make preparations as are in our power."[46]

Lee's worries were even more pronounced when he wrote to his sister: "The indications at present are that we shall have a hard struggle. General Grant is with the Army of the Potomac." From everything he had read and been told about Grant, his new opponent looked to be a lot more determined, and maybe a lot more competent, than any of his predecessors.[47] In another letter to Jefferson Davis, this one dated April 6, Lee expressed another concern. "Reinforcements are certainly daily arriving to the Army of the Potomac. . . . The tone of the Northern papers, as well as the impression prevailing in their armies, go to show that Grant with a large force is to move against Richmond."[48]

Lee was all wrong about this. Grant had no intention of moving against Richmond. There had already been too many failed "On to Richmond!" drives to suit him, beginning with George B. McClellan's disaster in 1862, and he was not about to attempt another one. Grant's target was to be the Army of Northern Virginia itself—he knew that if he destroyed Lee's army, Richmond would surrender soon afterward.

Lee never quite understood this. Someone once said that Lee developed a crick in his neck from constantly looking over his shoulder at Richmond, which is a perfect example of a true word being spoken in jest. His only real strategy was to defend Richmond against an attack that Grant had no intention of making. Later on in the war, William Tecumseh Sherman became concerned that Lee might turn south and attack his army, or at least send a large part of it to the Carolinas to reinforce Joseph E. Johnston's Army of Tennessee. If Lee did this, Sherman feared that the combined forces of Lee and Johnston could very well defeat him and then turn north against Grant. Sherman would write, "If Lee is a soldier of genius, he will seek to transfer his army from Richmond to Raleigh or Columbia; if he is a man simply of detail, he will remain where he is, and his speedy defeat is sure."[49] Lee would decide to remain where he was out of a sense of duty, which was one of his father's influences.

As the winter weather moderated, and the roads dried up and could once again be used by both armies as avenues for attack and retreat,

General Lee began making plans for the fighting he knew had to come. Along with the complications stemming from tactics and strategy and troop movements, he also had to concern himself with the issue of supplies and provisions. "My anxiety on the subject of provisions for the army is so great that I cannot refrain from expressing it to Your Excellency," Lee wrote to Jefferson Davis on April 12, 1864. "I cannot see how we can operate with our present supplies."[50]

Lee's would have two constant worries throughout the coming months: keeping his army supplied and U. S. Grant. Neither worry ever went away. The first problem, having enough food and ammunition and supplies to sustain the army, he always managed to resolve somehow. The men never had enough to eat—not enough to suit them, anyway—but they always had enough to keep fighting.

But Lee never solved the problem that was Lieutenant General U. S. Grant. Grant was always there: pounding and harassing and trying to get around his flank. He never gave up and never retreated, as his predecessors had done, not even when common sense would seem to dictate that he take his army back above the Rapidan River for resting and reorganizing.

Lee would learn that Grant was nothing like Ambrose Burnside, Joseph Hooker, George B. McClellan, or any of the other generals he had faced since 1862. But he would never really understand Grant. The patrician from Virginia would never quite fathom the rumpled, round-shouldered man from Ohio.

Chapter Three

NO TURNING BACK

MATTERS OF CONFIDENCE

While Colonel Orville Babcock was riding off toward the Confederate lines with General Grant's letter to General Lee, Grant and his party rode after him at a more relaxed pace—if anyone can be said to have been relaxed on that particular morning. General Philip Sheridan was anything but relaxed when Colonel Babcock came across him on his way through the lines. Sheridan paced back and forth, all nerves and anxiety. He had been informed of the impending surrender meeting between Grant and Lee, but he refused to be impressed by Lee or his offer. In fact, it was the news of the meeting that triggered Sheridan's case of galloping nerves that morning.

"Damn them, I wish they had held out for an hour longer and I would have whipped hell out of them," he grumbled at Colonel Babcock.[1] Sheridan did not want to discuss surrender terms with the rebels. He wanted to kill them, every damn one of them.

After Babcock rode off with Grant's letter, Grant's military secretary, Adam Badeau, followed closely behind. He ran into Sheridan as well, and he also had the unpleasant experience of receiving an earful from the irate general. Sheridan did not trust any of the rebels, including Robert E. Lee, and strongly suspected that all the talk about surrendering was nothing but a hoax designed to let Lee get away. "What do you think? What do you know?" he shouted at an alarmed Badeau. "Is it a trick? Is Lee negotiating with Grant? I've got 'em—I've got 'em like that!" he said, shaking his fist in Badeau's astonished face.

General Grant himself dropped by to see Sheridan shortly after-ward. He found Sheridan's men drawn up in line of battle, facing the Confederates, ready to whip hell out of them. They all shared Phil Sheridan's opinion of Lee and his offer to surrender: that the whole thing was a trick. "They said they believed that Johnston was marching up from North Carolina now, and Lee was moving to join him; and they would whip the rebels where they now were in five minutes, if I would only let them go in," Grant said.[2]

But Grant was confident that Lee was not trying to pull some sort of trick. Lee had already tried to get around the word "surrender" by suggesting a discussion of overall peace terms, which might have been an attempt at trying to trick Grant. It was probably just an attempt at postponing the inevitable. When Grant flatly rejected that notion, Lee realized that he had reached the end. Grant had no doubts that Lee's offer to surrender was genuine.

In spite of what Phil Sheridan had in mind, Grant did not want another pitched battle with Lee. Only a few weeks before, aboard the presidential steamer *River Queen*, President Lincoln had advised Grant, as well as General William T. Sherman and Admiral David Porter, of his hopes for the rest of the war. He wanted to destroy the Confederacy's ability to fight, he said, but he did not want to destroy the South. All Lincoln really wanted was for the seceded states to rejoin the Union. The end of the war seemed to be at hand, the Con-federate armies were on the verge of collapse—at least, that is what his generals were saying—and Lincoln wanted to avoid any more fighting and killing if it could be avoided. "Let 'em up easy," is the way Lincoln put it.[3]

Grant was in full agreement. As far as he was concerned, the fighting had gone on long enough. He wanted to end the war as soon as possible—today, if possible. He wanted to believe Lee's most recent communiqué, and he had confidence that it was not a trick.

Grant had as much confidence in Lincoln as President Lincoln had in him, which was a great deal. If it had not been for Lincoln, Grant knew that he would never have been appointed general-in-chief. Every one of Grant's predecessors—Hooker, Burnside, and especially McClellan, who was so convinced of his own genius—would have loved to have worn three stars on his shoulders. But Grant was the only general that Lincoln knew he could count on, who had the nerve and the grit to see the war through to the end.

Actually, Lincoln had entertained one doubt, one very disturbing doubt, but it had nothing to do with Grant's abilities as a general. During the summer of 1864, General Grant had been prominently mentioned as Lincoln's rival for president. Newspapers throughout the country were running editorials backing Grant. "Grant, the people's candidate," ran the New York *Herald*'s endorsement.[4] At the National Union Party's convention—the Republicans were calling themselves the National Union Party to accommodate the War Democrats who supported Lincoln's war aims—the Missouri delegation cast its twenty-two votes for U. S. Grant. (They later changed their minds and voted for Lincoln.) There had also been talk of dismissing Lincoln entirely and nominating Grant as the National Union candidate—Grant for president and either Admiral David G. Farragut or General William T. Sherman for vice president.

Lincoln heard all the talk about Grant for President and knew that Grant had the popular support—as well as some backing from the Republican Party—to derail his chances for reelection. The Democrats had nominated George B. McClellan as their candidate, and a good many Republicans wanted a general, as well. But General Grant also heard the talk, and he was almost as upset by all the gossip and rumors as Lincoln. He wrote to his old friend J. Russell Jones that he already had "a pretty big job" on his hands and wanted nothing to do with being president. In his letter, Grant said that he "could not possibly entertain the thought of becoming a candidate for the office, nor of accepting the nomination were it tendered him, so long as there was a possibility of keeping Mr. Lincoln in the presidential chair."[5]

Abraham Lincoln was a professional politician. In common with all politicians, he had two main goals in life: his first goal was getting elected, and his second goal was staying elected. Grant looked like somebody who might beat him out of staying elected, and Lincoln was not happy about it. He made up his mind to find out everything he could concerning U. S. Grant's political ambitions.

One of the people he questioned regarding Grant was Illinois congressman Elihu B. Washburne, who represented Grant's district of Galena and knew Grant personally. But when Congressman Washburne admitted that had no idea concerning U. S. Grant's thoughts on running for president, Lincoln asked if he knew of anyone else who might. Washburne suggested that he get in touch with J. Russell Jones, since Jones had also known Grant for years. Lincoln took the suggestion and lost no time in asking Mr. Jones to come to the White House for a private conversation.

Lincoln could not have invited a more reliable source on the subject. When Lincoln asked about Grant's ambitions, Jones knew exactly what he meant. He took Grant's "pretty big job" letter out of his pocket and handed it to the president. As soon as Lincoln read what Grant had to say about being a presidential candidate, Lincoln's mind was instantly put at ease. "My son, you will never know how gratifying that is to me," he said to Jones. "No man knows, when the presidential grub gets to gnawing at him, just how deep it will get until he has tried it; and I didn't know but what there was one gnawing at Grant."[6]

According to Grant, he had only one political ambition. "I aspire only to one political office," he said, tongue in cheek. "When this war is over, I mean to run for Mayor of Galena [his place of residence] and, if elected, I intend to have the sidewalk fixed up between my house and the depot."[7] He would eventually allow himself to be infected with White House fever and would accept the Republican nomination for president. But that would not happen for another four years. By that time Lincoln would be gone, and it would be a different world.

Now that his mind was at rest on the topic of Grant and the White House, President Lincoln was prepared to appoint General Grant to the rank of lieutenant general. Grant arrived in Washington to accept the commission on March 8, 1864, accompanied by his thirteen-year-old son, Fred. As usual, he looked rumpled, disheveled, nothing at all like the impending general-in-chief of all Union armies. Someone said that he looked like an Illinois wheat farmer who had come to town to cash a check. Nobody paid much attention to him—until they found out who he was.

The desk clerk at the Willard Hotel, which was Washington's premier hotel, consigned Grant and his son to a room on the top floor until he saw the general's name on the register. After regaining his composure, the clerk gave the Grants the best suite in the house. The poor man was understandably taken aback. The usual procedure for a general staying at the Willard was for the great man to be preceded by "a flock of aides who inspected the rooms and ordered the furniture changed around."[8] After all this fuss and display, "the general in full dress uniform would sweep in and disappear upstairs, surrounded by his escort." But this was not Grant's style. "There was none of this swankiness in Grant's behaviour."

A short while after Grant and his son disappeared upstairs to rest and relax for a while, they reappeared downstairs for dinner. It would not be an enjoyable meal. "A crowd formed around him," reported an onlooker, "men looked, stared at him."[9] Fred Grant remembered that somebody in the dining room stood up, hammered on the table with his knife to get everyone's attention, and announced that Lieutenant General Grant was now among them. Following this, pandemonium broke loose on a general scale. Diners lurched to their feet to get a better look at the general; people began chanting "Grant! Grant! Grant!" and someone else called for three cheers.

Some generals would have enjoyed all of this noise and attention. George B. McClellan, for instance, probably would have thought that he had it coming to him. But General Grant was embarrassed by the whole affair. He stood up and bowed, acknowledging the crowd, and tried his best to carry on as if nothing had happened. People were not prepared to leave him alone, though—they had a real, live celebrity in their presence and wanted to take full advantage of the situation. After a while, the two Grants went back up to their suite, probably wishing that they had ordered dinner in their room.

But Grant's evening was still far from over. Shortly after making his tactical retreat from the Willard's dining room, someone knocked at his door—former Secretary of War Simon Cameron, according to one account, Pennsylvania Congressman James K. Moorehead, according to another. Whoever it was informed Grant that a reception was in progress over at the White House and that it had been suggested that Grant might make an appearance—loosely translated, this meant that President Lincoln expected Grant to show up at his reception. Grant took the hint and set out for the White House, accompanied by his chief of staff, John A. Rawlins, and another member of his staff, Lieutenant Colonel Cyrus B. Comstock.

From what had happened to him in the Willard Hotel's dining room, Grant had a pretty good idea of what was to come. He was right. From the moment he walked into the White House, everybody gawked at him, made comments about his appearance, and moved out of his way as he walked across the room toward President Lincoln—"the crowd parted like the Red Sea waves," according to one account[10]. As Grant approached, the president stepped forward to welcome his obviously ill at ease guest.

Lincoln was no more interested in his appearance than Grant, although Grant had spruced himself up a bit before leaving the hotel. The president clearly had not given very much thought to the way he looked that night, even though he was hosting a formal reception. He came to his party wearing a black suit, which was his usual attire for all occasions, but with a collar that was a size too large for him, and a tie that was a bit too wide and had been tied awkwardly. He had once been described as looking like a boss undertaker. On this particular occasion, the description certainly fit.

Lincoln extended his long, bony hand and grasped Grant's much smaller hand, doing his best to put his guest at ease. "Why, here is General Grant," he exclaimed. "Well, this is a great pleasure, I assure you."[11] Everybody present was treated to the sight of two of the most famous men in the country shaking hands with each other—the Illinois wheat farmer and the boss undertaker.

Lincoln then introduced the general to Secretary of State William H. Seward. After shaking hands, Seward then took Grant off to meet Mary Todd Lincoln, the president's wife, and then escorted him to the East Room, where most of the guests were waiting. Grant's level of discomfort was about to increase exponentially.

The crowd let loose with a roar as soon as General Grant walked into the room. They shouted and cheered and clapped; some tried to do all three things at the same time. Men and women alike wanted to touch him and shake his hand. Grant was blushing like a schoolgirl, according to one onlooker. Major General U. S. Grant, the hero of Vicksburg and Fort Donelson, had reverted to Lieutenant Sam Grant, newly graduated from West Point and still smelling of his father's tannery in Ohio. He later said that he felt more pressure that night in the East Room than he ever felt in any battle.

"Stand up so we can all have a look at you!" someone shouted.[12] So Grant stood on a sofa, and everybody had a good look at him. Some people stood on tables, so that they could get an even better look at him. Lincoln took in the entire spectacle with a smile on his face, clearly enjoying himself. His guest of honor was just as clearly hating every second of what he was going through.

"It was the only real mob I ever saw at the White House," reporter Noah Brooks wrote. "For once at least the President of the United States was not the central figure in the picture. The little scared-looking man who stood on a crimson covered sofa was the idol of the hour."[13] He stood there for the better part of an hour before he was rescued from the mob and spirited into the Blue Room for a short meeting with the president and Secretary of War Edwin M. Stanton.

Lincoln instructed Grant to come back to the White House on the following day, when he would be formally presented with his commission as lieutenant general. It would be a small ceremony, nothing elaborate. Lincoln would make a short presentation speech. Grant, in turn, would say a few words of acceptance.

The president gave Grant a copy of what he was going to say—just a few lines, formal but to the point, designed to get the job done. He started out by saying that the nation's "appreciation of what you have done," along with "its reliance upon you for what remains to do," now combined in the presentation of this commission, "constituting you Lieutenant General in the Army of the United States."[14] The high honor brought with it a corresponding responsibility, the president continued. "As the country herein trusts you, so, under God, it will sustain you." Lincoln closed by saying that his own "hearty personal concurrence" accompanied the country's trust and sustenance.

Grant put the president's remarks in his inside coat pocket. Before he left, Lincoln had a few parting words on the subject of what he would like the general to include in his own speech of acceptance. He asked Grant to say something that would help to prevent any jealousy from other generals and also wanted some sort of mention "which shall put you on as good terms as possible with the Army of the Potomac"—and, presumably, with its commanding general,

George Gordon Meade.[15] Grant listened to the president, said good night, and went back to the Willard Hotel.

The White House was a very different place when Grant returned to it on the following afternoon. The crowd had disappeared, and the near hysteria of the night before had been replaced by a quiet, businesslike atmosphere. When Grant was admitted to the Executive Mansion at around one o'clock on March 9, accompanied by his son Fred and by John Rawlins, they were met by the president, members of his cabinet, and General Henry W. Halleck. Also present were a number of reporters, on hand to record the words of Lincoln and Grant for posterity.

As soon as all the hand shaking and formalities were out of the way, the general and the president took their places. President Lincoln spoke first, reading his remarks about the nation's appreciation of General Grant's accomplishments, along with his own hearty personal concurrence, in presenting the commission of lieutenant general to General Grant.

Lincoln's little speech lasted only a minute or so. When he finished, Grant faced the small gathering to deliver his own speech. He had written it in pencil, and it consisted of only three sentences.

"Mr. President," he began, "I accept this commission with gratitude for the high honor conferred. With the aid of the noble armies that have fought on so many fields for our common country, it will be my earnest endeavor not to disappoint your expectations. I feel the full weight of the responsibilities now devolving on me and know that if they are met it will be due to those armies, and above all to the favor of that Providence which leads both Nations and men."[16]

Grant did not like making speeches, especially not in front of the president of the United States and members of the press, and it certainly showed. He had jotted down his remarks very quickly the night before, when he was still recovering from the presidential reception, and had trouble reading his own handwriting. This only added to his embarrassment. Lincoln's secretary, John Nicolay, could see how embarrassed Grant really was.

It was actually Lieutenant Sam Grant who read the three sentences, the same Sam Grant who had blushed like a schoolgirl in the East Room the night before. He had only one thought regarding the speech—deliver it as quickly as possible and get it over with. The first sentence was so rushed that those present had trouble understanding what Grant was saying. After this rough start, he took a deep breath, gripped the paper with both hands, and ploughed ahead until he was finished.

When he finished rambling through his speech, and the ceremony was finally over, Ulysses S. Grant was officially general-in-chief of the US Army. He had not mentioned either point that Lincoln had requested, but no one seemed to notice. The jealousy of other generals would not concern Grant very much in the months to come, and he would find himself on excellent terms with the Army of the Potomac and with General Meade as soon as Meade and his army got to know Grant.

Shortly after receiving his third star, Grant did have a minor dispute with Secretary of War Stanton. The new general-in-chief had taken a good many of the troops that had been manning the defenses of Washington, DC, and turned them into infantry. Grant reasoned that the men were not accomplishing anything useful or constructive by hanging around Washington, and he would be needing all the men he could find in the coming fight against Lee and his army. Secretary Stanton did not see it that way at all. As far as he was concerned, Grant was taking vitally needed troops away from the capitol, leaving it vulnerable to attack.

The two men could not agree until Stanton announced that he was going to see the president regarding the matter. Grant was all in favor of taking the problem up with Lincoln. "That is right," Grant said. "The President ranks us both."[17] When they reached the White House, Stanton complained that Grant had exceeded his authority when he took the garrison troops out of Washington. Grant did not have anything to say on the subject. When Lincoln asked him to state his case, Grant told the president that he had no case to state.

Since Grant would not state his case, President Lincoln stated it for him. "Now, Mr. Secretary, you know we have been trying to manage this army for nearly three years, and you know we have not done much with it," he said. "We sent over the mountains and brought Mr. Grant, as Mrs. Grant calls him, to manage it for us; and now I guess we'd better let Mr. Grant have his own way."[18]

And that was that. Lincoln had enough confidence in Grant to let him run the army his way. If General Grant said that he needed the Washington garrison troops for the coming fight against Lee, that was good enough for him. Grant was Lincoln's general-in-chief, and he would continue to stand by him throughout the horrific months to come.

THE BIG SKEDADDLE

> ENEMY HAS STRUCK HIS TENTS. INFANTRY, ARTILLERY AND CAVALRY ARE MOVING TOWARD GERMANNA AND ELY'S FORDS.

General Lee sent this telegram to General Braxton Bragg on May 4, 1864. Later on the same day, he wrote to President Jefferson Davis, "You will already have learned that the army of Genl Meade is in motion, and is crossing the Rapidan on our right."[19]

The fact that the Army of the Potomac was on the move was certainly no secret. Thousands of wagons, and many more thousands of men, were heading south along unpaved roads, raising a cloud of dust that was visible for miles. Lookouts at the signal station on Clark's Mountain saw the dust—nobody for miles around could miss it—and spread the word with their signal flags: the enemy was on the move. Lee knew that Grant was coming by midmorning on May 4 and immediately began making plans of his own.

Lee had climbed up on the Clark's Mountain observation post himself only two days before and had taken his own look at the enemy on the other side of the Rapidan River. There seemed to be no end to their tents, which stretched as far as the eye could see. He told the officers who had come up with him that the enemy would be crossing the river at either the Ely or the Germanna crossing—"the fords that led into the Wilderness, where the ghost of 'Stonewall' Jackson walked."[20] In the coming weeks and months, General Lee would miss Stonewall more than he ever could have realized.

General Lee had a total of between 61,000 and 65,000 men to meet Grant's threat—although he usually referred to the Union forces as "Meade's army"—but these were scattered over "a large territory" across northern Virginia.[21] He ordered all of these units, including Braxton Bragg's division, to begin moving north toward the Germanna and Ely's crossings of the Rapidan River. Lee realized that it was going to take a while to move all of these troops into position.

It looked as though the enemy would be making its advance through the Wilderness, not far from the Chancellorsville battle-field of a year before, which fit right into General Lee's plans—the enemy's superior numbers would not matter as much if they were all tangled up in the dense underbrush and sapling trees of the Wilder-ness, which would give Lee a decided edge. The undergrowth was so dense that men could not see more than a hundred feet ahead, and usually less than that. Enemy troops could not be seen until they were almost in contact, and artillery was usually rendered useless at such short ranges. Also, there were not enough Confederate troops near the Rapidan to confront Grant as he crossed the river. Lee would not be able to attack Grant until General Longstreet's two divisions came up from the south.

"The Wilderness is a forest land about fifteen miles square," as described by General Longstreet, "lying between and equidistant from Orange Court-House and Fredericksburg."[22] This might be a nice enough physical description, but it does not even come close to describing what the Wilderness meant to the men who would fight there during the next few days. The Wilderness was a gloomy, ominous tangle of vines and brambles and underbrush. "The Confederates knew the region thoroughly. Where the roads led to, where the water was, where the natural line of defense was," a volunteer from New York reflected. "We knew nothing."[23] It was a spooky and disturbing place for both sides, but especially for the Northern troops.

The Union forces spent the night camped on the Chancellors-ville battleground, where more than three thousand men had been killed in May 1863. During the past year, rain had washed away the soil that covered the bodies of both the Union and Confederate dead that had been buried on the field, leaving the remains of the decayed corpses in full view. "The dead were all around us," one soldier recalled, "their eyeless skulls seemed to stare steadily at us." A soldier dug into a shallow grave with his bayonet and rolled a skull across the ground, saying, "This is what you are coming to, and some of you will start toward it tomorrow."[24]

General Lee was not troubled by the fact that the coming battle would be fought where so many men had been killed a year ago. If anything, it made him even more confident about his prospects. For one thing, having fought a major battle there gave him firsthand knowledge of the area. The ground was totally unfamiliar to Grant, who had still been at Vicksburg in May 1863. This would give Lee another advantage.

On the morning of May 5, General Lee was in the best of spirits. He made a few jokes at the expense of some of his staff officers during breakfast, which offended no one, and carried on with light conversation throughout the meal. In the course of the morning's conversation, Lee said that he was surprised that Grant had placed himself in the same predicament as Mr. F. J. Hooker had the previous spring. "He hoped the result would be even more disastrous than that which Hooker had experienced."[25]

Lee's instructions—officially worded suggestions is more like it— were that he preferred no general engagement to be started until General Longstreet's divisions arrived. But battles do not always go as planned. In spite of General Lee's directive, heavy firing was heard at around noon. An hour or so earlier, Federal troops had been spotted moving southeast; it looked as though they were trying to turn the Confederate right flank. No one, including Lee himself, could tell exactly what was going on. "The woods were so thick that the enemy could scarcely be seen at all," according to one account, "but the volume of his fire showed that he was in great strength."[26]

The full-scale battle that Lee had tried to avoid had started, whether he liked it or not. The two sides went at each other in dozens of separate fights. The two armies shot and stabbed and clubbed each other, but it was not a battle so much as an enormous brawl. No one had any sense of direction inside the maze of underbrush and brambles. Men sometimes fired on other men in the same regiment, not able to tell friend from foe in the tangle of trees and vines. "At times we could not see the Confederate line, but that made no difference; we kept on firing just as though they were in full view," one veteran remembered.[27]

General Lee had been riding in front of Henry Heth's division, along with A. P. Hill and General James Ewell Brown "Jeb" Stuart, his renowned cavalry commander, as confused as everybody else and still trying to determine exactly what was going on inside the impenetrable jumble of woods. All three officers dismounted near the farmhouse of a widow named Mrs. Catherine Tapp to hold an impromptu staff conference. They climbed down from their horses and were sitting under a shade tree to discuss the developing battle when a group of Northern skirmishers walked into the little clearing from behind a line of pine trees.

It would be difficult to say who was the most surprised, the Northern infantrymen or the Confederate officers. After gawking at each other for a moment, the three officers stood up. General Lee walked off, calling for his adjutant Colonel Taylor. A. P. Hill stayed where he was and stared at the intruders. Jeb Stuart stood still for a minute and then began walking toward the startled soldiers.

The Federals blinked, then backed into the pine trees and disappeared. None of them recognized the commanding general of the Army of Northern Virginia. Their only thought was that they had somehow wandered into the Confederate lines, and their most immediate impulse was to get away before they were either killed or captured. General Lee has been praised endlessly for his brilliance, for his genius, and for his audacity. On May 5, 1864, he was just plain lucky, which is probably the most valuable attribute of all. It can only be speculated what would have happened to the Confederate war effort, and to the war itself, if the Union soldiers had either shot Lee and his companions or had taken them prisoner.

By this time, which was after noon, two Union attacks had already been beaten back. General Gouverneur K. Warren's Fifth Corps had advanced against Richard S. "Baldy" Ewell's Second Corps but had to fall back in the face of a determined Confederate counterattack. A short distance to the south, along the Orange Plank Road, General Winfield Scott Hancock's Second Corps did not fare any better. The Federals fought to advance against General A. P. Hill's Third Corps from about four p.m. until nightfall, but for all their effort they were not able to gain much of an advantage.

A third and a fourth attack were also made during the afternoon of May 5, and a fifth charge was made against the extreme Confederate right just before sundown. General Lee was alarmed by the number and the ferocity of the attacks and wondered just how many times they could be driven back. He sent an urgent message to General Longstreet, who was still coming up from the south. It amounted to "come as quickly as you can." Without Longstreet's reinforcements, Lee doubted that his men could hold out much longer. He summed up the day in a single sentence: "The assaults were heavy and desperate," he said, "but every one was repulsed."[28]

Darkness finally put a stop to the fighting on May 5, but both armies stayed alert and tense all through the night. Wounded men who were stranded between the lines had to be left where they were. Any movement at all, including attempts to rescue the injured, drew nervous volleys of musket fire.

General Lee did not get very much sleep that night, either. He had plans for an attack in the morning, but he received word that Longstreet and his First Corps would not arrive until daylight. This was not good news. Lee was hoping that Longstreet would reach the lines long before that, so that he would be in position to move against the Union forces at dawn. He resigned himself to the situation, went to bed, and slept a restless four hours. Anxiety over the next day's activities did not help to put him at ease, and he had to get up before sunrise to get ready for what was to come.

General Lee had good reason to be anxious. Federal troops did not lose any time in renewing their attacks as soon as the sun came up. The firing began on a small scale but gradually rose to a steady rattle and then to a persistent cacophony. One soldier said that "the Confederate fire resembled the fury of hell in intensity, and was deadly accurate. Their bullets swished by in swarms."[29]

The Federals threw their full weight against the Confederate line until it broke. General Lee rode out and tried his best to rally the retreating soldiers, who were running down the road and across the fields. He was completely taken aback by the sight of the retreating men. "My God, General McGowan," he shouted to their commanding officer, "is this the splendid brigade of yours running like a flock of geese?"[30]

General McGowan was not flustered by the question. "General, these men are not whipped," he answered. "They only want a place to form, and they will fight as well as ever," In other words, they were not retreating, just heading to the rear to regroup. But they kept on running.

As Lee was watching McGowan's men run away, another group of men came running in the opposite direction, right through McGowan's refugees. This was the advance unit of John Bell Hood's Texas Brigade, now under the command of Brigadier General John Gregg. Sometimes referred to as shock troops, the Texas Brigade was also known somewhat romantically as the Grenadier Guard of the Confederacy. The Texans were the lead brigade of General Longstreet's First Corps. Longstreet had arrived, at long last.

"Who are you, my boys?" Lee asked as they ran past him.

"Texas boys," they shouted back.

With that, Lee lost control of himself. "Hurrah for Texas!" he shouted, waving his hat. "Hurrah for Texas!"[31] He did everything but jump up and down with excitement, not caring at all about the spectacle he was making of himself in front of his men. Longstreet was here, and Lee was almost hysterical with relief.

No one had ever seen Lee show so much enthusiasm before. "I have often seen General Lee, but never did I see him so excited, so disturbed—never did anxiety or care manifest itself before so plainly upon his countenance," a staff officer wrote. "If I mistake not, he was almost moved to tears." Here was the Marble Man himself, the very personification of detachment and aloofness, carrying on like a schoolboy on holiday.[32]

But his "Hurrah for Texas!" outburst was only the beginning. Lee carried on shouting words of encouragement to the men, who were all around him by this time. "The Texas Brigade has always driven the enemy back, and I expect them to do it again today," is one version of what he said. Someone else remembered hearing, "Texans always move them." This is the version that is most often repeated.[33]

Still carried away by the excitement of the moment, Lee indicated that he intended to lead the new arrivals against the enemy. According to one report, Lee said, "I want to lead the Texans in this charge." Another version quotes him as saying simply, "I will lead you, men." Other accounts give similar versions. Almost all of them include Lee using the word "charge."[34]

When those surrounding Lee saw that he meant what he said,

they were stunned. Lee did not seem to realize that if he carried out his plan he would be putting himself in grave danger. If he were killed in leading the attack, Lee's death would very probably mean the loss of the war—to the Army of Northern Virginia, as well as to most civilians throughout the South, Robert E. Lee *was* the Confederacy. Nobody could replace General Lee. The Texans determined to protect Lee from himself.

The men closest to Lee began shouting, "Go back, go back!" and "We won't go forward until you go back!" Others took up the chorus, "Lee to the rear!" One of the soldiers addressed Lee's horse, Traveller, saying, "Get out of the Wilderness with General Lee, you old loony."[35]

But Lee was not going back. He was determined to charge the enemy in spite of all the shouting. Colonel Charles Venable recalled that a sergeant took Traveller's reins and physically turned the horse around, pointing him toward the rear. Colonel Venable then tried his own method of persuading Lee to remove himself from harm's way. He tactfully advised the general to ride a short distance back to confer with General Longstreet and give him his orders.

Lee finally began to grasp what had been happening all around him—according to one account, he looked like a man coming out of a trance—and rode over to speak with General Longstreet. Longstreet promptly informed Lee that he should go back behind the lines even further.

Longstreet's arrival on the field changed everything. The advancing Union forces were stopped dead by Longstreet's counterattack, which pushed General Winfield Scott Hancock's corps back to their own trenches. General Longstreet rode forward along the Plank Road, toward the fighting, and ran into the men who had just met Hancock's men and sent them running. Some of these men thought that Longstreet and his party were Federal cavalrymen and opened fire on them. Longstreet was shot through the neck.

"I received a severe shock from a minie ball passing through my throat and right shoulder," Longstreet noted somewhat clinically in his memoirs.[36] "The blow lifted me from the saddle, and my right arm dropped to my side, but I settled back to my seat, and started to ride on, when in a minute the flow of blood admonished me that my work was done."

Longstreet lost quite a lot of blood, which made the wound look a lot worse than it really was. General Lee and his staff were shaken when they heard what had happened—Longstreet was the most experienced of Lee's corps commanders, and he was also well-liked by his men. The doctor attending Longstreet said that the injury might not be fatal, but the doctors had said the same thing about Stonewall Jackson, and he had been dead and buried for nearly a year. Jackson had also been shot by friendly fire, during the fighting at Chancellorsville, just four miles up the road. Everyone hoped and prayed that "Old Pete," as Longstreet was affectionately known, would not go the way of Stonewall Jackson.

The doctors got it right this time. Longstreet did not die, but his wound would keep him out of the fighting for five months. General Lee appointed General Richard H. Anderson as Longstreet's immediate replacement to command the First Corps. But Lee would miss his old war horse, as he called Longstreet, in the coming months.

The loss of General Longstreet brought no small amount of demoralization and discouragement to the Confederate forces. Many in the First Corps believed that Longstreet had actually died and that officers were spreading the story that he had only been wounded to raise morale. But there were still several hours of daylight left, and the battle was still not over. The First Corps would have to carry on without their commander.

General Lee shifted his attention to the Federal right flank and ordered an attack by General John B. Gordon's forces. Gordon carried out Lee's order with relish, or "with the impetuous ardor of youth," according to one colorful account. The thirty-three year-old general "swept a mile of the front of Sedgwick's [Sixth] Corps, cut off the Army of the Potomac temporarily from its base across the Rapidan, and captured some 600 prisoners."[37]

The attack had started at around six o'clock, less than an hour before sundown. The coming darkness stopped the advance more effectively than any Federal counterattack could have done. There was no course open to General Gordon other than to take his six hundred prisoners and withdraw before his men became totally lost and disorganized in the blackness of the Wilderness.

Both Lee and Gordon regretted that the attack had not been

made earlier in the day, which almost certainly "would have resulted in a decided disaster to the whole right wing of General Grant's army, if not his entire disorganization," as General Gordon would later lament.[38]

Lee felt the same way: that a golden opportunity had been missed. If only Stonewall Jackson had been there! Jackson would have pushed his divisions forward as soon as he saw the chance. He would not have waited until six o'clock. Richard E. "Baldy" Ewell was the commander of Jackson's old Second Corps, and Lee was very disappointed that Baldy Ewell had missed the opportunity. Not for the first time since Chancellorsville, and not for the last, Stonewall Jackson was conspicuous by his absence.

Throughout the night of May 6–7, the rebels dug trenches and fortifications against the attack they knew would be coming in the morning. By dawn, they had made a very strong and formidable defensive line for themselves. General Lee and everyone in those trenches hoped that Grant would come at them again—they were more than ready for him.

But when morning came, the Union forces had disappeared. There was some scattered firing from forward pickets making contact with each other, but nothing like the fighting of the past two days. By noon, it was clear that General Grant was not going to try making another assault. Jubal Early reported that the Federal troops in his area had abandoned their position. The enemy had pulled out.

The men in the front lines very quickly got the word that the Federals had left their works and were on their way out of the Wilderness—some mysterious grapevine always seems to inform the men in the ranks about such things, long before they are officially told by their officers. This could mean only one thing: Grant was giving up, going back north across the river. As soon as they heard the news, the entire Confederate line let loose with a massed, ear-splitting rebel yell. The shouting ran along the line's entire length. "Again, the shout arose on the right—again, it rushed down upon us from a distance of perhaps two miles," an officer noted. "Men seemed fairly convulsed with the fierce enthusiasm; and I believe that if at that instant the advance of the whole army upon Grant could have been ordered, we should have swept [him] into the very Rappahannock."[39]

So much for "Unconditional Surrender" Grant! He had turned out to be no different from Mr. F. J. Hooker, who skedaddled north across the river only a year before. Or from Ambrose Burnside or George B. McClellan or any of the others. That seemed to be the only thing these Yankee generals were any good at—the big ske-daddle. One whiff of gunpowder and they ran back home with their tails between their legs.

When General Lee received Jubal Early's report, he did not go wild with enthusiasm, but he certainly was intrigued. As understated by one of his biographers, "This was significant news for Lee."[40] A short while later, he received news that was even more significant: Federal cavalry had been spotted on the Brock Road, near Todd's Tavern, a few miles to the south.

If Grant was moving south, it was obvious that he was not retreating toward either the Rapidan or the Rappahannock crossing. Todd's Tavern was a little more than halfway to Spotsylvania Court House, a strategic crossroads on the road south. Lee knew that Spotsylvania was a good place for Grant to be—from Spotsylvania, he would be in a position to drive Confederate forces back toward Richmond. He also received word that Grant's artillery was moving in the direction of Spotsylvania as well.

All indications pointed toward Grant taking his army to Spotsyl-vania, not north across the Rapidan. On May 7, Lee ordered the First Corps to begin moving toward Spotsylvania after dark. The Second and Third Corps, under Generals Ewell and A. P. Hill respectively, would begin traveling south soon afterward, along with Jeb Stuart's cavalry.

Some accounts insist that General Lee's decision to send his army to Spotsylvania was based upon his genius and some sort of ability to read Grant's mind. But there was no mysticism involved. His decision was based upon solid intelligence, which is a lot more reliable than either black magic or clairvoyance.

Everything that Lee had read or been told boiled down to one unavoidable conclusion: Grant was not going to retreat. Up to this point in time, Lee entertained the notion—along with just about every-body else in the Army of Northern Virginia—that U. S. Grant was just like every other Northern general he had faced. He was just beginning to see that this was not even close to being the truth. "Lee did not yet understand Grant as he had McClellan, Burnside, and Hooker, who had always returned to lick their wounds after a sound whipping."[41] As another writer put it, "History was failing to repeat itself."[42]

Joe Hooker might have gone north across the Rapidan after what had happened on May 6 and 7, just as he had done after Chancellorsville, but Grant was not Joe Hooker. Lee did not quite fathom this, at least not yet. But he did grasp the fact that Grant was not going to retreat.

Another item that Lee did not comprehend was that Grant's ultimate goal was not Richmond. Earlier in the war, ages earlier in 1862, Richmond had been George B. McClellan's objective. But the war had changed since 1862.

There had already been too many failed "On to Richmond!" drives, and Grant was not about to attempt another one. His goal in the spring of 1864 was nothing less than the surrender of the Army of Northern Virginia itself. Lee had no idea that *he* was now Grant's primary target. He would continue to defend Richmond, always mindful to put his army between Grant and the Confederate capital, unaware that his opponent's objective had undergone a radical shift.

After Grant pulled his men out of the Wilderness on May 7, there was very little that Lee could do except watch and wait to see what his opponent was going to do next. He had not been painted into a corner, but his celebrated ability to outmaneuver and outflank the enemy, as he had done so brilliantly at Chancellorsville, had been completely nullified. "After the Wilderness," one writer noted, "the offensive was gone from Lee."[43] The initiative had gone over to Grant and would stay with him until the end of the war.

It probably never occurred to Lee, but in the months to come he would be playing General Santa Anna to Grant's Winfield Scott. During the Mexican War, Santa Anna had fought a defensive war against Winfield Scott and had been pushed all the way back to Mexico City. Santa Anna had found out, the hard way, that staying on the defensive was a losing proposition. By backing up steadily all the way from the Gulf Coast to the San Cosme Gate, Santa Anna not only lost Mexico City but also lost the war.

Lee did not realize that he had lost the initiative. As far as he was concerned, he had won the two-day battle in the Wilderness. On the evening of May 6, he informed the Confederate Secretary of War, James A. Seddon, that the enemy had "created some confusion," but that all lost ground had been recovered: "The ground lost was recovered as soon as the fresh troops got into position and the enemy driven back to his original line."[44] Other attacks followed, but "every advance on his part, thanks to a merciful God, has been repulsed." The way things looked to Lee, he had turned back Grant just as effectively as he had routed Joseph Hooker the year before. The only difference was that Grant was still south of the Rapidan and was about to begin moving even deeper into Virginia.

When the men in the ranks discovered that Grant was not retreating after all, that he was not going to execute the big skedaddle, they were disappointed. But they were not depressed. There would be other battles, they could be certain of that, and they would get old Unconditional Surrender Grant next time.

But there was now a note of doubt, which had never been there before. They knew they had given Grant a good whipping, but he refused to give up and go back north. By all accounts, Grant should be in full retreat, just like Joe Hooker. But he was not. Something new had taken place. Everyone could sense that, although they did not know exactly what. When Longstreet's First Corps, now General Anderson's, began walking south on the night of May 7, this was a new and slightly unsettling experience for them.

It was a new experience for General Lee, as well, but he did not dwell on it. He knew that he would have another confrontation with Grant, almost certainly within the next twenty-four hours.

TRUSTING ON GOD AND GENERAL GRANT

Colonel Horace Porter had never seen General Grant looking so resplendent before—"resplendent" was not a word usually connected with the normally untidy Grant. It was May 4, the first day of the campaign against Robert E. Lee and his Army of Northern Virginia—Grant called it the "Grand Campaign"—and he looked as though he had dressed for the occasion.[45]

Grant had turned himself out in the full-dress uniform of a lieutenant general, which included a frock coat over a blue waistcoat. "He wore a pair of plain top-boots, reaching to his knees," Colonel Porter noted with a hint of disbelief, "and was equipped with a regulation sword, spurs, and sash. On his head was a slouch hat of black felt with a plain gold cord around it."[46] He also wore a pair of dress gloves. Here was Zachary Taylor trying to pass himself off as Winfield Scott. Colonel Porter would not have been more surprised if the general had shown up wearing a top hat, white tie, and patent leather dancing shoes.

Porter was also impressed with the spectacle made by the Army of the Potomac as it made its way past General Grant and his staff, although in a completely different way. "As far as the eye could reach, the troops were wending their way to the front," he rhapsodized, after noting that a sun "as bright as the sun of Austerlitz" lit up the landscape.[47] "Their war banners, bullet-riddled and battle-stained, floated proudly in the morning breeze." He was just as impressed with the look of the men themselves. "The quick elastic step and easy swinging gait of the men, the cheery look upon their faces, and the lusty shouts with which they greeted their new commander as he passed, gave proof of the temper of their metal."

An officer on General George Gordon Meade's staff had thoughts of a different sort. As the army passed by, he wondered how it would look if every man who was to be killed in the fighting to come wore a large badge, some sort of emblem to indicate that he would not be coming back. Considering the number of men who would be lost in the not very distant future, it was just as well that there were no badges.

Elisha Hunt Rhodes, a lieutenant with the Second Rhode Island Volunteers, noted that on May 4, 1864, his unit, along with the rest of the Sixth Corps, left their pleasant winter quarters near Brandy Station at four a.m. After a march of about twenty miles, "in the heat and dust," the men "reached the Rapidan River and crossed to the south bank at Germania [sic] Ford."[48] General Grant himself crossed the Rapidan at Germanna ford a few hours later. He dismounted from his horse, Cincinnati, in front of a deserted farm house, sat down on the front porch, lit one of his ever-present cigars, and watched the Sixth Corps shamble past.

Even though he seemed to be thoroughly cool and collected, Grant was actually struggling to control his nerves. The full-dress uniform and the cigars were part of his attempt to cover up his nervous anxiety. Grant the stoic would never let on how nervous he really was, so he smoked endless cigars to help stay calm and wore a frock coat and sash to show the world that he was cool and confident.

While Grant was sitting on the porch, a courier arrived with the message Grant had been waiting for. It was an intercepted signal from General Richard S. "Baldy" Ewell, the commander of Lee's Second Corps, which began: "We are moving."[49] The dispatch meant that Lee had already put his army in motion and was setting out to block Grant's line of march.

Grant seemed relieved by the news. "That gives us just the information I wanted," he said. "It shows that Lee is drawing out from his position and is pushing across to meet us." He wrote a dispatch of his own to General Ambrose Burnside, commander of the Ninth Corps. "Make forced marches until you reach this place," he said, in his own colloquial manner. "Start your troops now in the rear the moment they can be got off, and require them to make a night march."[50] Now that he had put his own troops in motion, Grant felt a little more at ease.

Grant's plan for confronting Lee was fairly straightforward: move his army of about 116,000 men south through the Wilderness—he had heard about the Wilderness, although he had never actually seen it himself—and meet Lee and his army in the open country beyond. The Wilderness sounded a lot like the Pedregal, from his Mexican War days, with dense underbrush and thorn bushes instead of volcanic rock. From what he had heard of it, the Wilderness also sounded like the worst place in the world to fight a pitched battle. Grant was hoping to get his army in one side of it and out the other as quickly as possible.

Several hours later, after dinner, Grant and General Meade sat in front of a fire made from dried fence rails, talking and smoking cigars. A wind was blowing, and Meade had trouble lighting his. General Grant always carried a flint-and-steel lighter, which was not affected by wind, and offered it to Meade. While the two of them were talking, and trying their best to relax, Grant dictated a message to inform Washington that his crossing of the Rapidan had been a success. General Meade retired to his own headquarters a short time later, and Grant also decided to turn in for the night. Both generals knew that tomorrow would be a long day.

In the morning, General Meade began moving south, into the Wilderness, along the Germanna Road. General Grant had sent him another one of his colloquial messages at around 8:20: "If an opportunity presents itself for pitching into a part of Lee's army, do it without giving time for dispositions."[51] He wanted to pitch into Lee first, if at all possible, before Lee had the chance to pitch into him. A short while after this, he sent a note to General Burnside, telling him to move up as quickly as possible and join with John Sedgewick's Sixth Corps. Having disposed of his paperwork, at least for the time being, Grant hurried off toward the fighting front—he did not want to miss anything.

Nothing much happened until about noon, when the sharp sound of small arms fire disrupted the peace and quiet. "We remained in line until between 3 and 4 o'clock p.m. when we were ordered to advance to the attack," Elisha Hunt Rhodes wrote.[52] The firing from the front was "terrible," killing and wounding men by the hundreds. "The line surged backwards and forwards, now advancing and now retreating until darkness put an end to the carnage." "Blood," 'killing,' and "carnage" are the most repeated words used in reports of the day's fighting.

By the time the shooting began, Grant had found himself a knoll near the Germanna Road, and was carrying on a conversation with General Meade involving troop movements and about the developing battle in general. While they were talking, the fighting intensified and the firing kept getting louder. From the sheer volume of the noise, it was becoming obvious that this was not a small skirmish between forward patrols. It seemed to General Grant that Lee intended to fight a full-scale battle in the depths of the Wilderness, which was exactly where Grant did not want to fight.

As soon as Grant figured out what Lee had in mind, he immediately took action to counter Lee's threat. He ordered General Hancock to bring his Second Corps up as quickly as he could and also issued orders for the Sixth Corps, under General John Sedgwick, to hurry all of his troops into position. If Lee had his heart set on fighting in the middle of that God-forsaken patch of weeds, scrub-pine, and saplings, Grant was not about to disappoint him.

While couriers went pounding off with the new orders, Grant set about to calm his nerves before the battle intensified into the full-blown killing match that it would become. He sat down on a tree stump, lit a cigar, picked up a twig, took out a penknife, and started whittling. He kept whittling and smoking, smoking and whittling—"and would at times walk slowly up and down," according to one version—while he continued to give orders that sent more and more troops into the battle.[53] Outwardly, Grant was still the picture of calm and tranquility, but inside he was a bag of nerves.

"Many men were lying on the ground dead or wounded," Lieutenant Rhodes noted in his diary. "The woods and brush were so thick and dark that the enemy could not be seen, but we knew they were in our front from the terrible fire we received."[54] A cavalryman remembered, "In that almost impenetrable forest it was next to impossible for one regiment to know what was going on among neighbors to the right or the left."[55]

Soldiers on both sides reported that this battle was more confusing and disorientating than any fight they had ever been in before. Firing seemed to come from all sides at the same time. No one could see more than a few feet in front of them. Some units wandered off into the tangle of underbrush, lost their way, headed into the Confederate lines, and were taken prisoner.

The muzzle flashes from countless muskets set fire to the dry leaves on the ground. A rising wind propelled these little fires through the underbrush and stoked them into a major firestorm. The wind also drove the fire toward the wounded who were lying on the ground but were too badly injured to move out of the way. Disabled soldiers from the Fifth Maine Regiment shouted for help as the flames moved toward them. Two soldiers ran forward to pull the unfortunates away from the fire, but they were shot by Confederate troops. A Union general estimated that at least two hundred Federal soldiers were burned to death by the raging fires that day because they were not able to move and not lucky enough to be rescued.

The fighting went on all afternoon. Smoke from the fires was now making it even more difficult to see. Men simply fired in what they hoped was the direction of the enemy. The underbrush tore their clothing, scratched their faces, and tripped them when they walked. One veteran recalled, "The troops were so scattered and disorganized . . . that there was no central discipline to bind the men together."[56] The Wilderness itself was doing as much damage as the enemy.

"The uproar of battle continued through the twilight hours," a Union soldier remembered. "It was eight o'clock before the deadly crackle of musketry died grudgingly away, and the sad shadows of night, like a pall, fell over the dead in these ensanguined thickets."[57] Both sides kept going at each other until it was too dark to see.

General Grant managed to keep up the impression of being calm and composed. All throughout the battle, he whittled and smoked—something like twenty cigars—and issued orders and read dispatches. All day long, he seemed as detached and unconcerned as ever. But when the day ended, and the fighting came to an unwilling stop, Grant's cool demeanor finally cracked.

He gave some last-minute instructions to a few waiting officers, issuing orders that were needed for the next day, and went into his tent. As soon as he was inside the tent, Grant threw himself "face down on his cot" and "gave vent to his feelings."[58] In other, more direct words, the iron General Grant lost control and broke into tears.

As Civil War historian Shelby Foote put it, he "went to his tent, broke down, and cried very hard. Some of the staff members said they'd never seen a man so unstrung." The tension inside him had to break sometime. "Well, he didn't cry until after the battle was over," Foote said, "and he wasn't crying when it began again the next day." After his mini breakdown, Grant felt relieved and unburdened and went back to being his stoic iron self. "It just shows you the tension that he lived with, without letting it affect him," Foote added. Maybe it did not affect his judgment, or his outward expression, but being under that much tension had to take something out of him and exact some sort of toll on his psyche.[59]

General Grant and his entire staff were roused out of their sleep at four o'clock the next morning, May 6, by the arrival of Ambrose Burnside and his Ninth Corps. While Burnside's men clambered along the Germanna Road, moving toward the uncertainty that was waiting for them at the front, Grant's staff indulged in a very quick breakfast. Grant himself had an unusually light meal: he sliced a cucumber, poured some vinegar over it, and washed it all down with a cup of strong army coffee.[60] The meal, and especially the coffee, did not help his already frazzled nerves.

After finishing breakfast, Grant turned his attention to something much more important than food: his daily supply of cigars. His black servant, Bill, brought him two dozen, Grant promptly lit one with his flint-and-steel lighter and stuffed the rest in various pockets. Cigar in mouth, the general walked off toward the nearby knoll where he had spent much of the previous day. It was still only about five o'clock in the morning, but the shooting had already begun by the time Grant reached his knoll. He would be hearing a lot more of it before the day was over.

Winfield Scott Hancock's Second Corps had begun its attack on the rebel lines by five a.m., which was the noise that Grant was hearing, and they pushed the enemy about a mile and a half. But when Longstreet's First Corps arrived, the rebels took the initiative away from the advancing Federal troops and drove Hancock's men back—rolled up his line like a wet blanket, Hancock would later say. General Grant was becoming anxious about Burnside's men, especially over when they would be making their presence known to General Hancock. Hancock needed all the help he could get, and he needed it right away.

Colonel Horace Porter rode over to check on General Burnside and to advise him to "connect with Hancock's right at all hazards."[61] He came across the general sitting at the side of the road, eating lunch out of a "champagne basket." The affable Burnside invited Colonel Porter to join him. Porter immediately accepted, explaining that he was acting upon "the recognized principle of experienced campaigners, who always eat a meal wherever they can get it, not knowing where the next one is going to come from." It was known as the "eating for the future" diet.

After having lunch with General Burnside, Porter rode to the front to check on the progress of the Ninth Corps. What he saw was not encouraging. The men had to fight their way through the Wilderness itself before they could even get close to the enemy. They made the last fifty yards or so of their advance on their hands and knees, groping their way through a pine thicket, before coming face-to-face with Confederates behind a picket fence. Although Burnside's men gave the enemy a fight they would remember, they could not stop Hancock's line from going to pieces. General Hancock did manage to rally his men, form a new line of battle, and drive back a new Confederate advance. But none of this had anything to do with the Ninth Corps. "Burnside made an attack at half past five, but with no important results," as reported by Colonel Horace Porter.[62]

General Grant did not receive very many encouraging reports that day. The next piece of bad news came from the opposite end of the line. Confederate units under John B. Gordon managed to find a soft spot on the extreme right, which was manned by inexperienced New York troops. These men were part of the Sixth Corps, commanded by the indomitable John Sedgwick. General Sedgwick brought up reinforcements and reorganized his section of the line before disaster had the chance to set in. But Gordon's attack scared the hell out of everybody until Sedgwick stepped in and took control of the situation.

Through everything that had happened that day, the reports regarding Hancock and Sedgewick and all the other bad news, Grant's expression did not change at all. At one point, he was informed almost hysterically (and falsely) that General Sedgwick had been taken prisoner. Grant took it all in his stride. He just sat on a stool in front of his tent, smoking cigar after cigar. If he had been back at the Willard Hotel, listening to a not-very-interesting conversation, he could not have seemed more detached or indifferent.

At one point, Grant was interrupted by a general who came storming into camp with what he considered very bad news. "General Grant, this is a crisis that cannot be looked upon too seriously," the overwrought general declared. "I know Lee's methods well, by past experience; he will throw his whole army between us and the Rapidan, and cut us off completely from our communications."[63]

Grant listened to everything the general had to say before losing his temper. Or, as Colonel Porter phrased it, Grant spoke to the general "with a degree of animation which he seldom manifested." He even took the cigar out of his mouth. "Oh, I am heartily tired of hearing about what Lee is going to do," he shouted. "Some of you always seem to think that he is going to turn a double somersault, and land in our rear and on both of our flanks at the same time. Go back to your command, and try to think what we are going to do ourselves, instead of what Lee is going to do."

This story has been told many times over, but is worth retelling because it illustrates something significant about Grant. It not only shows his frame of mind concerning the battle itself but also illustrates his attitude toward Robert E. Lee.

When U. S. Grant became general-in-chief in March 1864, Robert E. Lee's dominance over Union commanders came to a dramatic end. Lee was not able to panic or intimidate Grant because, as Grant had said himself, he had known Lee personally and knew "that he is mortal."[64] Grant was not content to wait and see what Lee was going to do and then try to stop him, like his predecessors had done. He had made up his mind to go after Lee and keep after him. Once Grant set an objective, he would not stop or give in until he reached it. U. S. Grant was certainly Jesse Root Grant's son. He knew that Lee could be beaten, and he was determined to do exactly that.

"Darkness again put an end to the fighting," Elisha Hunt Rhodes wrote, "and we lay down among the dead and wounded."[65] When General Sedgwick's Sixth Corps finally beat back General John B. Gordon's attack, the Battle of the Wilderness was over. General Grant admitted that his losses "were very severe," but he thought "those of the Confederates must be even more so."[66] He was wrong. The total of Union killed, wounded, and missing or captured during the two-day battle is usually given at between 15,000 and 18,000. Confederate losses are estimated to have been about 8,000.[67]

When the sun came up on the morning of May 7, no one knew exactly what was going to happen that day. No one except Grant, and he was not saying. The day turned out to be warm and hazy, with smoke from the brush fires still in the air. Not very much was happening, to everyone's immense relief. Nervous pickets shot at each other throughout the day, but that was about all the shooting that took place. "Today we have had comparative quiet with only skirmishings going on in our front," Elisha Hunt Rhodes said. "We have entrenched ourselves the best we can with logs and earth and are waiting events."[68]

It did not take very long for events to make themselves known. At about four o'clock in the afternoon, hundreds of wagon crews began stirring and forming their teams and vehicles into a long, extended train, getting ready to make a head start on the infantry. A night march was on, that soon became clear enough. The question on everyone's mind was the same, throughout every corps, every division, and every regiment in the Army of the Potomac: exactly where was Grant taking them?

Veteran units remembered very well what had happened the year before, after Chancellorsville—Joe Hooker had conceded defeat to Bobby Lee and marched them back across the river. It seemed a fairly safe bet that Grant would do the same thing: retreat, reorganize, reequip, and then start planning another move against Lee in a few weeks or months. After all, the battle was fought nearly on the same ground, against the same enemy, with nearly the same result. The night march looked like another skedaddle. A soldier in a Massachusetts regiment said, "Most of us thought it was another Chancellorsville."[69] It looked like they were going to give up and go back north.

When night came, the men got ready to move out. They slung their packs, picked up their muskets, left their trenches, fell into something resembling a column, and started walking. Nobody could see very far, and they could not tell where they were going for a while. But all of this changed when they reached the crossroads by the old Chancellor house. Instead of heading north, as expected, the column turned south. Everyone instantly realized what this meant— they were not going to retreat after all. There was not going to be a skedaddle, not this time. They were not running away from Bobby Lee; they were going after him.

The word began to filter down through the column—they were not heading back toward the river crossings. They were going south, right out the other side of the Wilderness. Some of the men caught a glimpse of General Grant leading the way, all round shouldered and hunched over, sitting a big horse. The combination of the sight of Grant and the news that they were not going back north had an effect on the troops that was electric.

"Wild cheers echoed through the forest, and glad shouts of triumph rent the air," Horace Porter remembered. "Men swung their hats, tossed up their arms, and pressed forward to within touch of their chief, clapping their hands, and speaking to him with the familiarity of comrades."[70] The tired column sprang to life, forgetting all about their aches and pains and fatigue, and kept on yelling and cheering. Maybe they had won the battle after all! A young lieutenant would recall in old age that "the most thrilling moment of the whole war" came when his unit turned south at the Chancellorsville crossroads, and the men realized that they were advancing instead of retreating. One historian declared that Grant's decision to move south was "one of the most important decisions in American history."[71]

Grant's big horse, Cincinnati, became agitated by all the excitement and began rearing and prancing, much to Grant's annoyance. After regaining control of his horse, he ordered the men to stop cheering. Old Iron Man Grant was unhappy about all the noise, or at least he pretended to be unhappy. "This is most unfortunate," is the way that Colonel Porter remembered what he said. "The sound will reach the ears of the enemy, and I fear it may reveal our movement."[72]

Staff officers rode out and told the men to quiet down, so as not to alert the enemy. But the men kept cheering and shouting just the same, and kept it up until Grant had ridden out of sight. Some regiments even started singing. "If we were under any other General except Grant, I should expect a retreat," Elisha Hunt Rhodes entered in his diary, "but Grant is not that kind of a soldier, and we feel that we can trust him."[73]

During the First World War, the British army was described as lions led by asses—brave soldiers sent to their deaths on the Western Front by inept and bungling generals. The men of the Army of the Potomac felt the same way about themselves. They were a better army than their battlefield record, they were certain of that. All they needed was a halfway decent commander, a capable general who would lead from the front, and they would show old Bobby Lee what they were really made of. But all they had had so far was a steady stream of incompetents.

Somebody wrote a set of lyrics, sung to the tune of "When Johnny Comes Marching Home," which gave the prevailing view of the army's string of highly unsuccessful generals:

We are the boys of Potomac's ranks,
Hurrah! Hurrah!
We are the boys of Potomac's ranks,
We ran with McDowell, retreated with Banks,
And we'll all drink stone blind—
Johnny fill up the bowl.[74]

General Irvin McDowell commanded the Union forces at the First Battle of Bull Run/Manassas on July 21, 1861, which was a rout. General Nathaniel P. Banks was outmaneuvered and outgeneraled by Stonewall Jackson at the Battle of Cedar Mountain in August 1862.

They gave us John Pope our patience to tax,
Hurrah! Hurrah!
They gave us John Pope our patience to tax,
Who said that out West he'd seen naught but grey backs.
He said his headquarters were in the saddle,
But Stonewall Jackson made him skedaddle.

John Pope came east after a minor victory in Missouri in 1861, but was outgeneraled by both Stonewall Jackson and Robert E. Lee at the Second Battle of Bull Run/Manassas in August 1862. The verse mentions John Pope's boast that his headquarters were in the saddle. Some army wit cracked that General Pope had his headquarters where his hindquarters should be.

Then Mac was recalled, but after Antietam
Abe gave him a rest, he was too slow to beat 'em.

General George B. McClellan, "Little Mac," was relieved of his command by President Lincoln after the Battle of Antietam/Sharpsburg in September 1862, when he would not pursue the retreating Army of Northern Virginia.

Then Hooker was taken to fill the bill,
But he got a black eye at Chancellorsville.
Next came General Meade, a slow old plug,
For he let them get away at Gettysburg.

Nobody had yet written a verse about General Grant. For one thing, he was still too new—nobody knew enough about him. Also, there were those who had the feeling that this man Grant was not going to be like all the others. When Elisha Hunt Rhodes first set eyes on Grant, he was impressed by the look in the general's eye. A good many others agreed with him, although they said so in different ways.

On May 7, Sergeant Major William Burroughs Ross wrote to his father in New Jersey, "The First New Jersey Brigade lost heavily yesterday. The First Regiment half their men and 11 officers. I will write more when I have an opportunity for I think trusting in God and General Grant we are sure to be successful."[75]

In spite of his losses, General Grant was convinced that his army had won the battle. "Our victory consisted in having successfully crossed the formidable stream, almost in the face of the enemy, and in getting the army together as a unit." As far as Grant was concerned, just getting across the Rapidan—and staying there—constituted a victory. Seventeen years before, when Sam Grant was a lieutenant in Mexico, General Winfield Scott felt the same way about landing at Veracruz. Now Grant would push his way south, just as Winfield Scott had driven his army inland toward Mexico City. Grant had Scott's gift for strategy—he had learned it from Scott along the way from Veracruz to Chapultepec. Both knew exactly what they wanted to accomplish, as well as how to go about accomplishing it. Scott's goal had been the capture of Mexico City. Grant's was the grinding down of Robert E. Lee's army.

At least one military historian agreed with General Grant. British major general J. F. C. Fuller wrote, "Strategically, [the Wilderness] was the greatest Federal victory yet won in the East, for Lee was now thrown on the defensive—he was held. Thus, within forty-eight hours of crossing the Rapidan," General Fuller went on, "did Grant gain his object—the fixing of Lee."[76]

Others attributed the Army of the Potomac's refusal to retreat to Grant's force of personality. One historian wrote, "The battle of the Wilderness was no defeat, simply because Grant refused to accept that it was a defeat."[77] Grant would keep on forcing his way south because it went against his nature to do anything else. "He would keep moving on . . . and he would move in the direction that made continued fighting inevitable."

President Abraham Lincoln did not hear anything from General Grant until the second day of the fighting. All throughout May 5 and 6, Lincoln haunted the War Department's telegraph office, riffling through all the "flimsies"—the telegrams—trying to find out anything he could about what was going on in the Wilderness. These short reports did not say very much, at least not nearly as much as the president wanted to hear. On May 6, he finally received the cryptic message, "Everything pushing along favorably." This did not really say very much, either, but at least it was better than nothing.[78]

During the early morning hours of May 7, a young reporter from the New York *Tribune* named Henry E. Wing had an interview with President Lincoln. The president kept odd hours. Sometimes he stayed up all night long, pacing the corridors of the White House, agonizing over the future of the war and of the country. Henry Wing saw Lincoln at two o'clock in the morning, not an unusual time for the president during those tense days.

The meeting between Lincoln and young Mr. Wing went on for two hours. It was an unusually long session, considering that Henry Wing was only a junior reporter. But the president asked as many questions as Henry Wing. The president wanted Wing to tell him everything he could remember about the battle, everything he saw and heard. The reporter complied, answering every question fully and patiently.

After the interview ended, Wing conveyed a personal message from General Grant. Grant had specifically asked Wing to deliver this particular message for him. "If you see the president," the general said, "see him alone and tell him that General Grant says there will be no turning back."[79]

The president was visibly relieved to receive Grant's message. This was exactly what he wanted to hear. He was so pleased that he put his arms around the startled reporter and gave him a kiss on the forehead. Grant was not going to give up. He was not going to turn back, the way all of his predecessors had done. He was going to keep pressing, and keep on fighting until Lee gave up.

Lincoln had finally found the general who would stand up to

Lee. He had gone through McClellan and Burnside and Hooker, and he was satisfied that Grant was nothing like any of his predecessors. As the Army of the Potomac had already found out, and Robert E. Lee was about to find out, Lincoln discovered that Grant was not the kind of person who gave up and turned back. If he needed any further reassurances, Grant's "no turning back" message confirmed that he had appointed the right man as lieutenant general.

Robert E. Lee could not possibly have known about Grant's message, but the "no turning back" proclamation would apply to him, as well. He would no longer have the luxury of resting his army while his opponent retired across the river to regroup and re-equip. "No turning back" would mean hard and unrelenting pounding—at Spotsylvania, Cold Harbor, Petersburg, and all the way to Appomattox.

Chapter Four

ADVANTAGES AND DISADVANTAGES

INSPIRATION BY EXAMPLE

General Grant was having as much trouble with his own officers that morning, April 9, 1865, as with the enemy. First, Phil
Sheridan decided that Lee's offer to surrender was a hoax, and he
had to be restrained from launching a full-scale attack. Next, General
George Gordon Meade refused to recognize a flag of truce. He had
his men lined up to attack the rear of the stalled Confederate army,
and he was not about to call off his charge just because somebody
came riding into his lines with a white flag, asking for a ceasefire.

"Hey! What!" Meade shouted, edgy and agitated. "I have no
authority to grant such a suspension. General Lee has already refused
the terms of General Grant. Advance your skirmishers, Humphreys,
and bring up your troops." General Andrew A. Humphreys served as
Meade's chief of staff. "We will pitch into them at once!"

The advance began, with General Humphreys giving the order
to begin moving forward. Only when an officer attached to General
Philip Sheridan's staff rode up, carrying a note from Colonel Babcock,
did Meade begin to reconsider his order. The note from Colonel
Babcock was to the point. "I am with Gen'l Lee for the purpose of
conducting him to an interview with Gen'l Grant on the matter of his
surrender," General Meade read, "will you please maintain the truce
until you hear from General Grant."[1]

Because the communiqué had indirectly come from General
Grant, Meade had no choice but to comply. He emphatically did
not want to. Like Phil Sheridan, Meade knew he had Confederate

general John Gordon "like that!" But he reluctantly gave the order to stop the attack before his troops made contact with the enemy.

General Grant was glad that he had commanders like Meade and Sheridan, generals who drove their troops and had the killer instinct. Grant was a driven commander as well, as everyone in the Army of the Potomac—and the Army of Northern Virginia—had found out. But he knew when to let up, when to stop. He knew that time had now arrived—the time for fighting had ended. Now it was time to talk, time to discuss surrender terms with General Lee.

Grant was every bit as aggressive as either Meade or Sheridan. His determination and single-mindedness were traits he had inherited from his father, Jesse Root Grant, who became a successful tanner and businessman in spite of his limited education. They would turn out to be Grant's most valuable assets, and they were attributes that General Lee never did quite understand.

Ulysses S. Grant owed much of his success as a general to his upbringing in Point Pleasant, Ohio, and to his father. Neighbors in Point Pleasant probably called Jesse Root Grant's work ethic and single-mindedness bull-headedness, but they gave the future lieutenant general the determination and drive—and bull-headedness—he needed in Virginia against Robert E. Lee.

Among the things that young Ulysses learned from his father were not to give in, not to be discouraged, and never give up or stop trying. Jesse Grant taught these things by example. He was a tanner by trade and had become a partner in a Ravenna, Ohio, tannery by 1817. The public's need for bridles and harnesses and all manner of leather goods rose steadily, the tannery thrived, and Jesse Grant prospered. He managed to save about $1,500—about $60,000 in today's currency—and became one of the pillars of Ravenna society. But he came down with some sort of fever, known as "the ague," which left him bedridden and unable to work for some months. As the result of his long illness, Jesse Grant not only lost all of his savings but also his partnership in the tannery.[2]

As soon as he was strong enough, Jesse went back to work. He did not let his bad turn of luck, or his lost savings, get him down—or if they did, he did not let it show. Instead of feeling sorry for himself, Jesse Grant got a job with a tannery in Point Pleasant, Ohio, where

Ulysses was born on April 27, 1822. He went to work every day, saved his money, and worked his way back to financial solvency. "My father was, from my earliest recollection, in comfortable circumstances," U. S. Grant would later write, "considering the times, his place of residence, and the community in which he lived."[3]

Jesse Root Grant did not let the times, the community, his long illness, or anything else get in the way of his success and prosperity. He made up his mind that he would succeed, and he was not about to let anything or anybody stop him. His son picked up this determination to keep pushing until he reached his goal and put it to very effective use in places like Shiloh, Vicksburg, and the Wilderness.

One of Robert E. Lee's biographers wrote that Grant's campaign against Lee was a constant hammering, a single-minded pounding that did not let up until Lee finally cracked.[4] General Grant did not learn this relentlessness at West Point. He learned from his father that the secret of success was sometimes nothing more than the unwillingness to admit defeat. This is what happened at the Wilderness; Grant simply refused to be beaten.

Jesse Root Grant was also responsible for his son becoming an army officer in the first place. Going to West Point was Jesse's idea, not Ulysses's. Young Ulysses never even considered the army as a career. He knew that he did not want to be a tanner like his father; he hated the trade and everything about it. But a university education had only a vague appeal for him—he had no real idea which university might be suitable for him, or might even accept him as an undergraduate.[5]

On the other hand, Jesse Grant had a very definite idea of which university would be suitable for his son—the United States Military Academy at West Point, New York. Not only would West Point assure Ulysses of a decent future but, best of all, it would not cost him anything. In 1838, Jesse told Ulysses that he would be receiving an appointment to West Point, sponsored by his congressman, Thomas L. Hamer. He had arranged for the appointment himself. Ulysses would be entering the military academy in 1839.

To say that Ulysses was less than thrilled by the news of his appointment would be a colossal understatement. He wanted nothing to do with the army or with West Point and emphatically informed his father that he was not going. Jesse Root Grant was not a person to take no for an answer, especially not from his son. He informed Ulysses, even more emphatically, that he certainly *was* going to West Point and there would be no further discussion. For one of the few times in his life, Ulysses Grant backed down. In May 1839, he began the long journey—the trip took about two weeks—from Ohio to West Point, New York.

Cadet Grant settled into life at the military academy, but it took some time. His father may have dragooned him into going to West Point, but Ulysses still did not like it very much. "A military life had no charms for me," he grumbled, "and I had not the faintest idea of staying in the army even if I should be graduated, which I did not expect."[6]

In December 1839, Congress debated a bill that would abolish the military academy. Some well-meaning congressmen feared that West Point might produce an elite corps of officers that might one day overthrow the elected government and establish a military dictatorship. Grant read all about the debates "with much interest"—if Congress passed the bill, "I saw in this an honorable way to obtain a discharge."[7] But the bill did not pass, and Cadet Grant graduated with his class in 1843.

Twenty one years later, when Lieutenant General Grant had Robert E. Lee pinned down at Petersburg, the three-star general wrote to his father. From the tone of the letter, anyone might be led to believe that Jesse Grant was general-in-chief of all Union forces and that Ulysses was writing a situation report to his commanding general. "We are now having fine weather and I think will be able to wind up matters about Richmond. I am anxious to have Lee hold on where he is a short time longer so that I can get him in a position where he must lose a great portion of his army," Grant reported.[8] "The rebellion has lost its vitality, and if I am not much mistaken there will be no Rebel army of any great dimensions a few weeks hence. Any great catastrophe to one of our armies would of course revive the enemy for a short time. But I expect no such thing to happen."

When Jesse Root Grant died in 1873, at the age of seventy-nine, Ulysses—who had been elected president of the United States by that time—was almost overcome with grief. With good reason.

During Ulysses's formative years, Jesse had not only been his inspiration, but he had also been his driving force. Without his father's influence and his example, Ulysses would never have become the victor of Donelson, Vicksburg, or Appomattox. U. S. Grant's famed single-mindedness—and Jesse Root Grant's—would be very much in evidence during the coming months in Virginia.

PUSHING THE ENEMY

"Make all preparations during the day for a night march to take position at Spottsylvania C.H. [Court House] with one army corps," Grant wrote to General Meade during the early hours of May 7, "at Todd's Tavern with one, and another near the intersection of the Piney Branch Road and Spottsylvania Road with the road from Alsop's to Old Court House."[9] These were clear, concise orders—get to Spotsylvania as quickly as possible, wagons and all. (The town was spelled "Spottsylvania," with two *t*s, in the 1860s.) The idea was to get moving as quickly as possible, without alerting the enemy, and to reach Spotsylvania before Lee.

But issuing an order is one thing, and having it carried out is something else again. The men were more than willing to follow Grant's orders, and they were certainly in good spirits—they were walking south, going right after Bobby Lee, and their morale was probably higher than it had ever been before. Unfortunately, they were also attempting an all-night march after a grueling two-day battle. Walking ten miles in pitch darkness following that fight in the Wilderness would prove to be too much stress and strain and fatigue, in spite of everyone's high spirits. It is impossible for an army to move with anything resembling haste, or even cohesion, when it is dead on its feet.

If the Army of the Potomac could get to Spotsylvania ahead of Lee, it would then be situated between Richmond and the Army of Northern Virginia. Which would mean that Lee would have to attack the dug-in Union forces, either that or concede the Confederate capital to Grant—something that Lee would not even consider. If the Confederates charged the entrenched Federal troops, the result might be just as disastrous as it had been for General George E.

Pickett at Gettysburg. But the Union army, with Major General Gouverneur K. Warren's Fifth Corps in the lead, was having more than its share of problems. The main problem was with the Brock Road, which was the army's main road out of the Wilderness. The Brock Road was narrow, too narrow to accommodate an entire army, especially an army in a hurry. There were just too many men, too many horses, and too many wagons for such a small country road.

In addition to the problems caused by the width of the Brock Road, a fist fight that broke out between two cavalry units added to the difficulties. During the night move, the Third Pennsylvania Cavalry Regiment happened to pass a brand-new cavalry regiment that was straight out of the equipment depot in Washington, DC. The Pennsylvanians were a veteran unit—they had fought at Fredericksburg, Gettysburg, and Antietam/Sharpsburg, as well as in many other battles. The other regiment was made up entirely of green troops, with brand-new equipment and fresh horses. Because they were veterans of so many battles, the Pennsylvanians had nothing but contempt for the new recruits. When they saw that the green troops all had fresh horses, they decided to swap their worn-out mounts for the new horses—whether the new recruits liked it or not.

None of the replacement troopers wanted to change horses, as might be expected. When the grizzled Pennsylvanians forced the issue by pulling the rookies off their horses and climbing aboard themselves, the resulting brawl tied up the Brock Road for over an hour. Nobody could get past the fight, which held up the entire Army of the Potomac. Eventually, the Pennsylvanians rode off on the fresh horses, leaving their old mounts behind. By the time the rest of the army could start moving again, several hours had been wasted.

The combination of the exhausted troops, the narrow road, the darkness, and the brawling cavalrymen created "one of the most expensive traffic tie-ups in American history," according to one source.[10] The clogged road delayed the Union forces just long enough to allow the Confederates to get to Spotsylvania first. The result of this cost the lives of thousands of northern troops.

By the time Warren's Fifth Corps reached the vicinity of Spotsylvania, the rebels had already dug themselves an impressive series of fortifications. The lead division, the Second Division, was com-

manded by General John B. Robinson, a bearded veteran of countless battles, who rode ahead to see the situation for himself. He could
not help being impressed by the Confederate works. They ran right
along the top of the hill in front of him, known as Laurel Hill, which
would make any sort of attack an extremely hazardous proposition.
The Confederates continued to dig as Robinson looked on, making
their trenches deeper and even more formidable.

Robinson's orders were to take the hill, in spite of any and all
trenches and obstacles, but Robinson had his doubts. For one thing,
there was the question of those damned fortifications. But most of
all, he could see that his men were tired beyond all endurance. He
asked General Warren for a bit more time, so that his men could get
at least a little rest and also so that he could regroup and reorganize
his men. But Warren said no. He was under the impression that only
cavalry was defending Laurel Hill and wanted the attack to begin as
soon as possible.

General Robinson knew that his division would do their best to
break through the Confederate line, in spite of everything. After all,
the trenches were probably unfinished, and the enemy troops were
certainly as worn out as his own men. If he could get past the men in
the trenches, the village of Spotsylvania would be his for the taking,
along with its famous court house and its strategic crossroads.

But even though the rebels were tired, they could still shoot. It
was easier for the exhausted Confederates to stay in their trenches
and shoot at the enemy than it was for Robinson's men to walk across
several hundred yards of open ground. As Robinson's division began
climbing up the hill, almost stupid with fatigue, they walked right
into a solid line of musket fire.

Near exhaustion did not stop the rebels from hitting their targets,
either. They shot down the advancing troops at an alarming rate.
Those who were lucky enough to survive the first volleys threw themselves to the ground, which at least gave them a small measure of protection, and waited for reinforcements. But when supporting troops
from Robinson's Second Brigade finally did arrive, mostly men from
Maryland, they did not fare any better. The Confederates took aim
from inside their new trenches and cut down the Marylanders as they
came into range. Instead of falling flat, the advancing line turned

and ran—or at least they moved as quickly as they were able in their exhausted state.

General Robinson himself came forward on horseback to rally his discouraged men, waving his hat and shouting encouragement. But a minie ball struck him in the left knee, shattering his leg. When they saw what had happened to their commander, Robinson's men resumed their shamble toward the rear.

But the fighting was far from over. More Confederates came up on the flank of the men who were lying on the ground. The rebels immediately opened fire, killing and wounding hundreds. This unexpected attack encouraged the men to get up and charge the rebel fortifications in front of them—if they were going to get killed anyway, they might as well get killed attacking the enemy. Which is exactly what happened; hundreds more were shot down in their slow walk toward the trenches.

Some of Robinson's men actually made it as far as the enemy fortifications, and promptly found themselves in a bayonet fight with the defenders. But they were just too tired to do very much, and they had already lost too many men to do any effective damage to the enemy, anyway. After an agonizing hand-to-hand melee, with bayonets and clubbed muskets as the main weapons, the men backed off and began walking down the hill. One of the officers later said that he tried his best to run but could only move forward at a sort of shuffling walk, using his sword as a cane.

Laurel Hill finished Robinson's division as a fighting unit. About two thousand men had either been killed or wounded, including many officers. General Robinson's horribly mangled left leg had to be amputated. He did receive the Congressional Medal of Honor for his performance at Laurel Hill. The remains of his division were broken up and assigned to other units within the Fifth Corps.[11]

General Warren watched what was happening at Laurel Hill with increasing alarm and anxiety. He sent the rest of his corps forward, which were followed by John Sedgwick's Sixth Corps. The fighting went on throughout the day, a series of attacks and counterattacks, but the Federals did not make any gains. The men were just too tired to make an all-out charge that might overwhelm the Confederate position. Also, the rebels were too well dug-in for a frontal assault to succeed without incurring horrific casualties.

General Warren informed General Meade of what had taken place and concluded his summary by reporting, "I cannot gain Spotsylvania Court House with what force I have."[12] General Meade was not happy to hear what Warren had to say. And when Meade was not happy, the world soon knew all about it—he was not called the goddamn old goggle-eyed snapping turtle because of his easy-going disposition. On this particular occasion, he decided to take his unhappiness and bad temper out on General Philip Sheridan instead of Warren.

He made up his mind that today's fiasco was all the fault of Phil Sheridan and his cavalry. The cavalry had stalled on the Brock Road, which stopped the infantry from getting through and had fouled up the entire advance. As it turned out, Meade had ordered Sheridan to take his cavalry off the Brock Road so that the infantry could pass, but Sheridan never received the order. Either that, or Meade, or someone on his staff, never bothered to tell Sheridan. When Meade summoned Sheridan to his headquarters to complain that the cavalry had blocked Warren's infantry, the meeting was anything but pleasant.

"He had worked himself into a towering passion regarding the delays encountered in the forward movement," according to an eyewitness of the encounter.[13] Meade went at Sheridan "hammer and tongs, accusing him of blunders, and charging him with not making proper disposition of his troops, and letting the cavalry block the advance of the infantry."

Phil Sheridan was not the type who would have taken that kind of tongue-lashing from anybody. He went right back at Meade, in the same tone of voice and with the same vocabulary, according to the same eyewitness: "His language throughout was highly spiced and conspicuously italicised with expletives." In other words, he cursed right back at General Meade, matching him obscenity for obscenity.

The tangle on the Brock Road was Meade's fault, not his, Sheridan bellowed. If Meade had not countermanded his orders without letting him know, there would not have been any mix-up and no troops would have been put in danger. Furthermore, Sheridan went on "with great warmth," if he had his way he would concentrate all the cavalry under his own command, move out in force against Jeb

Stuart and his celebrated cavalry corps, and whip it properly. If only Meade would stay the hell out of his way, he could beat Jeb Stuart.

Meade did not appreciate being told off by one of his own subordinates. Phil Sheridan may have been commander of Meade's entire cavalry corps, but George Gordon Meade was the commanding general of the Army of the Potomac. Only Lieutenant General Grant outranked Meade. Following the shouting match, General Meade stomped over to Grant's tent to report Sheridan for insubordination.

Grant did not seem all that interested in what Meade had to say about Phil Sheridan. As far as he was concerned, the quarrel sounded like a schoolyard argument between two ten-year-olds. But when Meade mentioned Sheridan's claim that "he could move out with his cavalry and beat Stuart," Grant immediately brightened. "Did he say that?" Grant asked. "Well, he generally knows what he is talking about. Let him start right out and do it."[14]

General Meade did not expect that sort of reaction from Grant—he thought that Sheridan should have at least received a reprimand for his outburst. But he did what he was told and issued new orders for Phil Sheridan: Sheridan was to take his cavalry corps south, all 13,000 troopers plus horse-drawn artillery, create as much mischief as possible, and take care of Jeb Stuart when he came out to stop him.

Grant thought that Sheridan's planned venture would be well worth the effort. Phil Sheridan was just the man for this particular job—he would take his cavalry all the way to Richmond and back if the opportunity presented itself. At very least, Sheridan would disrupt Lee's supplies. And Grant had no doubts at all that Sheridan would get the better of Jeb Stuart, just as Sheridan had said he would. Sheridan had just one thing on his mind—destroy the enemy. He would especially like to put a stop to Jeb Stuart's colorful career.

James Ewell Brown Stuart had been the stuff of myth and legend ever since his cavalry had ridden around the entire Army of the Potomac in June 1862, capturing Union prisoners, horses, and supplies along the way, and he had been a mortal nuisance to every commanding general since George B. McClellan. Jeb Stuart was the Stonewall Jackson of the Confederate cavalry and was just about as famous as Jackson had been. When Sheridan was told to move out and engage Stuart, it was an order that he would carry out with relish. The way Sheridan saw it, Meade's directive was, "A challenge to Stuart for a cavalry duel behind Lee's lines, in his own country."[15]

At about 6:30 a.m. on the following morning, May 9, General Meade issued another order, which was a lot less popular than the one he issued to Phil Sheridan—he effectively put General John Sedgwick in command of Gouverneur Warren's Fifth Corps. Actually, Meade's order put Sedgewick in charge of any operation that might involve his own Sixth Corps and Warren's Fifth Corps. This was obviously a reprimand—Meade was not pleased with Warren's performance the day before, and he no longer trusted him as much as he once had. But Sedgwick was not comfortable with Meade's order and had no intention of carrying it out. Instead, he decided to drop in on General Warren to let him know that he should carry on commanding his own corps, as usual.[16]

Sedgwick's men called him "Uncle John"; they not only trusted him but also liked him. He was a good commanding officer but, just as important in the eyes of the Sixth Corps, he was also fair-minded. One of his officers said that Sedgwick was like a kindly father to his men. The reason he was so well-liked is apparent in his treatment of Gouverneur Warren. Other corps commanders might have welcomed an order to take over someone else's command, but not John Sedgwick. He showed a lot more consideration for Warren than Meade had done.

General Grant was up by 6:30 that day, as well, and came to visit Sedgwick at about eight o'clock, along with Colonel Horace Porter and two other staff officers. Grant was riding a little black pony named Jeff Davis instead of Cincinnati, his usual mount. The smaller and gentler horse was much more comfortable for the general. Grant was suffering from a bad case of boils, and Jeff Davis had a much easier gate than the larger and more vigorous Cincinnati.

The two generals, both on horseback, discussed preparations for the fighting that was still to come. Sedgwick seemed to be in good spirits and was confident that the Sixth Corps would make a good record for itself. The men of the Sixth Corps, including their commanding general, thought they were the best unit in the army. When their conference ended, Grant left camp and Sedgwick rode off toward the front lines.

Only a very short while later, Grant was informed that Sedgwick was dead, killed by a rebel sniper. "General Sedgwick commanding our Corps was killed about half an hour ago," Sergeant Major William Burroughs Ross wrote to his father in New Jersey. "He was standing right by our Regiment and was shot directly under the left eye, the blood flying on some of our boys. I saw him fall as he stood about ten feet in advance of my position."[17]

General Grant was completely stunned by the news. "Is he really dead?" he asked twice in disbelief. "His loss to this army is greater than the loss of a whole division of troops," he said.[18] Grant may have been the implacable iron man in battle, but he felt the loss of his friends as much as anyone, probably a lot more than he let on. Major General Horatio G. Wright was named as the Sixth Corps' new commander.

General Philip Sheridan's column, including supply wagons and artillery, stretched for about thirteen miles. As soon as Jeb Stuart found out that Sheridan was on the move, he got behind the Federal column and stayed there. Sheridan's rearguard and Stuart's advance columns came violently in contact with each other in the middle of the afternoon on May 9, at a place called Mitchell's Shop. The battle lasted several hours, resulted in a few dozen casualties on each side, and had no lasting effect on Sheridan's advance.

Sheridan's lead column, the Sixth Michigan Cavalry of General George Armstrong Custer's brigade, reached Beaver Dam Rail Station, ten miles south of Mitchell's Shop, about five hours later. They arrived at the same time as nearly three hundred Union prisoners, mostly men from the Fifth Corps who had been captured at Laurel Hill the day before. The prisoners were due to be shipped to prison camps further south. Two trains were waiting at the station, both filled with supplies. The original plan had been to unload the supplies, board the prisoners in the same boxcars, and depart for points south via the Virginia Central Railroad. These plans changed, quickly and dramatically, when the cavalry arrived.

The first order of business for Custer's men was to disarm the Confederate guards and free the Union prisoners. This was carried out quickly and effectively, much to the delight of the former captives, who were soon walking back toward the Union lines. Next, the two trains were captured at gunpoint along with their cargoes—bacon, rations, and medical supplies. The troopers confiscated as much bacon and food as they could carry, and set fire to everything that was left. They also burned the station buildings, along with both locomotives and all of the freight cars, ripped up between eight and ten miles of railroad track, and tore down miles of telegraph lines.

Phil Sheridan had been on the loose for less than a day, and he had already done no small amount of damage to the Confederate war effort. Nearly all of General Lee's desperately needed medical supplies had literally gone up in smoke at Beaver Dam Station. There had not been a full-scale confrontation with Jeb Stuart, at least not yet. But Stuart was still right behind Sheridan, and it would only be a matter of time before the two sides met head to head.

The fighting on May 9 had been spotty and sporadic, with a good deal of time and effort spent digging trenches and preparing for more fighting—there would be a lot more fighting, everyone was sure of that. On the following day, Grant planned an overall attack against the entire Confederate line that was to begin at five p.m. But because General Warren was having trouble reforming his corps, the attack did not actually begin until six o'clock. Warren had already made another attack at Laurel Hill, which resulted in high casualties and not much else. At six o'clock, the battle finally began.

During the fighting in the Wilderness, Grant told some of his staff officers that he could not help thinking about the first battle he had ever seen, the Battle of Palo Alto during the Mexican War. At Palo Alto, General Zachery Taylor commanded about three thousand men, which Lieutenant Grant thought was a "fearful responsibility."[19] Casualties from the battle were reported to be "nearly sixty in killed, wounded, and missing." In young Sam Grant's eyes, these were terrible losses, and the battle itself assumed a magnitude that was "positively startling." Now, during the current fighting, "such an affair would scarcely be deemed important enough to report to headquarters." Sixty casualties in 1864 would be considered nothing more than a glorified skirmish.

Grant often thought about the time when he was a junior officer in Mexico. But that was another time and another place. Now both sides used rifled muskets that could kill a man at a range of several hundred yards. Before the day was out on May 10, 1864, a good many men on both sides would be killed and wounded by rifled muskets.

But a good many men would also be killed by bayonets in the day's main attack. That attack would be led by a New York colonel named Emory Upton, against a position known as Doles's Salient. Brigadier General George P. Doles from Georgia commanded the brigade that manned that section of the Confederate line. At about 6:30 p.m., Colonel Upton rode to the front of five regiments, usually described as about five thousand hand-picked men, and began the advance. Doles's position was part of the Mule Shoe Salient, a bulge in the Confederate line that looped northward. Somebody looked at the map and decided that the U-shaped bend looked like a mule shoe, and the nickname held.

Colonel Upton had the idea of charging the enemy lines in a column instead of having the men strung out side-by-side in a line a mile wide. If the men came at the Confederate trench in the usual way—in a linear, shoulder-to-shoulder formation—they would be chopped down by the dug-in rebels before they could get anywhere near the enemy trenches. He wanted to push his men forward in a narrow front, like a battering ram, which might just break the rebel trenches. The idea appealed to Upton's superiors, including General Horatio G. Wright, commander of the Sixth Corps, and Upton was given permission to put his plan into effect.

On the afternoon of May 10, Colonel Upton's hand-picked regiments formed into a column and started walking toward Doles's Salient. Every man in the advancing column was given specific instructions: have your bayonet fixed and your musket loaded but not capped—having no copper detonation cap in place meant that the weapon could not be fired. Everyone was also told to keep moving forward. Keep moving until you reach the enemy trenches, Upton's men were told, and then use your bayonet.

As they reached the last few hundred yards, the men began to run, shouting and screaming at the top of their lungs. The fight that broke out at the edge of the trenches is usually described as short, sharp, and desperate. It was also murderous. The first soldiers that reached the rebel lines were either shot or bayonetted. But they kept coming, faster than the Confederates could shoot or thrust their bayonets. Upton's men jumped into the trench, using their own bayonets and the butts of their muskets with lethal effect. A soldier from a Georgia regiment waved his unit's flag in defiance at the charging Federal troops. Soldiers from Upton's column bayonetted him fourteen times.

The defenders were overwhelmed. About three thousand Confederate prisoners were taken, including General Doles himself, and the seemingly impenetrable entrenchments were firmly in Union hands, at least in the section that had been under Doles's command.

But capturing the rebel works turned out to be only half of the problem. After overrunning the enemy's line, Upton's men now had the unenviable job of holding it. A division under General Gresham Mott was supposed to come up and reinforce Upton's columns after they had taken Doles's position, but they never came within a quarter mile of the rebel line. Confederate artillery units had been forced to stand by and watch the battle so far; they had not been able to fire at Upton's troops without hitting their own men. But they had a clear field of fire with Mott's division, and they opened fire with gusto. The gunners blew gaps in the union line as it advanced, first stopping it and then driving it back in panic. Mott's superiors later blamed Mott himself for failing to support Upton, but nothing could have stood up to the determined fire from twenty artillery crews.

Because Mott had not been able to reach Upton's regiments, the men were completely isolated and had to be withdrawn before counterattacking rebels killed or captured them. By about 7:30 p.m., when Upton ordered his men to fall back, the sun had almost gone down and it was nearly dark. He estimated that he had lost about a thousand men in storming Doles's Salient. But he had also captured about a thousand prisoners and had killed several hundred more of Doles's brigade.

Upton's attack had not been a total loss for the Union side, but the prevailing attitude was that it should have accomplished a lot more. Many were convinced that John Sedgwick would have sent his reinforcements forward in spite of the enemy artillery, which would have allowed Upton to hold the section of entrenchments that he had captured. But John Sedgwick was dead, killed by a rebel sniper, and he had been replaced by Horatio Wright. General Meade had placed Mott under General Wright's direct command. If Uncle John had been in command, the thinking went, he would have seen to it that Mott reached Upton somehow.

General Grant was certainly impressed by Colonel Upton's charge, even if was not the overwhelming success he had been hoping for. "Upton had gained an important advantage, but a lack in others of the spirit and dash possessed by him lost it to us," Grant later wrote.[20] He had been given the authority to promote officers on the field "for special acts of gallantry" before he left Washington with his third star: "By this authority I confirmed the rank of brigadier-general upon Upton on the spot, and this act was confirmed by the President."

Darkness ended the fighting on May 10. No major engagements took place on the following day—that is, no battles that involved the entire army. "On the eleventh, there was no battle and but little firing," is the way Grant put it, "none except by Mott who made a reconnaissance to ascertain if there was a weak point in the enemy's line."[21] But Elisha Hunt Rhodes saw things in a different light—lieutenants tend to see things differently than generals. "Constant skirmishing going on in our front and both Armies are evidently preparing for another death grapple," was Lieutenant Rhodes's very perceptive comment regarding the day's activities.[22] "Shot and shell are constantly passing over us, and we are fast adding to the toll of dead and wounded. Will it ever end. I hope for the best." This is not quite the "no battle and but little firing" observed by General Grant.

Phil Sheridan would have agreed with Lieutenant Rhodes. May 11 was not a day of "no battle and but little firing" for him or his cavalry, either. There would be quite a lot of firing from his troopers, who were armed with seven-shot Spencer repeating carbines. Sheridan was still set on beating the hell out of Jeb Stuart, and an opportunity to fight the flamboyant Confederate cavalry commander presented itself on the morning of May 11. The fighting began with a charge led by the colorful George A Custer, who was almost as showy and flamboyant as Jeb Stuart himself. Custer's Michigan regiments came up against Confederate pickets at a place called Yellow Tavern, about six miles north of Richmond, and drove them off. But in spite of this early success, Jeb Stuart directed a counterattack that stopped the Union cavalry and forced them to retreat.

But Phil Sheridan was not about to be put off—he still had the rest of the day, and Jeb Stuart was still north of Yellow Tavern. At about four p.m., he sent Custer and his Michigan regiments to attack Stuart again. Custer rode against Stuart's left flank, while the rest of his cavalry dismounted and began moving toward the Confederate right and center.

Custer went right at the rebels, yelling and shouting as he rode at the head of his column. The Sixth Virginia Cavalry counterattacked, and the two sides fought it out with clanging sabers. But in spite of the rebel counterattack, the Michigan brigade captured two cannons and shattered the Confederate left. The dismounted troopers continued their advance, while Phil Sheridan rode among them shouting encouragements.

Jeb Stuart was also shouting words of encouragement to his own men, sitting on horseback and firing at the enemy with his nine-shot revolver. A passing soldier from the Fifth Michigan Regiment spotted Stuart, who would have been hard to miss—a bearded officer wearing a plumed hat, sitting tall on his cavalry mount. Private John A. Huff was an expert marksman, probably the best shot in his regiment. Stuart was about forty feet away, which was an easy target for a sharpshooter of Huff's ability. Private Huff stopped, took aim at Stuart with his .44 caliber revolver, and fired one shot.

Stuart crumpled in his saddle from the bullet's impact but stayed on his horse. Private Huff saw that he had hit his target and resumed his interrupted walk, moving out with the rest of his regiment. He could not have known it at the time, but Stuart would die from his wound on the following day.

While Jeb Stuart was being taken to Richmond by ambulance, Phil Sheridan's cavalry continued its assault on Stuart's regiments and gave his vaunted cavalry corps a mauling. Yellow Tavern turned out to be a disaster for Stuart's corps—Stuart himself had been mortally wounded, his horsemen had been routed, and Richmond itself was now in danger. Church bells in Richmond sounded the alarm, while its residents held their breath. Phil Sheridan had an idea that he might attack Richmond, but he thought better of it. He knew that he could take the city but was convinced that he would not be able to hold it.

General Grant's faith in Phil Sheridan had been more than justified. Little Phil, as he was sometimes called (although not to his face), certainly did know what he was talking about. He had beaten Jeb Stuart at his own game, which no other Union commander had been able to do. One of Sheridan's divisional commanders, Brigadier General James H. Wilson, put it succinctly: "We captured his guns, crumpled up his dismounted line, and broke it into hopeless fragments."[23] They had also disposed of Jeb Stuart himself, which represented no small victory for the Federal cavalry all by itself, even without taking anything else into consideration.

Besides killing Jeb Stuart and scattering his cavalry, Yellow Tavern also increased the Federal cavalry's confidence in itself. Northern cavalry units had generally thought of Southern horsemen as superior—superior riders with superior mounts. The rebels always seemed to be able to outfight and outshoot and outride them. And their leader, Jeb Stuart, had seemed almost invincible. Now Stuart was dead and his invincible cavalry had been routed. It gave the Union cavalrymen new faith, not only in themselves but also in Phil Sheridan. They now thought of themselves as being just as good as the Southern cavalry, if not better.

General Grant also had confidence in the Army of the Potomac and what the army was accomplishing, but this was nothing new. He always seemed to be confident, in his quiet, self-possessed way. On the morning of May 11, his friend and patron Congressman Elihu Washburne asked Grant to write a letter to President Lincoln, some sort of statement advising him of the situation in Virginia. The president had been getting many different accounts from many different sources, not all of them reliable, and he would like to have an account from his general-in-chief.

Grant was not all that enthusiastic about the idea. For one thing, he knew that anything he said would reach the newspapers, which meant that he would have to be very careful about what he wrote. But Congressman Washburne was returning to Washington that day, and Grant did not want to disappoint his old friend. He decided to send a communiqué to Major General Henry Halleck, who was Chief of Staff of the Army. He knew that Halleck would pass his message along to the president.

Grant's dispatch to Halleck overflowed with confidence. "We have now ended the 6th day of very hard fighting. The result up to this time is much in our favor," he began, and went on to explain that he had lost eleven general officers killed, wounded, or missing, and that total casualties were "probably twenty thousand men."[24] This was a very conservative estimate. The National Park Service estimated Federal losses to be about 18,000 from the Battle of the Wilderness alone, which did not count the fighting between May 8 and May 10. "I think the loss of the enemy must be greater," Grant continued. This was another underestimate. Confederate casualties given by the National Park Service are estimated to be 8,000 in the Battle of the Wilderness, not counting the fighting around Spotsylvania.[25] But Grant was giving his figures with the Northern press in mind—he wanted to give the public in the North some encouraging news concerning the war in Virginia.

After giving his account of the losses on both sides, Grant arrived at the heart of his message. "I am now sending back to Belle Plain all my wagons for a fresh supply of provisions and ammunition, and propose to fight it out on this line if it takes all summer." This sentence was meant for the general public as well as for Lincoln—he wanted everyone to know that he did not intend to retreat.

The message went on in the same general tone for two more paragraphs. Grant mentioned the arrival of reinforcements and how beneficial this would be for the morale of the army. He also said that he was satisfied that "the enemy are very shaky" and were being kept "up to the mark" in the front lines by the efforts of their officers. This was just plain wishful thinking. The enemy was anything but shaky, and Confederate morale was high, as he would find out the hard way during the coming weeks and months.[26]

But Grant was right about the Northern newspapers picking up his remarks. Some papers printed every word of his communiqué to General Halleck, but most editors only ran the most quotable parts. Especially popular was the sentence about Grant intending to fight all summer. Many editors changed it so that the phrase would stand on its own: "I propose to fight it out on this line if it takes all summer."

The phrase instantly became famous, printed in every newspaper in every town from Illinois to Delaware. It became a sort of signature phrase for Grant's determination to win the war. The *New York Times* said, "It is believed here, in the best informed military circles, that when Gen. GRANT announced his intention 'to fight it out on this line if it takes all Summer,' that he meant what he said."[27] Everyone in the North tended to agree with the *New York Times*—Grant would not be scared off by Robert E. Lee the way his predecessors had been.

When Jesse Root Grant read his son's remarks back in Galena, Illinois, he certainly agreed with the sentiment. It was the sort of thing he might have said himself, especially when he was a young man in Point Pleasant, Ohio, after he had lost his partnership in a tannery business because of illness. Jesse Grant's single-mindedness and drive to succeed, a drive never to give in or give up, had certainly rubbed off on Ulysses. It had taken a lot longer than a summer for Jesse Grant to reach his objective, but he had finally fought his way back to financial solvency in spite of all hardships.

Jesse Root Grant was understandably proud of his son's success as a battlefield general, but he was not above using his son's name and reputation to his own advantage. He wrote an advertising jingle that used his famous son to promote his leather goods store in Galena:

> Since Grant has whipped the Rebel Lee
> And opened trade from sea to sea
> Our goods in price soon advance
> Then don't neglect the present chance
> To Call on GRANT and PERKINS.[28]

"Grant and Perkins" was the name of Jesse's store. Ulysses had worked there as a clerk from May 1860 until Fort Sumter—"I took a clerkship in my father's store," was the way U. S. Grant himself put it.[29]

Jesse kept track of his son's progress in Virginia by reading the newspapers, which he did every day, and he was the type who basked in the reflected glory of Ulysses's success—unlike his mother, Hannah Simpson Grant, who never said anything about her famous son or any of his accomplishments, even after he became president. It was clear to Jesse Root Grant that Ulysses had inherited his father's determination and drive. There could be no doubt in his mind that Ulysses would combine this inherited determination with his own willpower to overcome Robert E. Lee, if not this summer then at some point in the near future. West Point may have provided the training, but he had given Ulysses the genes.

On the morning of May 12, General Grant was up early. Colonel Horace Porter found him wrapped in his overcoat and trying to keep warm by the anemic heat of his headquarters campfire. Torrents of rain were falling, and the fire was fighting both the downpour and a steady wind, but Grant seemed to be in good spirits in spite of the weather. "We have just had our coffee, and you will find some left for you," he told Colonel Porter.[30] Porter had just come back from observing General Winfield Scott Hancock's Second Corps moving toward the front lines through a steady rain, and he was soaked to the skin. After looking at Porter's drenched uniform and generally bedraggled appearance, Grant added, "But perhaps you are not hungry." Porter recognized that this was Grant's attempt at being funny and responded by downing his coffee "with the relish of a ship-wrecked mariner."

With the coffee—and the joke—safely out of the way, Colonel Porter began making his verbal report on the movements of General Hancock's troops. Before he could finish, "the sound of cheers and the rattle of musketry from Hancock's front" shattered the early morning stillness.[31] The main assault on the Confederate line had started.

Grant had been highly impressed by Emory Upton's attack on May 10, which showed that the apparently invulnerable Confederate trenches could be broken after all. Grant reached the conclusion that if a single brigade could crack a line of enemy entrenchments, then a full corps should be even more effective. With that in mind, he decided to try Upton's technique with a much larger force—General Hancock's Second Corps, with Ambrose Burnside's Ninth Corps and Horatio Wright's Sixth Corps in support. There were to be no half measures this time.

Everyone was full of enthusiasm that the plan would succeed, including General Hancock. As he watched his Second Corps heading off toward the Mule Shoe, he was confident that his men would over-whelm the Confederate position. The only officer who seemed to have any reservations was General Francis Barlow, commander of the First Division. His division would be leading the attack, forming the first wave, and he feared the worst for his men. But General Barlow was a lawyer by trade—he had joined a New York volunteer regiment as a private back in 1861—and he had a natural tendency toward pessimism.

Barlow's men stepped off into the early morning fog and quickly overran a line of rebel pickets. In spite of Barlow's pessimism, the advance was succeeding. His division actually hit the very tip of the Mule Shoe, which was their objective. The rest of Hancock's corps, along with those of Burnside and Wright, swarmed over the Confed-erate trenches, capturing about three thousand prisoners, two gen-erals, and twenty cannons. And all of this took place in spite of an on-and-off rain that turned the ground into the kind of slick mud that would have slowed the advance of a single infantry squad, let alone three massed infantry corps.

At about 5:30 a.m., an officer came bursting into General Grant's headquarters to announce that General Hancock had captured the first line of enemy works. Other news soon followed. At about 6:15, General Burnside reported that he had driven the enemy two and a half miles along his front. Messengers kept arriving one after the other with encouraging information, bringing reports of increasing numbers of prisoners and even more success against the rebel entrenchments.

"The scene at headquarters was now exciting in the extreme," Colonel Porter remarked.[32] Every time another messenger rode in with more news from the front, all hell would break loose—all the staff officers would stop whatever they were doing and begin cheering at the top of their lungs. Only General Grant remained silent. Through all the cheering and the shouting, Grant sat quietly in his camp chair. He did not give any indication that he was even aware that a battle was being fought anywhere within a hundred miles. The inscrutable General Grant preferred being alone with his thoughts.

When reports came in that thousands of Confederate prisoners had been taken, Grant's composure changed instantly. "That's the kind of news I like to hear," he said. "I had hoped that a bold dash at daylight would secure a large number of prisoners. Hancock is doing well."[33]

One of the prisoners was Major General Edward Johnson, commander of the renowned "Stonewall Brigade." General Johnson rode into Grant's camp at about 6:30 a.m., looking very much the worse for wear—covered with mud and with a hole in the crown of his felt hat that let a tuft of hair poke through "like a Sioux chief's war lock."[34]

Both Grant and General Meade had known Edward Johnson for many years. Meade and Johnson had been cadets together at West Point. As soon as Meade recognized Johnson, he extended his hand and greeted his erstwhile enemy like a long-lost friend.

General Grant was just as glad to see Johnson, who was another link with his days in the "old army." The two of them had served together in the Mexican War as junior officers, a time that Grant remembered fondly. "How do you do," Grant said as he shook hands with Johnson. "It is a long time since we last met."[35] Johnson agreed, and went on to say that he never expected to meet a fellow Mexican War veteran under such circumstances. "It is one of the many sad fortunes of war," Grant said, as he offered his old friend a cigar.

The three of them, Grant, Meade, and Johnson, sat in camp chairs by the fire, smoking and reminiscing. While they were talking about old times, a messenger rode up with a dispatch from General Hancock: "I have finished up Johnson and am now going into Early."[36] General Grant did not read Hancock's communiqué to the other officers, as he normally would have done. Instead, he passed it around so they could read it themselves. He did not want to hurt the feelings of his guest, who was also his prisoner.

Grant received another message a short while later, this time from General Burnside, he had lost contact with Hancock's corps and was doing his best to connect with it. Although Grant did not seem very upset by the news, his reaction to it was typical. "Push the enemy with all your might," he replied, "that's the way to connect."[37] This was vintage Grant: be considerate of your friends, even though they may have been trying to kill you only a short time before, but keep pushing your enemy until he breaks.

The morning was going the way Grant wanted it to go, but it was not over yet. While Barlow's men were pushing their way through the rebel trenches, the torrential rain began to fall again. The Confederates also came at the massed Federal troops in a torrent of their own. The savage counterattack drove the Federals out of the trenches, but they quickly regrouped and came right back at the rebels.

Men shot each other through the spaces between the log emplacements, stabbed each other with their bayonets, and clubbed each other with the butts of their muskets. The most savage fighting came at a chink on the west side of the Mule Shoe, where the line of trenches made a sharp indentation. This notch in the lines was originally referred to as the Western Angle, but it quickly became known as the Bloody Angle, the name by which it will always be known.

Not all of the fighting was done by infantry. A battery of artillery was rolled up by hand, "close by the famous Angle," and fired without let up at the Confederate entrenchments. A soldier who wrote a report on the incident thought this was "the only instance in the history of war" when a battery of artillery charged an enemy position. "We were a considerable distance in front of the infantry," an artillery sergeant named William E. Lines recalled. Sergeant Lines's gun fired fourteen rounds; the crew on his left fired nine rounds. "The effect of our canister upon the Confederates was terrible," he reflected.[38]

But while the gun crews were firing double charges of canister at the enemy, the rebels kept shooting back at them. Only Sergeant Lines himself and the lieutenant in command of the battery managed to avoid being shot. Of the twenty-four men who went into the fight, seven men were killed outright and the rest were wounded, some severely. The two cannon themselves were also badly damaged by the intense musket fire. The gun carriages were so badly riddled by minie balls that they could no longer support the weight of the guns.[39]

The carnage at the Bloody Angle was so horrific that even veterans of many past battles were sickened by what they saw. "Nothing can describe the confusion, the savage blood-curdling yells, the murderous faces, the awful curses, and the grisly horror of the melee," one soldier recollected. "Of all the battles I took part in, Bloody Angle at Spotsylvania exceeded all the rest in stubbornness, ferocity, and carnage."[40] Elisha Hunt Rhodes of the Second Rhode Island Volunteers agreed: "I never saw even at Gettysburg so many dead Rebels as lay in front of our lines."[41] Lieutenant Rhodes was wounded twice at the Bloody Angle, once in the arm and once on his forefinger, but both injuries turned out to be minor. Thousands of others were not nearly as fortunate.

General Grant went out to see some of the fighting for himself, riding from headquarters on Jeff Davis to get his own impression of what was happening at the tip of the salient. "During the day I was passing along the line from wing to wing continuously," is the way he described his inspection tour of the front lines.[42]

In the course of one of his swings across the lines, Grant came across a house that was occupied by an old lady and her daughter. The lady of the house was very happy to see the Union troops, and was especially glad to look at the Union flag again. She told Grant that she had not seen the Stars and Stripes in a long time and that it did her heart good to see it, and she also showed other "unmistakable signs of being strongly Union."[43] Among other things, she told the general that her husband and son had to leave the area early in the war because of their pro-Union sympathies, and the only thing she knew about either of them was that they were somewhere in one of the Union armies if they were still alive. She also said that she and her daughter did not have very much to eat.

Grant listened to what the woman had to say with sympathy. When she had finished, he ordered rations to be sent to her and her daughter, and he also promised to find out exactly where her husband and son were. This was another instance of the implacable iron man Grant being touched by someone else's trouble and misfortune.

From what he observed during journeys back and forth along the lines, Grant seemed to be favorably impressed by the results of the day's fighting. He summed up his impressions in a telegram to General Henry Halleck in Washington.

May 12, 1864, 6:30 p.m.

Major-General Halleck

The eighth day of the battle closes, leaving between three and four thousand prisoners in our hands from the day's work, including two general officers, and over thirty pieces of artillery.

The enemy are obstinate, and seem to have found the last ditch. We
have lost no organizations, not even that of a company, whilst we
have destroyed and captured one division (Johnson's), one brigade
(Doles's), and one regiment entire from the enemy.
    U. S. Grant
    Lieut.-General[44]

Grant was wrong about Doles's brigade. Although it had certainly
been very badly mauled, the entire unit had not been captured. But
Grant had the right to be overly optimistic. For one thing, an enormous
number of prisoners had been taken since the Army of the Potomac
had crossed the Rapidan River, somewhere in the vicinity of five thousand to six thousand. He could afford to be pleased about that. Prisoners were more valuable to him than dead Confederates. Prisoners
often yielded valuable information about what units he was facing and
other important intelligence, while the dead told him nothing.[45]

But Grant was also well aware of how many men he had lost—
besides observing the movements of his troops during his ride along
the lines, he also saw the accumulating piles of dead and wounded.
When he mentioned all the killing he had seen to General Meade,
Meade replied, "General, we can't do these little tricks without heavy
losses."[46] He was not trying to trivialize what had happened that day;
he was only doing his best to make Grant feel better about the terrible casualties the day's "little trick" had cost.

The men who did the fighting and the killing were not quite as
casual about the day's losses as General Meade. They had seen the
dead in the trenches, Federal and Confederate—which were stacked
four and five deep in places—from a close-up and personal point of
view. "I don't expect to go to hell," one soldier said, "but if I do, I
am sure that Hell can't beat that terrible scene."[47] Lieutenant Elisha
Hunt Rhodes spoke for thousands of survivors of the slaughter at
Spotsylvania when he said, "Thank God I am still living."[48] Both sides
continued to shoot at each other until it was too dark to see.

After notifying General Halleck about the fighting on May 12,
Grant sent a telegram to his wife, Julia, just to let her know how things
were going. He reported that all the advantages were on his side, as
far as he could tell, that he never felt better in his life, and that he had

absolutely no doubts about how the war was going to end. His losses were heavy, but General Lee's losses were even heavier. In short, he was positive that the Union armies were going to win the war.

By this time, Grant had come to the conclusion that the fighting in Virginia was not the same as it had been in the West and that Robert E. Lee was a far different general than John C. Pemberton, his opponent at Vicksburg, or any other adversary he had faced. But he was not intimidated. He had every confidence both in himself and in the Army of the Potomac, and he was certain that the war would end in triumph for the Union armies. It might not happen that summer, it might not happen until several more terrible battles were fought, but Grant had every confidence that Lee's surrender was only a matter of time.

Even though the war was not being won quickly enough to suit many people throughout the North, there were an increasing number who were beginning to share Grant's optimism. Even the *Times* of London was beginning to look at Grant's strategy in a favorable light. The editors at the *Times* had always been blatantly pro-Confederate, ever since Fort Sumter, but now they had nothing but praise for the aggressive Union general who refused to retreat.

"Grant has stamped a new character on the tactics of the Federals," the *Times* declared. "No other general would either have advanced upon the Wilderness after the severe battle of the 5th or followed up an almost victorious though retiring enemy after the still harder fighting of the 6th. None but he again would have attacked his adversary so resolutely on the 8th and on the 9th or held his ground so tenaciously in spite of failure. Under his command the Army of the Potomac has achieved in invading Virginia an amount of success never achieved before except in repelling invasion."[49]

This was nothing less than a ringing endorsement. Here was one of the leading newspapers in Britain saying good things about Grant for having stamped his aggressive personality on the army, a paper that rarely had anything complimentary to say about Lincoln or any of his generals. It is not very likely that General Grant ever read what the *Times* had to say about him, but he probably would not have been fazed by the article even if he had read it. He would have hunched his shoulders, taken another puff on his cigar, and walked silently away.

General Grant had other things to worry about. The rebels had retreated from the Mule Shoe, and Grant was afraid that Lee might be trying to get away. It turned out that Lee had reformed his lines at the base of the salient. Eighty years later, British general Bernard Montgomery would describe such a move as "tidying up" his lines. Instead of a bulge pointing northward, the new Confederate front now ran along an east-west line. The dead remained where they were.

"There was no fighting on the 13th, further than a little skirmishing between Mott's and the enemy," Grant wrote.[50] Some of the men might have expected a rest after such a grueling fight, even a short one, but Grant was not the type to give anybody any time off. Resting his own men would also have meant giving the enemy time to catch its breath. Grant sat down and wrote the order for the army to move out—begin moving by the left flank again.

The entire army began to stir, without a lot of enthusiasm, but without much complaining, either. Since old Grant had taken over, the men had resigned themselves to the fact that they would always be either marching or fighting. Morale was surprisingly high, considering what they had just been through. They knew that there would be more of the same just ahead, if not tomorrow then the day after tomorrow or the day after that. "Today we were relieved at daylight by other troops," Elisha Hunt Rhodes commented, "and we formed in the rear of the 9th Corps."[51] He went on to say, "Our battery and the Rebel guns have made a great noise today, but very little has been accomplished." The guns on both sides would begin making a lot more noise before long, and the killing would begin again.

Only the weather—constant rain that literally turned the roads into rivers of mud—stopped the fighting from starting sooner. It could not start soon enough to suit Grant, who waited impatiently for the rain to stop so that he could restart his drive against Lee. On May 16, Grant sent a message to General Halleck that sounded almost apologetic: "You can assure the President and Secretary of War that the elements alone have suspended hostilities and that it is in no manner due to weakness or exhaustion on our part."[52] It was an unnecessary communiqué. Neither President Lincoln nor Secretary of War Stanton needed any reminder when it came to General Grant's aggressiveness.

UNFORTUNATE DAY

On May 8, 1864, General Robert E. Lee telegraphed Confederate Secretary of War James A. Seddon: "The enemy has abandoned his position and is moving towards Fredericksburg."[53] Actually, Grant was not retreating; it just seemed that way to General Lee. As Colonel Horace Porter put it, "When Lee found our wagon-trains were moving in an easterly direction, he made up his mind that the army was retreating."[54] Lee was not intimidated by Grant any more than Grant was intimidated by Lee, but from his message to Secretary of War Seddon it was obvious that he did not know Grant. If he had known his opponent better, he would have realized that Grant would never even have considered withdrawing. It was just not part of Grant's nature.

Notions of a Federal withdrawal did not last very long. On the afternoon following his communiqué to Seddon, Lee received reports that enemy skirmishers had made contact with one of his divisions in the vicinity of Spotsylvania, where the rebel army had already dug a line of trenches. News of enemy activity kept coming in throughout the day on May 10, as well, informing Lee that several unsuccessful attacks had been made against a bulge in the Confederate line. Artillery fire began hitting the western side of this bulge, the Mule Shoe, late in the day—troops on that side of the salient claimed that it was probably the worst barrage they had ever been through—but the steady fire ended abruptly at about 6:30 p.m. About ten minutes later, a burst of shouting and musket fire gave warning that the Federals were mounting another attack. Grant was definitely not moving toward Fredericksburg.

A short time after General Lee heard the firing, a courier rode up and handed him some startling and unexpected news—the section of line commanded by General George Doles had been broken. One Confederate general would later remark that the enemy troops "poured through the gap" in Doles's trenches. Another soldier compared the Union attack to an avalanche.[55] The courier went on to report that several cannon had also been taken, along with many prisoners, including several officers.

When he heard the news of what had happened at Doles's Salient, General Lee immediately mounted Traveller and set out to rally his beleaguered troops. Fortunately, cooler heads prevailed, in the persons of Charles Venable and Walter Taylor. The two of them managed to persuade Lee that riding off to rescue Doles and his men was not a very practical idea and might very well prove fatal. But even though Lee had been persuaded not to make a mad dash to the salient, his blood was still up, and he wanted something to be done about the situation right away. "Then you must see to it that the ground is recovered," Lee answered Taylor and Venable. The men got on their horses and "galloped into the fury of the fight" before Lee had the chance to change his mind.[56]

Another variation of the story tells a slightly different version. According to this variation, it was General John B. Gordon who intervened to stop General Lee. The general had already begun to ride off toward Doles's Salient when General Gordon spoke up. "General Lee, this is no place for you," he said. "Do go to the rear. These are Virginians and Georgians, sir—men who have never failed—and they will not fail you now. Will you, boys?" he shouted to the men closest to him. "Is it necessary for General Lee to lead this charge?"

"No! no!" came the resounding reply. "General Lee to the rear! We will drive them back if only General Lee will go to the rear." The chorus of "General Lee to the rear, General Lee to the rear" was taken up by the men, just like at the Wilderness.[57] Also just like at the Wilderness, somebody turned Traveller toward the rear and led both horse and rider away. "I verily believe that had it been necessary or possible, they would have carried on their shoulders both horse and rider to a place of safety," General Gordon later reflected.[58]

For the second time in a week, General Lee had to be restrained from needlessly putting himself in peril. In both instances, at the Wilderness and at Spotsylvania, the level-headed, imperturbable General Lee had become an irrepressible romantic. In this instance, at least, he copied his father, Henry "Light-Horse Harry" Lee—boldness and brashness were among the few of Light-Horse Harry's traits that Robert E. Lee thought fit to imitate.

The word most often used to describe Harry Lee is "dashing." When he was a twenty-three-year-old major, he was awarded a gold medal by Congress for his part in the capture of the British fortifications at Paulus Hook, New Jersey. Later during the War of Independence, Harry Lee was just as dashing in the Carolinas, under the command of General Nathaniel Greene. George Washington asked Lee to become his aide, but Lee declined. He preferred building up his reputation in the South with his cavalry. Woodrow Wilson would compare Light-Horse Harry with Prince Rupert of the Rhine, a legendary seventh-century cavalry commander—highly strung, impetuous, and romantic. When Robert E. Lee decided to charge the enemy in spite of the implications—fully aware that his death would amount to a mortal blow to the Confederate cause—he was certainly his father's son.

The fighting at Doles's Salient continued to run its murderous course: "The fire by this time [late evening] was as violent as any that had ever been heard in the battles of the Army of Northern Virginia."[59] But Colonel Upton did not receive the reinforcements that had been intended, and his men were pushed out of the Confederate works. The line was restored. General Lee and everyone else could breathe a sigh of relief.

But there was still another problem. Federal cavalry under General Philip Sheridan had gone around the flank of the Confederate army and destroyed the Beaver Dam Creek rail station. Critically needed supplies had also been burned—"most of the reserve stores of the army and 504,000 rations of bread and 904,000 of meat had been destroyed" at Beaver Dam.[60] Jeb Stuart was right behind Sheridan, but General Lee knew that Stuart and his men were both tired and hungry. To catch up with Sheridan, they would have to push themselves to the limit.

Stuart's cavalry finally confronted Sheridan at Yellow Tavern on May 11, but the resulting battle did not go the way General Lee had hoped. Jeb Stuart's rout at the hands of Phil Sheridan came as a shock. Some would claim that Yellow Tavern was the turning point of the cavalry wars between North and South—up to that point in time, everything had gone the Confederates' way, but afterward the Union cavalry would have the upper hand.

The most unsettling news of all from Yellow Tavern concerned the death of Jeb Stuart. Stuart was extremely popular throughout the army, not just his own cavalry corps. He was admired for his good-natured personality as much as for the damage he had done to the enemy during his widely publicized cavalry raids and skirmishes. Word of his death shook morale in every unit of the Army of Northern Virginia. "I never saw such a distressed body of men," one observer wrote, "many of them shedding tears when they heard that our gallant general had been shot."[61]

General Lee was also shaken by the news. He probably had more admiration and respect for Jeb Stuart than for any other of his officers, especially since Stonewall Jackson's death. A member of Lee's staff recalled the general's reaction when he first heard what had happened to Stuart. "I was sitting on my horse very close to General Lee," he wrote, "when a courier galloped up with the despatch [sic] announcing that Stuart had been mortally wounded and was dying. General Lee was greatly affected, and said slowly as he folded up the despatch, 'General Stuart had been mortally wounded: a most valuable and able officer.'"[62] Lee was actually a lot sadder and more affected than he let on at the time. He had not only lost a "most valuable" and popular officer, but also an irreplaceable commander. There would be no replacement for Jeb Stuart, any more than there would be another Stonewall Jackson.

General Grant did not attack on May 11, which came as something of a surprise. General Lee received reports that Federal wagons were on the move and that the army was sending its wounded back to Belle Plain. It looked as though Grant "was taking another step toward Richmond." He issued orders that his army should begin making immediate preparations for a quick march. Because he would have to move very quickly to keep up with Grant, Lee ordered two artillery batteries to be removed from the Mule Shoe salient "with as much caution as possible to prevent observation" by the enemy.[63] When the army began to move, speed would be very much of the essence. The slow and bulky artillery would only slow everything down, so they were removed from the lines.

Once again, Lee guessed wrong. As one biographer put it, he "outsmarted himself."[64] When the general heard heavy firing during the early hours of May 12, the first sign of an enemy attack, he mounted Traveller and rode toward the sound of the guns. He had not gone very far when he came across men running toward the rear at full speed. At that point, it was evident that Grant was not moving south toward Richmond after all. Instead, he had launched another full-scale attack, which threw the Confederates into a near panic.

As soon as he realized what had happened, General Lee did his best to rally the men. He took off his hat, so that they would be able to recognize him, and began shouting at everyone within earshot. "Hold on!" he barked at them. "We are going to form a new line!" Some of the men listened to him and stopped, some of them kept running right past him. "Shame on you men, shame on you," he called out to the ones who did not stop. "Go back to your regiments; go back to your regiments!"[65]

The reason behind the panic soon became obvious: Grant's attack hit the Mule Shoe like a tidal wave. "The whole thing happened so quickly that the extent of the disaster could not be realized at once," according to Confederate general E. M. Law.[66] General Edward Johnson reported that the Union regiments came at the salient "in great disorder, with a narrow front, but extending back as far as I could see."[67]

The Federal attack quickly overran the Confederate position. Winfield Scott Hancock's Second Corps captured twenty pieces of artillery, as well as most of the famous "Stonewall Brigade," which was part of Edward Johnson's division. General Johnson himself was also taken prisoner. Because most of its men were now prisoners of war, the Stonewall Brigade officially ceased to exist after Spotsylvania.

A great deal of romantic myth and legend has been written about "the last stand of the Stonewall Brigade," but the reality is not nearly as romantic. The brigade surrendered practically as a unit when their position was overrun; many did not fire a shot. Like General Lee, General Johnson tried to encourage the men to stand and fight, stomping about and shouting and waving his famous hickory club. But no one paid any attention. When the brigade was disbanded, its survivors—only about two hundred men out of three thousand—became part of General William Terry's regiment for the rest of the war.

Some of the cannon that had been captured were those that had been withdrawn by General Lee. When it became obvious that Grant was not heading south toward Richmond, they were rushed back to the salient—just in time to be captured by the onrushing Federal attack. The troops carried on as best they could without the missing artillery pieces, firing their muskets into the massed enemy troops at point blank range. But a .57 caliber minie ball was no substitute for a double charge of canister, no matter how determined the defenders might be.

The fighting went on all afternoon, in spite of a heavy rain. Confederates called this part of the Mule Shoe the "Bloody Angle," the same as the Union troops, and for the same reason. "All day long and until far into the night the battle raged with unceasing firing, in the space covered by the salient and the adjacent works," a Confederate general remembered.[68] Union troops ran at the Confederate works, while the defenders desperately tried to beat them back. Sometimes, troops threw rifles with bayonets fixed, like harpoons. "The hostile battle-flags waved over different parts of the same works, while the men fought like fiends for their possession."

General Lee rode along the lines to observe the situation for himself, just as General Grant was doing at that very moment, giving orders and offering words of encouragement. When long-range Federal artillery began firing at the Confederate position, the bursting shells frightened Lee's horse, Traveller, which began rearing up on its hind legs. General Lee tried his best to quiet the horse, but the exploding shells terrorized the animal. As Traveller was jumping and rearing, a solid shot passed underneath the horse only a few inches from the stirrup. If he had not reared up at that particular moment, General Lee would have been hit by the cannon ball. Once again, luck came to Robert E. Lee's rescue. It was the closest he had come to being killed since the Mexican War, when he was nearly shot by a sentry at Veracruz.

By this time, General Lee had made plans to evacuate the Mule Shoe and withdraw his troops to a line of trenches across the base of the salient. But before the men could be withdrawn, the new line of trenches had to be finished. Lee went to supervise the progress of the new works himself. As the men built the entrenchments, felling trees, hauling them into position, and covering them with dirt, Lee was on hand to watch and encourage. While all this was going on, the relentless fighting continued only eight hundred yards away.

Lee's veteran units had been ordered to hold the salient, and they managed to hold it throughout the day.

At about midnight, Lee finally gave the order to withdraw to the new lines. Several thousand men climbed out of their entrenchments and began walking the eight hundred yards to the trenches at the base of the salient. The move took the rest of the night—the last of the men did not take up their new positions until early dawn on May 13. They left behind thousands of dead and wounded lying in the mud of the Mule Shoe.

It had not been a good day, and General Lee knew it. Even Lee's optimistic young adjutant, Colonel Walter Taylor, was forced to admit that not very much had gone right. "The 12th was an unfortunate day for us—we recovered most of the ground lost but cd [*sic*] not regain our *guns*," he reflected. "This hurts our pride—but we are determined to make our next success all the greater to make amends for this disaster."[69] Lee had managed to keep Grant and his army from plowing their way through the Confederate lines, but it had cost him more than he had intended to part with. If he had won any sort of a victory at all, it had been a pyrrhic victory.

On the day following the Bloody Angle, Lee sent this sparsely worded telegram to Confederate Secretary of War James Seddon:

"THE ENEMY TODAY HAS APPARENTLY BEEN ENGAGED IN BURYING HIS DEAD & CARING FOR HIS WOUNDED. HE HAS MADE NO ATTACK ON OUR LINES. THE LOSS OF ARTILLERY YESTERDAY IS ASCERTAINED TO HAVE BEEN TWENTY PIECES."[70]

He did not mention the loss of Jeb Stuart.

The war had certainly changed since 1862, when Lee had first taken command of the Army of Northern Virginia, and he was all too aware of it. Back then, he had completely dominated the Army of the Potomac as well as its commander, General George B. McClellan. He had put McClellan on the defensive almost immediately after taking command and had retained dominance over every other general that had come after him. McClellan had been overly cautious. His successors were all basically inept and incompetent.

All that ended abruptly when Grant crossed the Rappahannock River. The initiative had abruptly passed to Grant, who immediately put Lee on the defensive. Now all General Lee could do was wait to see where Grant was going next. There was no doubt in his mind as to *what* Grant was going to do—he was going to attack and keep on attacking. The war was now beyond his control; he could see that.

Everything Lee had learned from Winfield Scott during the Mexican War, which he had used to such effectiveness until now—keep moving, stay on the offensive, do everything possible to keep the enemy off balance—had been negated by Grant's strategy of relentless attack. There was no real way for him to stop Grant, short of a miracle. Or short of Grant making some kind of colossal blunder that would cost him the confidence of President Lincoln and the population of the North.

Chapter Five

HOLDING ON LONGER

AGONIZING DECISIONS

General Lee continued to wait for a reply from General Grant throughout the morning of April 9, 1865. He had already sent a note asking what terms Grant was proposing with reference to the surrender of the Army of Northern Virginia. But by late morning he had still not received any reply to his note, which was making him very anxious. Federal forces were advancing toward the place where Lee was waiting. One of his staff officers noted that "Federal troops in our immediate front were advancing, and I knew that in a few minutes they would meet the skirmishers of our rear guard." If that happened, "'the fat would be in the fire' as far as a suspension of hostilities was concerned."[1] After a while, Lee was forced to ride back behind the Confederate lines, where he continued to wait alongside the men of General James Longstreet's First Corps. Lee found that General Longstreet was waiting as well, except Longstreet was waiting for a Federal attack.

Finally, sometime after ten o'clock, Lieutenant Colonel Charles Whittier rode up with a white flag, and also with a note from General George Meade. General Meade had finally given his reluctant approval for a truce, but only for an hour's duration. In response to this, General Lee sent Grant another note, which restated his desire to come to terms. The last sentence of the note came to the point: "I therefore request an interview at such time and place as you may designate, to discuss the terms of the surrender of this army in accord with your offer to have such an interview contained in your letter of yesterday."[2]

The tone of this letter seemed a lot more worried and apprehensive than his previous communiqué. Lee was becoming increasingly anxious that Grant would demand stricter surrender terms than Lee would be willing to accept. He mentioned this to General Longstreet, who did his best to put the general's mind at ease. He knew Grant well enough, he told Lee, to say that Grant would ask for conditions similar to any terms that Lee himself might ask for if the situation was reversed. Longstreet could certainly speak with authority—he probably knew U. S. Grant better than anybody in the Confederate army. But General Lee was not calmed by what Longstreet had to say. He was still concerned that General Grant might demand unconditional surrender or would draw up some other unreasonable terms.

Longstreet had a quick answer for this. If Grant should become belligerent, he suggested, Lee should break off the interview at once and tell General Grant to do his worst. This suggestion of carrying on with the fight seemed to encourage Lee. He rode off in a much better state of mind than he had been only a few minutes earlier.

General Longstreet had a discussion of his own that morning on the subject of surrender. Actually, it was not a discussion as much as a verbal skirmish. Soon after the truce went into effect and the fighting stopped, Longstreet was approached by twenty-five-year-old General George A. Custer and his entourage. Custer "came in a fast gallop," with his "flaxen locks flowing over his shoulders," and spoke directly to Longstreet: "In the name of General Sheridan, I demand the unconditional surrender of this army."[3]

Longstreet refused to be impressed, either by Custer's flaxen locks or by his demand. He bluntly informed Custer that he was addressing a superior officer in a disrespectful manner, and also that he was within the Confederate lines without authority. Longstreet also pointed out that he was not the commander of the Army of Northern Virginia. But even if he had been the commanding general, Longstreet went on, he would not receive such a message from Phil Sheridan, who was not his equal in rank.

Custer was clearly taken aback by Longstreet's scolding and responded to the rebuke by saying that it would be a pity "to have more blood on the field."

"As you are now more reasonable," Longstreet responded, "I will

Top left: U. S. "Sam" Grant before the Mexican War. He learned a great deal about tactics and strategy in Mexico—and also learned that Robert E. Lee was mortal. (Library of Congress)

Top right: Robert E. Lee, circa 1848. Although he met U. S. Grant during the Mexican War, he claimed that he did not remember Grant. (Library of Congress)

Bottom left: Thomas J. "Stonewall" Jackson, in a photo taken shortly before his death in 1863. During General Lee's campaign against Grant in 1864 and 1865, General Jackson's presence was missed. (Library of Congress)

Bottom right: President Abraham Lincoln stood by General Grant throughout the terrible fighting of 1864 and 1865, in spite of criticism that Grant was a "butcher." The president had confidence that Grant possessed the nerve to see the war through to the end. (National Archives and Records Administration)

Above: The Army of the Potomac crosses the Rapidan River on May 4, 1864. One Union officer wondered how it would look if each man who would be killed in the coming months wore a badge, indicating that he would not be coming back. (Library of Congress)

Right: General Grant whittling to calm his anxieties on the first day at the Battle of the Wilderness. Grant was doing his best to give the impression of being calm and collected, but he was actually a bag of nerves. (Library of Congress)

Federal soldiers rescuing their comrades from fires at the Battle of the Wilderness. During the fighting, muzzle flashes from muskets set fire to leaves and underbrush. These fires killed several hundred wounded soldiers who were not lucky enough to be rescued. (Library of Congress)

When the Army of the Potomac turned south after the Battle of the Wilderness, soldiers cheered General Grant until he was afraid that the noise would alert the enemy. The men knew they were not running away from General Lee, as they had done after Chancellorsville a year earlier. Instead, they were going after Lee. A young lieutenant would recall that this was the most thrilling moment of the war. (Library of Congress)

Top: Units of the Army of the Potomac crossing the North Anna River in May 1864. On the other side of the river, General Lee did not take advantage of the opportunity to attack Grant's badly divided army. (Library of Congress)

Bottom left: U. S. Grant during the summer of 1864. Both stress and determination are evident in his expression. He informed his chief of staff that he proposed to fight it out on this line if it took all summer, a message that raised morale throughout the North and encouraged President Lincoln regarding the outcome of the war. (National Archives and Records Administration)

Bottom right: General Grant with his wife, Julia, and his son Jesse, at Grant's headquarters, City Point, Virginia. The general did his best to seem calm and composed throughout the battles of 1864 and 1865, but he was under daily tension and anxiety. Visits by his family helped to ease the stresses of war. (Library of Congress)

Top: Some of the dead of Cold Harbor being reburied in 1865. An increasing number of people in the North were beginning to wonder if the war was worth the cost in dead and wounded. But General Grant never lost faith in his ability to win the war. (Library of Congress)

Bottom: A Pennsylvania artillery unit at Petersburg, in June 1863. During the nine-month siege of Petersburg, artillerymen fired thousands of rounds into the city. When General William T. Sherman captured Atlanta in September 1864, General Grant ordered a hundred-gun salute to be fired into the Confederate works at Petersburg using live ammunition. (Library of Congress)

Left: At the end of January 1865, Confederate president Jefferson Davis confirmed Robert E. Lee as general-in-chief of all Confederate armies. The appointment had come much too late to help the Confederate war effort. (National Archives and Records Administration)

Below: A Union wagon train winds its way through Petersburg in April 1865, bringing food and supplies to troops that were pursuing General Lee's army toward Appomattox. (Library of Congress)

Right: General Lee, with his son G. W. C. Lee (left) and his aide Colonel Walter Taylor. Colonel Taylor's comments regarding General Lee tended to be frank and honest and sometimes presented a less-than-flattering portrait of the general. (Library of Congress)

Below, left: The ruins of Richmond, Virginia, in 1865. General Lee never understood that Richmond was not Grant's objective. (Library of Congress)

Below, right: The Wilmer McLean House in the village of Appomattox Court House. In McLean's parlor, General Grant followed President Lincoln's inclination to be generous to the defeated former enemy, to "let 'em up easy," and offered the best and most generous terms possible to General Lee. (National Archives and Records Administration)

Above left: General Robert E. Lee waits for General Grant in Wilmer McLean's house, as imagined in a painting by Thomas Nast. General Lee wore a full-dress uniform for the surrender, complete with a sword "of considerable value," while General Grant wore his everyday uniform, which was dirty and spattered with mud. The two generals made a striking contrast. (Library of Congress)

Above right: The well-known photograph of Robert E. Lee, taken by Matthew Brady a short time after the war ended. This is the General Lee of legend: calm, composed, resolute, and wearing a full uniform. General Lee had fought against several Union generals prior to 1864 and managed to get the better of every one of them. But he met his match in U. S. Grant. (Library of Congress)

Above, center: General Lee rides away from the McLean house on the afternoon of April 9, 1865. Although he had surrendered his army, he had done his best for his men, and he was touched by the generosity of General Grant's terms. (Library of Congress) say that General Lee has gone to meet General Grant, and that it is for them to determine the future of the armies." Custer had nothing to say to this. He turned his horse around and rode back toward the Union lines.

A short time after General Lee sent his note to Grant regarding Grant's terms of surrender, Lieutenant Colonel Orville Babcock rode up with another letter from General Grant. After the preliminary introductions and salutes were exchanged, Lee read what Grant had to say: "I am at this writing about four miles west of Walker's church, and will push forward to the front for the purpose of meeting you."[4] Colonel Babcock added that he had been advised by General Grant to make any arrangements for the coming interview that would suit General Lee, within either the Union lines or the Confederate lines.

Colonel Babcock's message instantly put General Lee's mind at ease. General Grant's note made no mention that harsher surrender terms would be demanded, which could only mean that the terms he offered the day before were still valid. Also, Colonel Babcock's manner was so courteous that it must be a reflection of Grant's attitude. It seemed that General Longstreet was right—it looked as though General Grant was going to offer conditions that would be as generous as Lee could reasonably expect.

General Grant had also offered Lee the option of sending another officer to surrender the Army of Northern Virginia, a courtesy meant to spare Lee the humiliation of surrendering the army himself. But General Lee rejected this option. He had said that he would accept all responsibility and was not about to delegate this unpleasant duty to a junior officer. He would go and face General Grant in person, come what may, and he would face any consequences that had to be faced.

Colonel Charles Marshall, an officer on Lee's staff, thought that the general made up his mind to surrender the army himself because of something his father had said in his *Memoirs*. Harry Lee had been at Yorktown when Lord Cornwallis surrendered his army to George Washington, and he was surprised that Cornwallis had elected not to attend the surrender ceremony himself. Instead, he sent a subordinate, General O'Hara, to represent him. Light-Horse Harry was disappointed that "Cornwallis held himself back from the humiliating scene, obeying emotions which his great character ought to have stifled."[5] He went on to write, "The British general in this instance deviated from his general line of conduct, dimming the splendour of his long and brilliant career." Because of his father's "unfavorable reference" to Cornwallis's behavior at Yorktown, Robert E. Lee decided not to do what Cornwallis had done. He felt duty-bound to attend the surrender ceremony himself. Light-Horse Harry's influence was still with his son, even at such a time.[6]

General Lee, Colonel Babcock, and their escorts rode off to meet with General Grant. Colonel Walter Taylor asked if he could be excused from attending the surrender ceremony. The excuse he gave was that he had already ridden through the lines twice that morning, but the real reason was that he did not want to be present at the surrender. Lee sensed the real reason and let Taylor off the hook, "with his usual consideration for the feelings of others."[7]

General Lee had a consideration of his own. He asked Colonel Babcock if the truce that had been granted by General Meade would last long enough to cover his interview with Grant. The last thing he wanted was for some hot-headed lieutenant on either side to start shooting while he was in the middle of negotiating a peace agreement with General Grant. Colonel Babcock immediately wrote an order, in Grant's name, extending the truce until further notice.

With these items of business out of the way, Lee, Babcock, Colonel Marshall, and the other members of the group started up the road. Lee's horse, Traveller, stopped for a drink at a stream, but this was only a short pause before the riders continued on their way "past the silent line of battle on the hillside."[8]

Surrendering the Army of Northern Virginia was the most difficult and anxious decision General Lee had been forced to make since he resigned his US Army commission four years earlier. In 1861, he had agonized for days over whether or not he should remain in the "old army" after a lifetime of service, or whether he should join the armed forces of his native Virginia.

Virginia seceded from the Union on April 17, 1861, three days after Fort Sumter surrendered. Robert E. Lee—Colonel Robert E. Lee, United States Army, at the time—underwent three days of "severe mental trouble," in the words of one of Lee's most trusted staff officers, while trying to make up his mind. Lee's wife, Mary Custis Lee, wrote, "what a sore trial it was for him to leave the old army, to give up the flag of the Union, to separate from so many of his old associates (*particularly* General Scott, from whom he always felt the greatest regard) and to be censured by many whose good opinion he valued."[9]

Mary Custis Lee also mentioned "interviews" (actually only one interview) with fellow Virginian General Winfield Scott, during which General Scott "used every argument he could bring to bear to induce him to remain with the Union."[10] Among other things, General Scott suggested that Lee would become overall commander of all Union forces within a few years, when Scott himself retired, if Lee did not resign his commission. According to Mrs. Lee, Scott also advised the "Government" to do everything possible to persuade Lee not to leave the US Army, saying, "Robert Lee would be worth fifty thousand men to them."

Immediately before his three-hour interview with Winfield Scott, Colonel Lee also had a conversation with Francis P. Blair, one of President Lincoln's advisors, on the same subject. Blair said to Lee, "I come to you on the part of President Lincoln to ask whether any inducement that he can offer will prevail on you to take command of the Union army?"[11]

"If I owned four million slaves," Lee responded, "I would cheerfully sacrifice them to the preservation of the Union, but to lift my own hand against my own State and people is impossible."

Two days after these conversations, on April 20, 1861, Robert E. Lee tendered his resignation to General Winfield Scott. "General: Since my interview with you on the 18th Inst. I have felt that I ought not longer to retain my Commission in the Army," his letter began.[12] He went on to ask General Scott to recommend his resignation for acceptance and explained that he would have presented it at once if it had not been "for the struggle it has cost me to separate myself from a Service to which I have devoted all the best years of my life." He had resigned his commission and left the army, just as his father, Light Horse Harry Lee, had done.

Colonel Lee also expressed his indebtedness to General Scott himself, for his kindness and consideration: "I shall carry with me to the grave the most grateful recollections of your kind consideration, and your name and fame will always be dear to me."

"Save in the defense of my native state I shall never desire again to draw my sword," he concluded his resignation. "Be pleased to accept my most earnest wishes for the continuance of your happiness and prosperity and believe me, most truly yours, R. E. Lee."

Lee sent similar letters to his sister, Mrs. Anne Marshall of Baltimore, and to his brother, Sidney Smith Lee, on the same day. In both letters, he tried to explain the reason for his resignation from the army and also used the same basic phrasing. He told his sister, "With all my devotion to the Union and the feeling of loyalty and duty of an American citizen, I have not been able to make up my mind to raise my hand against my relatives, my children, my home. I have therefore resigned my commission in the Army, and save in defense of my native State, with the sincere hope that my poor services may never be needed, I hope I may never be called on to draw my sword."[13] He went on to say, in the way of an apology, "I know you will blame me; but you must think as kindly of me as you can, and believe that I have endeavoured to do what I thought right."

Lee's letter to his brother said essentially the same thing: "After the most anxious inquiry as to the correct course for me to pursue, I concluded to resign, and sent in my resignation this morning." He went on to insist that he was now a private citizen and that he had no ambition except to remain at home. "Save in defense of my native State, I have no desire ever again to draw my sword. I sent you my warmest love."[14]

Lee repeated the statement that he had no desire to draw his sword in all three letters. But he had a fairly good idea that the State of Virginia was not going to let him sit at home and lead a quiet life as a private citizen, not with his military background and his West Point training. He was asked to take command of Virginia's armed forces after the state seceded from the Union, and he accepted the Virginia Convention's commission on April 23, 1861.

"Trusting to Almighty God, an approving conscience, and the aid of my fellow citizens," he concluded his reply to the Convention, "I will devote myself to the defense and service of my native State, in whose behalf alone would I ever draw my sword."[15]

Virginia was now Robert E. Lee's country and his allegiance. Virginia had been the homeland of the Lee family long before the United States of America even existed. The Lee family's power and influence extended back into Virginia's past for generations, ever since it was a British colony. Robert E. Lee's great-great-grandfather, Richard Lee, lived in Virginia as early as 1642. He had owned about 16,000 acres of land, which made him one of the wealthiest and most influential men in the colony. Lee's grandfather and great-grandfather were also men of wealth and influence, along with just about every one of his ancestors—two of them signed the Declaration of Independence and three were members of the Continental Congress. His father, Henry "Light-Horse Harry" Lee, was a bona fide war hero and one of George Washington's most celebrated officers. Washington himself declared, "I know of no country that can produce a family all distinguished as clever men as our Lees."[16]

By "country," Washington meant Virginia, not the United States. Light-Horse Harry considered himself a Virginian, not an American. Or at least a Virginian first and an American second. When he was offered command of an army that was to be sent off to Ohio to put down an Indian uprising, Harry Lee wrote that he did not want to leave "my native country, to whose goodness I am so much indebted."[17] In fact, he often referred to Virginia as his country, a sentiment that rubbed off on his son.

Dedicating himself to the defense and service of Virginia was another influence of Light-Horse Harry Lee that would affect Robert E. Lee's life. Surrendering to General Grant not only meant that Lee would be giving up his army and the dream of Confederate independence. It also meant that he would be giving up on his native country, which had been the home of his ancestors for over two hundred years.

STRIKING THEM A BLOW

On the morning of May 21, 1864, General Lee finally began receiving reliable reports on General Grant's activities. For the past week, he had been trying to find out if Grant was planning a new attack on Spotsylvania or was going to move out on another one of his flanking maneuvers. There had been some enemy movement since the Bloody Angle, and a cavalry raid had burned Guiney's Station, a railway station on the Richmond, Fredericksburg, and Potomac Railroad, on May 18 and had also cut the rail line—Grant had not been sitting still and burying his dead all that time. It looked as though Grant was up to something, but nobody could say exactly what. Lee was upset by the almost total lack of information. If Jeb Stuart had still been in command of the cavalry, he lamented, he would know all about what the enemy was doing.

All of this changed on May 21. The Confederate signal station at the Catlett family's farm, about seven miles southeast of Spotsylvania, began wig-wagging flag warnings that the Yankee army was on the move. A soldier with the 44th Alabama regiment had managed to get close enough to the Federal troops to hear them saying, "On to Richmond, boys, we'll be there in three days." He was able to get back to his own lines without being discovered, where he promptly reported what he had seen and heard. The signalmen at the Catlett farm kept sending the warning.[18]

As soon as he heard the news, General Lee rode to the front to see the situation for himself. He stopped near a battery of artillery to take a look at a series of Federal entrenchments across the way, trying to determine if the enemy was still there or if they had moved out. Although he gave the trenches a good long look with his field glasses, he was not able to tell if they were occupied or not. He ordered the battery commander to fire on the enemy position. Return fire soon followed, and Lee had his answer.

Lee continued to study the enemy position while the firing continued; mounted on Traveller, he made an especially inviting target. A nearby soldier shouted, "Won't somebody take that damn fool away from here?" Lee heard what the man said but did not take any offense—or at least he pretended not to. He simply put his glasses down and rode off.[19]

Now that he knew that Grant was "changing his base," as he phrased it, General Lee also realized that he would have to reach the North Anna River, which was the next natural barrier on the road to Richmond, before the enemy. Grant had the Mattaponi River between him and the Army of Northern Virginia, which would protect him from attack, at least for the time being. Lee sent a telegram to Secretary of War James Seddon to report the situation.

To: James A. Seddon
Secretary of War
Telegram
Spotsylvania Court House

May 21, 1861
8:40 A.M.

THE ENEMY IS APPARENTLY AGAIN CHANGING HIS BASE.
THREE GUNBOATS CAME UP TO PORT ROYAL TWO DAYS
SINCE. THIS MORNING AN INFANTRY FORCE APPEARED AT
GUINEY'S. HIS CAVALRY ADVANCED AT DOWNER'S BRIDGE,
ON BOWLING GREEN ROAD. HE IS APPARENTLY PLACING
THE MATTAPONY BETWEEN US, AND WILL PROBABLY OPEN
COMMUNICATION WITH PORT ROYAL. I AM EXTENDING ON
THE TELEGRAPH ROAD, AND WILL REGULATE MY MOVE-
MENTS BY THE INFORMATION [RECEIVED. THE CHAR-
ACTER] OF HIS ROUTE I FEAR WILL SECURE HIM FROM
ATTACK TILL HE CROSSES THE PAMUNKEY.
R. E. LEE[20]

If Grant managed to cross the North Anna River before him,
Lee was all too aware that the enemy would have a head start to
Richmond. He would still have to cross the South Anna River to
get to Richmond, the river that joins the North Anna to form the
Pamunkey River, but he would have a distinct advantage if he crossed
the river unopposed. If they were going to reach the North Anna
before Grant, Lee's men would have to push themselves, and they
were already on the brink of exhaustion.

The men did push themselves, or at least they moved as quickly
as the muddy roads and their fatigue would allow. They kept walking,
plodding along toward the North Anna, somehow managing to
move fifteen miles in the course of the day. Sometimes their wea-
riness would get the better of them, and they would fall out to get
some desperately needed sleep. Stragglers could be found all along
the side of the road, some sleeping, some just taking time out to rest.

General Lee happened across a band of stragglers during the
early hours of May 22, all sprawled out in the darkness, and advised

them to get on their feet and start moving. "I know you don't want to be taken prisoners," he said to them, "and I know that you are tired and sleepy, but the enemy will be along before or by daybreak and if you do not move you will be taken."[21]

The men did not take kindly to being scolded, and some of them answered back from the safety of the darkness. "Well, you may order us to 'move on, move on,' when you are mounted on a horse and have all the rations that the country can afford," one of them grumbled, loud enough for the general to hear.

Some of the men recognized the mounted figure, and called out, "Marse Robert!" That was all it took. As soon as they realized that the man on horseback was none other than General Lee himself, the men stood up and began cheering. "Yes, Marse Robert," they called out, "we'll move on and go anywhere you say, even to hell!" General Lee thanked them quietly and moved on himself.

Lee's troops also moved on and kept moving until they reached the North Anna. Jubal Early's division, part of the Second Corps, approached the river on the morning of May 22, with General Early riding out in front. At about 8:30 a.m., General Lee himself crossed the Chesterfield Bridge. He had won the race to the North Anna.

When the men of General Early's division saw General Lee that morning, they were appalled by his appearance. The stress and strain of the past weeks were all too apparent; Lee looked worn and haggard. One officer thought that he looked like a very sick man. General Lee ordered Early to form his division into a defensive line, but Early disputed the order. He told Lee that his men were not ready and that they should be given some desperately needed time to rest before being put back into the line of battle. Lee was not in the mood to hear any complaints and told Early to carry out an order when he was given one. Early did not appreciate the reprimand and grumbled that the general was not well.

General Lee and his staff rode off to Hanover Junction, about three miles south of the river, where he set up his headquarters. He telegraphed Secretary of War Seddon to say that General Ewell's Second Corps was on its way, and that the First and Third Corps were also expected. The entire Army of Northern Virginia should be crossing the river with plenty of time to spare. Now all he had to do was wait for Grant.

The problem was that nobody knew exactly where Grant was going. General Lee sent another telegram to Secretary of War Seddon, admitting that he had no real idea of Grant's movements: "I have learned as yet nothing of the movements of the enemy north of the Mattapony."[22] For the second time in two days, Lee had lost contact with the enemy. The entire Army of the Potomac seemed to have disappeared. Colonel Walter Taylor noted from "Camp Hanover" on May 23, "For the first time since the 4th of the month, we are spared the sight of the enemy."[23]

At around noon on May 23, the enemy finally made its presence known. Federal troops were sighted on the north side of the North Anna, and Confederate artillery began shooting at them as soon as they came within range. The advancing infantry took cover behind some low ground, but the horse artillery began shooting back. Federal gunners kept up their fire for a while, then ceased fire when it became apparent that they were not doing any damage. They retreated toward the Union rear, out of range of the rebel gunners.

While the artillery duel was going on, General Lee rode up to the front in a carriage. The general was not feeling very well, certainly not well enough to ride Traveller, so he decided to make his rounds by carriage instead of horseback. He came to a stop next to the battery of a gunner named George Michael Neese. The Union forces were visible to the naked eye, but General Lee used his field glasses to get a better look. He leaned against a pine tree, not ten feet from where Neese was standing, and gave the approaching enemy his full attention.

After watching the troops move closer to the river for a short while, he turned and said to a horseman who had accompanied him, "Orderly, go back and tell General A. P. Hill to leave his men in camp; this is nothing but a feint, the enemy is preparing to cross below." Having seen everything he wanted to see, General Lee put his glasses back in their case, got back in his carriage, and rode back toward Hanover Junction.[24]

But General Lee had guessed wrong. His decision that Grant would "cross below" showed how little he had learned about his opponent since May 4. By this time, he should have known that Grant would attack him where he was and would not try to find a safe crossing somewhere several miles away.

Actually, General Gouverneur K. Warren's Fifth Corps did attack a few miles away from Gunner Neese's position, at Jericho Mills, but this was not what General Lee had in mind when he said that the enemy was preparing to "cross below"—he meant a lot further off than Jericho Mills. By 4:30 p.m., General Warren's entire corps had crossed the North Anna and was moving southeast toward A. P. Hill's Confederate Third Corps. Hill's troops went at the Federals with a determination that can only be called grim and drove General Lysander Cutler's Fourth Division back toward the river. But Warren's men counterattacked, and this time it was the Confederates who retreated in confusion. Casualties from this encounter were about the same—six thousand men—on both sides.

While Warren's men were attacking and counterattacking on the south side of the North Anna, the men of Winfield Scott Hancock's Second Corps were making their way toward the river from the north. They were stopped, briefly, by a South Carolina brigade just north of Chesterfield Bridge. The Confederates opened fire from inside a three-sided fortification, with a fire that was intense enough to stop the advancing column dead in its tracks. But Hancock's artillery began an intense fire of its own at about 5:30, which stopped the Confederate musket fire and allowed the advance to resume. Federal troops stormed the redoubt by climbing up each other's backs and by hauling themselves up the walls with bayonets stuck into the parapet. As the Federals swarmed over the fortification, mostly New York and Pennsylvania troops, the South Carolina brigade retreated across Chesterfield Bridge to the opposite side of the North Anna. Just a few hours after General Lee had ridden across the same bridge, it was firmly in the hands of Grant's troops.

The general had another close call that day, but it had nothing to do with Chesterfield Bridge. He had been invited to have a glass of buttermilk by the owner of a house just south of the river, an act of hospitality that very nearly resulted in Lee's death. While he was sitting on the porch, a cannonball missed him by only a few feet, startling the general's host and imbedding itself in the frame of his front door. General Lee did not even blink. He calmly finished his glass of buttermilk as if nothing had happened, thanked his host, and rode away. Once again, luck, or fate, or chance, had intervened on the side of Robert E. Lee.

By the afternoon of May 23, Lee had increasingly begun to feel the effects of what is usually described as an intestinal disorder. Biographers have supposed that this condition was brought on by bad food and long hours. Whatever caused it, the disorder was violent enough to give the general considerable pain and discomfort, which was the main reason he visited the front lines by carriage instead of on horseback. But no matter how sick he might have been, he obstinately refused to give in to his ailment and also refused to give up command of the army to any subordinate, even temporarily.

For one thing, Lee was just too stubborn to give up his command. Also, and probably even more significantly, he did not have enough faith in any of his officers. Stonewall Jackson was gone, Longstreet was recovering from his Wilderness injury, and there was no subordinate he felt he could trust with commanding the Army of Northern Virginia. General Lee made up his mind to suffer through his illness and to carry on the best he could under the circumstances. In his own mind, he did not have any other option.

General Lee had not been in the best of health for quite some time. His most serious medical disorder was a weak heart, which interfered with his ability to direct his forces in the field. His cardiac disorder was probably a major factor behind his ordering Pickett's Charge at Gettysburg nearly eleven months earlier. It has been suggested that he suffered a heart attack during the battle and that this affected his judgement.

In 1992, two doctors from the University of Virginia Health Services Center offered their opinion on General Lee's condition. "We believe that General Robert E. Lee had ischemic heart disease," they wrote, and went on to say, "It is our opinion that he sustained a heart attack in 1863 and that this illness had a major influence on the battle of Gettysburg." The two doctors conclude, "It often was stated that the loss of the war broke the heart of Lee, but in view of our modern day understanding, it probably is more accurate to say that advancing coronary atherosclerosis was the culprit."[25]

In May of 1864, General Lee was fifty seven years old. But because of the pressures and anxieties of the war he looked, and probably felt, much older. General Grant's constant hammering increased the strain he was feeling, wearing him down both physically and mentally, and adding to his health problems. Also, the general was really not looking after himself properly—he was not getting enough sleep, and he was pushing himself too hard. He seldom slept more than three hours on any given night. On the night of May 23, he had a light—and not very substantial—meal at three o'clock in the morning. After eating, he went to sleep until about five o'clock, when he got up and started south. At about 8:30, he rode across Chesterfield Bridge.

This daily routine of insufficient sleep and short, inadequate meals was intensifying the effects of Lee's intestinal troubles, which were already intense enough and getting worse. The pain and discomfort of his ailment were making the general cantankerous and bad-tempered; he snapped at subordinates and shouted at aides. After enduring one of the general's tirades, one officer told Lee that he was not fit to command the army and stormed out of his tent. The officer was right, and Lee himself knew it.

Lee did not reserve his bad temper just for junior officers. General A. P. Hill, a veteran of the Seven Days' Battle, Antietam/Sharpsburg, Fredericksburg, and Gettysburg, received a visit from the general, along with a few well-chosen words, on the morning of May 24. Lee was not happy that Gouverneur Warren's corps had not been pushed back across the North Anna the day before, and he was not very diplomatic in letting General Hill know about his unhappiness. "General Hill, why did you let those people cross the river?" he wanted to know. "Why did you not drive them back as General Jackson would have done?"[26]

Actually, Stonewall Jackson was best known for his flanking movements, which he employed with telling effect against "Fighting Joe" Hooker at Chancellorsville, not for mounting frontal attacks. But Lee was angry with Hill, and wanted to give him a good dressing-down. The pressures of battle, combined with his burning intestines, put the general in a particularly bad temper that morning. He decided to take his frustrations out on General Hill, who seemed to have accepted the tirade very calmly.

But instead of just invoking the name of Stonewall Jackson, General Lee would have been much better off if he had tried copying his tactics. If he had relieved his army of the thankless task of guarding Richmond, he would have been free to shift his position and range and maneuver his troops the way Jackson would have done. In U. S. Grant, Jackson would have been up against a completely different kind of general than Joe Hooker or Ambrose Burnside or John Pope. But he would have at least tried to employ tactics other than inflexibly defending the Confederate capital.

By tethering his army to Richmond, Lee was also disregarding the basic lesson he had learned from Winfield Scott in Mexico: outmaneuvering and outwitting the enemy was a lot more effective than trying to outfight him. General Scott had gotten the better of General Santa Anna by manipulating his much smaller force around the Mexican army and by maintaining the initiative all throughout his drive toward Mexico City. The effectiveness of fighting such a war was a lesson that Stonewall Jackson never forgot from his time in Mexico. If General Lee had allowed himself to abandon Richmond, and had detached his army from defending the approaches to Richmond, he would have been much better off—especially in view of the fact that the Army of Northern Virginia was Grant's primary objective, not Richmond.

Now that Grant's forces had crossed the North Anna, Lee had to find a way to stop them from going any further. And he had a very good chance of doing exactly that because Grant had unwittingly divided his army. Gouverneur K. Warren's Fifth Corps, which had crossed the river at Jericho Mills, and Winfield Scott Hancock's Second Corps, which was south of Chesterfield Bridge, were separated by several miles. The US Ninth Corps, commanded by General Ambrose Burnside, would attempt to bridge the gap by crossing the North Anna at a place called Ox Ford, which was about midway between Warren's and Hancock's forces.

But Lee had placed A. P. Hill's Third Corps and Anderson's First Corps (formerly Longstreet's) between the two Federal corps south of the river. The trenches occupied by the Confederates did not run in a straight line. The shape of the entrenchments is usually called an inverted V, but it actually looked more like a rough sketch of the Rock of Gibraltar than any letter of the alphabet. The trenches formed a salient, similar to the one at Spotsylvania. But the main difference between the North Anna line and the Mule Shoe salient at Spotsylvania was that the apex of the inverted V was anchored by the

North Anna itself, while the two down strokes were secured by the Little River on the west and by marshland on the east. There would be no open flank for the Federals to go around. Because the two Federal corps were separated by Anderson and A. P. Hill, Lee would have the chance to destroy the two units individually, with no threat of a counterattack by the remaining corps. If everything went Lee's way, he would be able to deliver a crippling blow to the Army of the Potomac without encountering overwhelming opposition.

But this opportunity would not last forever. General Grant was not just going to sit by and watch while one of his corps was being threatened. Whatever Lee was going to do to Grant would have to be done quickly. Because of his intestinal disease, Lee was not able to do very much, and he was not able to do anything quickly. He was very sick and getting worse. His adjutant, Walter H. Taylor, admitted that the general could "attend to nothing except what was absolutely necessary for him to know & act upon," and "his attack frightened all sickness away from me."[27]

When he learned that his father was unwell, Robert E. Lee Jr., wrote, "this terrible thought forced itself upon us: Suppose the disease should disable him, even for a time, or, worse, should take him forever from the front of his men! It could not be! It was too awful to consider!"[28] General Jubal Early said that Lee was the life and soul of the army, and he was absolutely right. Without General Lee, the Army of Northern Virginia could not even mount an effective attack against one of Grant's corps, much less win the war.

Lee had Grant right where he wanted him, but he was too sick to do anything about it. He could not even leave his tent, much less get on his horse and ride to the front. Just a little over a year earlier, which must have seemed like a thousand years to General Lee, he might have deputized either General Longstreet or Stonewall Jackson to take command—his war horse and his right arm. But Jackson was dead, and Longstreet would be disabled for several more months.

General Lee did his best to conduct operations in spite of his illness, but there was not a lot he could do in his present physical condition. "We must strike them a blow; we must never let them pass us again," he repeated again and again from his bed; "we must strike them a blow."[29] He had been pushed backward for the past three weeks, losing men he could not afford to lose, and now he had the chance to strike the blow he wanted, the chance to go on the offensive. But even though he had reports from the field brought to him throughout the day, and although he kept giving orders to his subordinates, Lee was not physically capable of throwing that longed-for knock-out punch. He could not even get out of bed. His aide, Colonel Charles S. Venable, wrote, "Lee confined to his tent was not Lee on the battlefield."[30]

The only good news that General Lee received all day came from Ox Ford, where Ambrose Burnside's Ninth Corps was trying to fight its way across the North Anna. Burnside's men found their way blocked by a Confederate division commanded by General William Mahone, which had dug itself in south of the river. Mahone's men sent the enemy troops scrambling back. Burnside decided that the rebels were too firmly entrenched for any attack to succeed and called off the offensive.

Toward the end of the day, General Lee began receiving reports that the two enemy corps south of the river had begun to dig trenches of their own. He immediately realized what this meant—Grant had discovered his army's predicament and was preparing for an attack. In other words, Lee's great advantage over Grant had disappeared. At that point, he knew that his opportunity to win a stunning victory had ended. This knowledge did not improve Lee's already-less-than-serene frame of mind.

Because of his medical condition, which was also not improving, General Lee moved his headquarters three miles south to Taylorsville. His doctor wanted him to get away from the front, to someplace that would provide him with a bit of rest and at least some respite from the stress and anxiety he was facing on a daily basis. Because he was still too unwell to ride a horse, he rode the Richmond, Fredericksburg, and Potomac Railroad southward, away from the battle, still fretting over his lost opportunity. He knew that he would not get another chance to "strike them a blow" anytime soon. Grant was too smart to let himself be trapped like that a second time.

On May 25, General Lee sent a message to Jefferson Davis in Richmond, a letter that was not exactly overflowing with optimism:

"We have been obliged to withdraw from the banks of the North Anna, in consequence of the ground being favorable to the enemy, and the stage of the water such that he can cross at any point."[31]

He went on in the same tone in a second paragraph: "The army yesterday moved around us in all directions, examining our position, and entrenching as he came, until he reached the Central Road above Verdon. I presume he has destroyed all within his reach. In the evening he fell back towards the North Anna."

On the following day, Lee began receiving reports that the enemy was on the move again. It looked as though Grant was planning to withdraw from the North Anna altogether, which meant he would be making another one of his flanking movements to the south. Lee thought that Grant would swing around the Confederate left flank, which would put him on a direct route to Richmond—he still thought in terms of defending Richmond—a move he would have made himself if he had been in Grant's place. He sent a telegram to Secretary of War James Seddon to report, "The enemy has made no demonstration against our position to-day. From present indications he seems to contemplate a movement on our left flank."[32]

Lee had guessed wrong again. Going around the Confederate left flank would have been a good, sound move on Grant's part, but it was not the maneuver that Grant had in mind. Instead, he planned on going around Lee's right flank—north across the North Anna, then southeasterly along the north side of the Pamunkey. After withdrawing across the North Anna, the Federal rearguard set fire to Chesterfield Bridge.

The weather on May 26 was filthy—rain and more rain filled the trenches with several inches of water and mud. General Lee was not really certain if Grant had pulled out or not until early on May 27. All those baggage wagons could not be kept secret for very long, and his pickets did not waste any time in reporting that the enemy was moving east. Later in the day, cavalry units sent word that Grant was crossing the Pamunkey at Hanovertown, about fifteen miles southeast of the spot where Grant crossed the North Anna.

By going around Lee's right flank and moving the army east, Grant was forcing Lee out of his North Anna trenches and also keeping in contact with his supply depot at White House Landing, about twelve miles down the Pamunkey from Hanovertown. But all Lee could see was that Grant had moved closer to Richmond—Hanovertown lies about fifteen miles northeast of Richmond, about eight miles closer than Grant had been at the North Anna. This meant that Lee would have to move parallel with the Union army in order to keep himself between Grant and Richmond.

As soon as he was absolutely certain where Grant was going, General Lee ordered his army to move out in pursuit. These orders were issued within the hour of receiving the cavalry dispatch from Hanovertown. General Richard S. "Baldy" Ewell and his Second Corps were the first to leave the North Anna entrenchments, with Richard Anderson's First Corps following and A. P. Hill's Third Corps bringing up the rear. The Battle of North Anna, as it has come to be known, resulted in about two thousand Confederate casualties and about the same number of casualties on the Federal side.[33] Compared with all the dead and wounded that had been carted off to cemeteries and hospitals since May 4, when Grant first started moving south—and compared with what was to come in the weeks ahead—this hardly amounted to anything at all. The North Anna was not a major battle, certainly not an Antietam/Sharpsburg, or even a Wilderness, where Grant first showed that he would not be intimidated by Lee and his renowned army. As far as General Lee was concerned, the battle was important because of what he did *not* accomplish: he did not stop Grant in his drive southward, and he did not attack Grant's army below the North Anna, when it was split into two sections.

That man Grant was turning out to be a hard man to stop, or even to discourage. Even Lee's adjutant Walter H. Taylor, who never had anything good to say about *any* northerner, especially U. S. Grant, grudgingly admitted, "He certainly holds on longer than any of them [his predecessors]. He alone of all would have remained on this side of the Rappahannock after the battle of the Wilderness."[34]

REALLY WHIPPED

At about 6:30 on the morning of May 22, General Grant received reports that General Lee and his army were heading south, down the Telegraph Road, toward the North Anna River. Grant had been hoping to get to the North Anna first, to catch Lee before he had the chance to dig in, but now there was no possibility of that. He was too far away, too far south, for Grant to catch up with him. Grant could see that the Confederates would be able to cross the North Anna well before any of his troops could get near enough to attack Lee on the north side of the river.

General George Gordon Meade was disappointed that Lee had managed to get away. He was hoping to catch the enemy out in the open and finish him off before he could take shelter on the south side of the river. But Grant was too optimistic—and too hardheaded, like his father—to let a minor setback get him down. He would catch Lee out in the open someplace else—there would be a lot more opportunities in the months to come.

"We were now to operate in a different country from any from any we had before seen in Virginia," Grant noted with confidence.[35] "The roads were wide and good, and the country well cultivated." He went on to say that the area "was new to us," and that they did not have reliable maps or guides to help them find the roads or to advise them "where they led to." But Grant was not at all fazed by these shortcomings. "Our course was south," he insisted, "and we took all the roads leading in that direction which would not separate the army too widely."

By and large, the army shared Grant's enthusiasm. Soldiers groused and grumbled about the marching and the rations, but soldiers in all the armies since the days of Julius Caesar had always griped about something, usually the food and the marching. Considering all that the Army of the Potomac had been through during the past two and a half weeks, the men were in excellent spirits. On May 20, Lieutenant Elisha Hunt Rhodes of the Second Rhode Island Volunteers wrote in his diary, "A mail arrived today, the first in several days. I received eighteen letters as my share." Well-fortified by many

letters from home, Lieutenant Rhodes went on to say, "We have finished our earthworks and now feel secure. Our works are strong and
built of large trees covered with earth. Let the Rebels try to take them
if they want to."[36]

General Grant himself had a lot to do with this way of thinking.
The men in the ranks had confidence in Grant, the kind of confidence that comes from getting the measure of someone after
watching them do their job competently. The army did not admire
him, the way they had admired General McClellan, their first commanding general. (Although there was an increasing number who
admitted that if Grant had been in command in 1862, the war would
probably be over by now.) And they certainly did not idolize Grant
the way Southerners idolized Lee—no one this side of Nazareth was
ever worshipped the way the Army of Northern Virginia worshipped
Robert E. Lee.

The Army of the Potomac rarely cheered General Grant. The
men would watch him as he rode past, usually without making any
noise at all, and then would talk about him after he disappeared.
Nobody ever gave him a colorful nickname, either, the way other
generals had nicknames, like "Baldy" Smith (William F. Smith), or
"Little Napoleon" or "Little Mac" (McClellan), or "Old Prayer Book"
(Oliver Howard), or "Old Woodenhead" (Confederate General
John Bell Hood), or even "Old Rough and Ready" (Zachery Taylor,
Grant's mentor from the Mexican War). Some of the men called him
"Useless," at least until they found out that he was anything but.

Nicknames are usually given on the basis of either affection or
animosity, and the Army of the Potomac neither loved nor hated
Grant. They accepted him (some with resignation), they respected
him, they tolerated him, but they did not love him. Which was a sentiment that suited the practical-minded Midwestern general perfectly.
He did not particularly want any of his men to love him, just to follow
orders. General Lee could have the adulation. All Grant wanted was
for his men to do what they were told. He was hardheaded enough
to realize that love was not going to win the war.

General Grant explained to Horace Porter that his main objective was to get Lee to come out of his trenches and attack him. He
was confident that his army could withstand any offensive that Lee

could throw at him. Ironically, Lee's best chance of getting the better of the Union forces was also Grant's best chance of catching Lee out in the open. So far, Lee had been much too cagey to go on the offensive except once, and that had been three days earlier. On May 19, Richard S. "Baldy" Ewell's Second Corps had attacked a newly arrived division commanded by Brigadier General Robert O. Tyler, and had been sent scrambling back to their own lines by the rookie division.

Most of General Tyler's men had been in "heavy artillery" regiments, gunnery units that manned the big guns that protected Washington, DC, and had spent the war in relative comfort until a few days earlier. Grant had decided that these regiments—some of which had as many as 1,800 men—were not doing any good sitting around Washington, so he took them out of their comfortable barracks and turned them into infantry units.

General Tyler's men had no experience at all as infantrymen. They had enjoyed a very nice life as garrison troops, with beds and good food and no marching, unlike most other units. When they joined Winfield Scott Hancock's Second Corps on May 16, the veterans did not exactly greet them with open arms. "How are you, heavies," someone called out. "Is this work heavy enough for you?" And, "If you keep on like this a couple of years, you'll learn all the tricks of the trade." These were some of the milder things that were hurled at the new arrivals.[37]

But when the fighting began on May 19, the new troops, in their brand-new uniforms and new muskets, fought with as much grit and determination as the veterans who had make fun of them. The fighting went on all day long, until about 9 p.m.—when it was too dark to see—and the Confederates had been driven back across the Ny River, in Spotsylvania County. The rebels lost over four hundred prisoners, and also suffered severe losses in dead and wounded, according to Horace Porter. General Tyler's "heavies" lost about six hundred killed and wounded.[38]

During the fighting, a staff officer came across a row of men stretched out along the ground, looking like they were taking a nap. The officer was annoyed by this obvious shirking of duty and got down from his horse to give the soldiers a good going over. "Get up! What do you mean by going to sleep at such a time as this?" When none of the men moved, he was shocked to discover that they were all dead, and were lying where they fell.[39]

General Grant was hoping that this attack meant that Lee was going over to the offensive. But Lee was not about to come out of his trenches and fight on Grant's terms, as Grant was about to find out. The Army of Northern Virginia kept moving south, heading for the other side of the North Anna River. On May 22, General Gouverneur K. Warren reported that his Fifth Corps had not been able to make contact with either Anderson's First Corps or Baldy Ewell's Second Corps, although they managed to pick up about fifty stragglers. He went on to say that a black civilian who had just come from Hanover Station informed him that the Confederates had "miles of troops and oceans of wagons and artillery" on the south side of the river. Warren correctly concluded that A. P. Hill's Third Corps "must have taken the route through Chilesburg or one farther west," but mistakenly said that the river they crossed was the Pamunkey instead of the North Anna.[40] (Hill's corps was actually several miles from the Pamunkey.)

General Grant ordered all of his corps commanders to be ready to march on the following day, May 23: "At that hour each command will send out cavalry and infantry on all roads to their front leading south, and ascertain if possible where the enemy is."[41] He wanted to make absolutely sure that Lee did not get too much of a head start, and, above all, wanted to keep on pushing south.

Winfield Scott Hancock's Second Corps made contact with the enemy at Henegan's redoubt, on the north side of the river, just in front of Chesterfield Bridge. Hancock thought that he had already crossed the North Anna and informed Grant that he was fighting on the south side of the river. Actually, he had only crossed a stream called Long Creek, which was not on the map. Hancock discovered his mistake a short while later, and also discovered that the North Anna was about five hundred feet away, just beyond the Confederate position.

Artillery was brought up, and began firing at the redoubt at around 5:30. The gunners kept the rebels pinned down inside their works. They also managed to hit a nearby farm house, much to the alarm of the inhabitants. The farmer and his family ran out of the house as fast as they could go, as the Yankees kept up their infernal shelling.

The men of General David R. Birney's Third Division were not at all alarmed by the artillery fire. They knew that they were going to need all the support they could get. As long as the gunners kept up their shelling, they would be able to attack Henegan's redoubt without running into any defensive fire from the rebel lines. At about 6:30, after an hour of artillery support, three thousand men from General Birney's division ran straight at the redoubt from three directions. The ditch surrounding the little fort stopped the charge, but only for a minute.

The men climbed out of the ditch and up the walls like an army of flies—they climbed on each other's shoulders, and the soldiers who reached the top pulled their mates over the walls. Some of the men were killed as soon as they set foot on the redoubt, but Birney's troops kept on coming. They not only charged the fort but also came at the two South Carolina regiments on either side of it. The rebels broke and ran, with Birney's men right behind them—either running across Chesterfield Bridge or splashing across the North Anna. It did not take long before that stretch of the river, along with Chesterfield Bridge, had been overwhelmed by the Federals.

About four miles to the west, General Gouverneur Warren's Fifth Corps crossed the North Anna at Jericho Mills. The river was deep and fast at that point. Some of the men were knocked off their feet by the current, and clambered onto the south bank soaked to the skin. As they began walking southward, some men from a Massachusetts regiment wandered into the garden of an elderly woman. The old woman roundly scolded the soldiers for trampling her garden.

As Colonel Horace Porter summed up the crossing: "Warren reached Jericho Ford soon after noon, seized it, laid a pontoon bridge, and by 4:30 p.m. had moved his whole corps to the south bank." The men of the Massachusetts regiment obviously did not benefit from the pontoon bridge.[42]

Sixteen cannon of Confederate Colonel William J. Pegram's artillery battalion began a withering and noisy barrage against the still disorganized Fifth Corps. On another part of the Union line, the men of the Second Corps found themselves under attack by Cadmus

M. Wilson's division. General Warren's right flank began to disinte-grate, driven back toward the North Anna by the Confederate attack.

But Warren's artillery north of the river began a withering barrage of its own, and sent round after round right through the ranks of Wilson's division. The gunners began taking their toll on the Confederate artillery units and forced them to pull back. Federal infantry counterattacked, inflicting heavy casualties on two South Carolina regiments until they broke and ran. The Fifth Corps had managed to beat off A. P. Hill's attack and had firmly established its position on the North Anna's south bank.

General Grant did not feel the need to visit the front lines and check on the progress of the battle in person. He read the communiques from his generals on the North Anna and listened to the sounds of the battle. All throughout the day and through the noise of the battle—veterans said that the firing was loud and continuous, as noisy as anything they had heard throughout the war, with the possible exception of Gettysburg—Grant remained quiet and calm, at least outwardly. Staff officers remarked about how cool and collected he seemed to be while the guns kept up their almost continuous firing.

Grant had good reason to be poised and confident. His Fifth Corps and his Second Corps had crossed the North Anna, and General Burnside's Ninth Corps was moving into position to cross at Ox Ford. Horatio Wright's Sixth Corps would be crossing at Jericho Mills in the morning, which would put the entire Army of the Potomac on the south side of the river, safe and dry, and ready to fight. As soon as this had been accomplished, Grant intended to continue his advance southward. He was in good spirits—the day had gone well, and the outlook for the following day seemed to be just as promising.

That night, May 23, General Grant sent a message to his chief of staff in Washington, General Henry W. Halleck. The entire tone of the communiqué almost overflowed with optimism. He explained that the two corps on the south side of the North Anna had been "violently attacked," but both corps had "handsomely repulsed the assault without much loss to us."[43] Grant concluded his message, "Everything looks exceedingly favorable for us."

General Halleck sent a message of his own to General Grant on the same day, a communique that was full of encouragement and advice regarding troop movements and the possible intentions of the enemy. But Halleck's main point came toward the middle of his dispatch: "Permit me to repeat what I have so often urged, that in my opinion every man we can collect should be hurled against Lee, wherever he may be, as his army, not Richmond, is the true objective of this campaign."[44] Warming to his subject, General Halleck went on to advise Grant, "When that army is broken, Richmond will be of little value to the enemy," and "If you succeed in crushing Lee, all will be well."

If General Grant had been a sarcastic person, he probably would have let Halleck know that making Lee and the Army of Northern Virginia "the true objective of this campaign" was not exactly an original thought on his part and that he had told General Meade exactly the same thing before the campaign had even begun. Henry Halleck was far from being General Grant's favorite person in the world, for a number of reasons. In 1862, Halleck had informed General George B. McClellan, who was general-in-chief at the time, that Grant had resumed his heavy drinking, and he had also reported Grant for leaving his post without permission—both of which were completely untrue.

But being a taciturn Midwesterner—people said that he had the talent and ability for being silent in several languages—Grant probably just put the message down somewhere and walked away. He had more important things to think about than well-meaning but inane messages from his chief of staff.

The most important thing on Grant's mind the next morning was the intentions of his opponent—what exactly was Robert E. Lee going to do? From all the reports he had read, it seemed to him that Lee was retreating. A couple of escaped slaves reported that the Confederates had pulled out of their lines during the night. General Meade sent this information along to General Grant as soon as he received it, along with the observation that opposition seemed to be thinning out south of the river, especially in Hancock's and Burnside's sector.

Some of the prisoners that had been taken on the previous day seemed to confirm the notion that Lee was falling back. These prisoners "were more discouraged than any set of prisoners I ever saw before," according to one account. "Lee had deceived them, they said, and they declared that his army would not fight again except behind breastworks."[45]

General Grant notified his chief of staff, "The enemy have fallen back from North Anna; we are in pursuit."[46] At long last, the Confederates were on the run. Grant did not know if Lee was going to cross the South Anna and make a stand there, or if he intended to move farther south. But it did not really make any difference—wherever Lee went, Grant was determined to be "in pursuit."

The only real opposition seemed to be against General Burnside's Ninth Corps at Ox Ford, and that did not seem to be anything more than a rear-guard action—slowing the Federal advance while the rest of the army got away. General Warren ordered one of his brigadiers "to move out a small detachment as far as you think it safe," to try to get some idea of what the enemy was up to.[47] But as Warren and Wright and Hancock tried to push their way south, the enemy's actual intentions become apparent.

General Hancock informed Grant that he had a very large enemy force in front of him, possibly the entire Army of Northern Virginia, certainly a lot more than just a rear-guard detachment. At noon, Grant notified General Halleck in Washington, "The enemy are evidently making a determined stand between the two Annas. It will probably take two days to get in position for a general attack or to turn their position, as may favor best."[48]

Grant had also made the upsetting discovery that his army was split into two sections, and that it was not only badly divided but was also alarmingly vulnerable to attack. Warren and Wright's corps were on the right side of the divide, Hancock was on the left, and Lee's entire army was between them. "Lee could reinforce any part of his line from all points of it in a very short march," Grant noted, "or could concentrate the whole of it wherever he might choose to assault. We were, for the time, practically two armies besieging."[49]

Another item that upset Grant was the fact that if he continued driving his way south, he would actually be splitting his already-divided army even further. His famous hammering, which had been so successful so far, would now work against him. Lee's line was shaped like a wedge, with the tip on the North Anna and the two sides diverging as they moved south. Which meant that the Union forces would also diverge as they moved south. Grant the hammerer would have to switch over to the defensive.

Grant ordered Hancock to start digging trenches, just in case Lee decided to attack, and told Burnside to keep his Ninth Corps on the north side of the river. This was not a move he enjoyed making, but he could see that he was in no position to continue his offensive. Because he could not attack, he would have to go around Lee, just as he had done at Spotsylvania.

Skirmishers from Warren's corps and A. P. Hill's corps shot at each other throughout the morning of May 25. Grant had ordered the railroads in the North Anna vicinity to be destroyed, or at least put out of action for several weeks. The army spent much of the day carrying out this order with relish and began destroying tracks, bridges, culverts, and anything else they could wreck. At the same time, preparations were being made to send the Army of the Potomac across to the north side of the river. A few of Grant's advisors, including General Warren, suggested moving west after the army crossed to the north bank. Lee would be expecting Grant to march to the east, just as he had done after the Wilderness and Spotsylvania, and moving west would fool the Confederates, at least for a while, giving them a head start before Lee came charging after them.

But General Grant decided to move the army to the east, so that he could cross the Pamunkey. Moving west would have meant having to cross three separate rivers, the New River, the Little River, and the South Anna, while going eastward would leave just the Pamunkey to negotiate—it was the lesser of two evils. He had already moved his headquarters to the North Anna's north bank, ready to start the next phase of his campaign against Robert E. Lee and his army.

"Direct Generals Warren and Wright to withdraw all their teams and artillery not in position to the north side of the river to-morrow," Grant instructed General Meade from his new headquarters.[50] He went on to say that this movement should be accomplished "without attracting attention to the fact"—without attracting the attention of Lee, he meant.

All of this bustle and activity began on May 26. The army crossed the North Anna on pontoon bridges that had been set up by engineers and then were taken down again after the crossing. "The withdrawal from the North Anna had now been successfully accomplished," according to Colonel Horace Porter.[51] Heavy rain on May 26 helped to conceal the crossing from Confederate scouts.

Every soldier in every unit throughout the Army of the Potomac was relieved to get away from the North Anna, including General Grant. Grant knew that Lee had been in position to attack his army when it had been divided, and to inflict considerable damage. But for some unknown reason he did not. As Grant put it, Lee "did not attempt to drive us from the field."[52]

As far as Grant was concerned, there could be only one reason for Lee's failure to attack him: the Army of Northern Virginia was too tired and too discouraged. Lee had Grant right where he wanted him, but he did not do anything about it. If the situation had been reversed, Grant never would have let Lee get away. He would have demolished at least one of Lee's corps and would have pounded the other two until they were shattered. But Lee did nothing.

Grant had no idea that Lee was sick, or that his reason for letting the Army of the Potomac escape was that his burning intestines were keeping him confined to his tent. All Grant could see was that Lee did not attempt to drive him from the field when he had the chance. The problem must be with Lee's army, Grant decided. Lee did not attack because he could not depend upon his army to carry out such an offensive.

"Lee's army is really whipped," Grant informed Halleck on May 26: "The prisoners we now take show it. And the action of his army shows it unmistakably. A battle with them outside of entrenchments cannot be had. . . . I may be mistaken, but I feel that our success over Lee's army is already assured."[53]

Some of this was for the benefit of the press. Grant knew that reporters would get hold of this statement, and that they would proceed to put it on front pages all over the North—just as they had done with "I propose to fight it out on this line if it takes all summer." But General Grant believed every word of it. It seemed to him that the Army of Northern Virginia was on its last legs, run down and dispirited from the constant hammering he had inflicted on it, and was on the verge of collapse. Maybe one more good fight, one more all-out attack, would convince General Lee that his army was finished and that it was time for him to give up.

Chapter Six

STRIKING AND MANEUVERING

LIKE A PRIVATE SOLDIER

"**A**bout one o'clock the little village of Appomattox Court-house, with its half-dozen houses, came in sight, and we soon were entering its single street."[1] Colonel Horace Porter rode into the village right behind General Grant. He could see enemy troops, "with his columns and wagon-trains," in the low ground beyond. Federal cavalry and infantry occupied the high ground to the south and west of the Confederate columns, completely heading them off.

As Colonel Porter, General Grant, and the other riders approached the town, they could see a group of Federal officers standing by the road. Porter recognized General Philip Sheridan among the group. Phil Sheridan had calmed down by this time and no longer suspected that Lee's offer to surrender was some sort of trick. His face showed confidence that everything was going the way he wanted it to go—that Lee really did intend to surrender, in other words.

General Sheridan and the other officers saluted Grant when he rode up, all covered with dust. "How are you, Sheridan?" Grant asked.[2]

"First rate, thank you; how are you?" Sheridan replied in his very best top-of-the-morning voice.

"Is Lee over there?" Grant wanted to know, nodding his head in the direction of the village.

"Yes, he is in that brick house, waiting to surrender to you," Sheridan said, without a trace of suspicion.

"Well, then, we'll go over." Grant, Sheridan, and the others headed up the road toward Appomattox, with Grant leading the way.

General Grant might have compared his entry into Appomattox with General Winfield Scott's procession into Mexico City all those years ago, but the comparison probably never occurred to him. It would not have been much of a comparison anyway, more like a study in contrasts. General Scott did not just ride into the city's Grand Plaza, he entered it like a one-man procession. Scott looked every bit the conquering hero, complete with full-dress uniform, dress sword, gold braid, brass buttons, and fore-and-aft hat. Grant did not even bother to change out of his everyday field uniform and looked more like a private soldier than a three-star general. Putting on a clean uniform never entered into his mind. Like his old mentor from the Mexican War, Zachary Taylor, he never cared very much about appearances, only results.

Grant, Porter, and the rest of the group did not travel very far before they came across a rider sitting in front of a two-story brick house. The rider turned out to be an orderly sent by Orville Babcock to keep an eye out for General Grant and to let him know where General Lee was. He told Grant that General Lee and Colonel Babcock had gone into the brick house about a half an hour before and that they were waiting for him.

Later, General Grant would find out that the brick house belonged to Wilmer McLean. In 1861, McLean had lived about a mile from the battleground at Manassas and moved to Appomattox, about 150 miles to the southwest, to get away from the war. But Mr. McLean was about to find out that the war could not be avoided quite that easily.

Grant dismounted, walked up the wide wooden steps and across the porch, and entered the house.

AT LAST ACCOMPLISHING SOMETHING

The entire Army of the Potomac was filled with optimism at the end of May 1864. They had been through more hard fighting during the past three and a half weeks than they ever could have imagined, and had seen their friends killed and wounded in horrible numbers since they crossed the Rapidan. But it also seemed that everything they had done had been for a purpose. The enemy was still full of fight, but they were being pushed back steadily in spite of how stubbornly they fought. What was even more important, they were not being pushed back themselves. The men from New Jersey and New Hampshire and Maine had stood their ground against Lee's veterans and had a growing confidence in themselves, as well as in General Grant. Old Grant may have been scrubby and shabby and unglamorous, but he had the nerve to stand up to Bobby Lee. Behind him, they were convinced that they were finally on the verge of ending the fight, once and for all. As a member of a New Hampshire regiment put it, when he heard that his unit would be assigned to the Army of the Potomac. "We are going up to help Grant finish up the job with Lee."[3]

General Grant could not have agreed more. His war of constant hammering seemed to be paying off. It seemed to him that Lee's army was really whipped, and it was about time to finish it off. It would have gone against Grant's personality, his way of thinking, and everything he had learned since he was a boy in Point Pleasant, Ohio, if he had changed his strategy, especially since it seemed to be working.

In the course of a conversation with an army surgeon, Grant explained his philosophy regarding strategy, tactics, and his thoughts concerning war generally. He told the surgeon, "the art of war is simple enough; find out where your enemy is, get at him as soon as you can, strike him as hard as you can, and keep moving on."[4] When the surgeon wanted to know what was to prevent the enemy from attacking his rear while he was doing all of these things, the reply he received was typical U. S. Grant. "He's not thinking of that," Grant said, "we'll keep the front busy."

Grant had certainly struck Lee at the North Anna, although not nearly as hard as he had intended, and now it was time to move on. Which meant another move around Lee's left flank—another sidling movement. On May 29, Grant sent Winfield Scott Hancock's Second Corps, Gouverneur K. Warren's Fifth Corps, and Horatio Wright's Sixth Corps on a reconnaissance in force to find Lee's exact position. They found it on the following day. Hancock encountered the enemy in a "strongly fortified" position, according to General Grant, as his corps approached the Totopotomoy River, a few miles closer to Richmond. Jubal Early's Confederate Second Corps attacked Warren's Corps "with some vigor," and Ambrose Burnside's Ninth Corps was ordered to join the fight. With the help of Burnside's reinforcements, Warren repulsed Early "and drove him more than a mile."[5]

Now that Grant knew where Lee was, which was northeast of Richmond, in the vicinity of Cold Harbor, he began making preparations for the coming battle. General William F. "Baldy" Smith's Eighteenth Corps was temporarily detached from the Army of the James and ordered to reinforce Grant's corps. Baldy Smith was a hot-tempered, acid-tongued professional officer, and a graduate of West Point, who had briefly commanded the Sixth Corps. Phil Sheridan's cavalry was also brought up. "Sheridan ought to be notified to watch the enemy's movements well out towards Cold Harbor," Grant notified General Meade on the evening of May 30.[6]

Cold Harbor is usually described as a "strategic crossroads." Grant knew that controlling Cold Harbor meant controlling the roads heading south toward the James River as well as toward Richmond. General Lee was also well aware of Cold Harbor's strategic importance—he knew a lot more about the Virginia landscape than Grant did—and sent a cavalry division commanded by his nephew Fitzhugh Lee to hold the crossroads. Lee's cavalry got there before Phil Sheridan's. But Sheridan's men used their rapid-firing Spencer carbines to good effect and pushed Fitz Lee out of the crossroads.

On the following morning, June 1, a brigade of infantry from Richard Anderson's Confederate First Corps arrived at Cold Harbor to dislodge Phil Sheridan. But Sheridan's cavalrymen had dug themselves in by that time, and their magazine-loading Spencers were as effective against Anderson's infantry as they had been against Fitzhugh Lee's cavalry. The result of the fighting was the same as it had been the previous day; the Confederates withdrew with heavy losses.

Horatio Wright's Sixth Corps arrived to reinforce Sheridan's cavalry and began digging their own line of trenches. Grant had instructed Wright to arrive at daylight, but his men were so exhausted that the lead columns did not start arriving until about 9 a.m. Gouverneur Warren's Fifth Corps was also sent in, along with about 13,000 men from the Eighteenth Corps, which had been transferred from the Army of the James to support the build-up at Cold Harbor. But the Eighteenth Corps had been sent to New Castle Ferry by mistake and had to double back in order to reach their objective. By the time they finally arrived, the men were as covered with dust and as exhausted as Wright's men.

Weary or not, both corps began moving forward to the attack at about 6:30 p.m. Emory Upton's brigade also took part in the advance—Upton had just found out that he had been promoted to brigadier for his activities at Spotsylvania. He stood in the front lines, first leading an attack and later trying to beat back a Confederate counterattack. The counterattack was successful, in spite of Upton's attempt to rally his men, and the brigade was pushed back toward its original position.

A short distance from Upton, a brigade commanded by Colonel William S. Truex charged through a gap in the Confederate line. In a firefight that can only be described as brutal, Colonel Truex and several other officers were wounded and several hundred Confederates were killed, wounded, and captured. Truex and his men were also forced to withdraw to their starting point.

The day had been encouraging for General Grant, although hardly an overwhelming success. His army had stood its ground and had given as good as it got. The newly arrived Eighteenth Corps had acquitted itself well against Lee's veterans. Just as important, the army was in a good position for another attack on the following day. And Grant had already determined that there was going to be another attack on June 2.

"There has been a very severe battle this afternoon and as I write, now 9 o'clock at night firing is still continued on some parts of the battle line," Grant wrote to his wife, Julia, on the evening of June 1.[7] "The rebels are making a desperate fight and I presume will continue to do so as long as they can get a respectable number of men to stand." General Lee would be putting a more respectable number of men in the trenches than Grant seemed to realize.

Grant was hoping to maneuver his army to a position between Lee and Richmond. If he could do that, Lee would be forced to dislodge the Federal army from the approaches to Richmond—in other words, Lee would have to attack him instead of the other way round. This would give Grant a decided advantage and would also allow him to turn the tables on Lee. He would be able to face Lee from the safety of prepared trenches, while Lee came at him across open ground—just the opposite of what had happened at Spotsylvania.

The Federal and the Confederate lines paralleled each other for several miles, running from Cold Harbor off toward the northwest. Grant reached the conclusion that the southernmost part of Lee's line, the end closest to Cold Harbor, was the weakest part and also decided that a major attack against that section stood a good chance of succeeding. To strengthen this section of the line, Grant ordered Winfield Scott Hancock to move his Second Corps to reinforce the three corps—General Warren's Fifth, General Wright's Sixth, and Baldy Smith's Eighteenth—that were already in position.

Hancock's men, all 25,000 of them, left their trenches at the northern end of the line after dark on and began walking south. The lead columns arrived at Cold Harbor at around 6 a.m., with the rest of the men straggling behind for several miles. Grant had hoped to begin his attack at daybreak, but Hancock's men were in no condition to take part in a major assault, not after making a night march of about ten miles. When Hancock finally arrived at Cold Harbor, he notified General Grant that he would not be ready to attack for at least several more hours.

The men were absolutely worn out, both physically and mentally, from the constant fighting and incessant marching of the past several weeks. This state of exhaustion did not apply just to the Second Corps, but to every man and every regiment throughout the Army of the Potomac. One officer thought that the men had aged twenty years in the past twenty days.

Veterans remembered Cold Harbor from another June day, three years earlier. The Battle of Gaines's Mill, sometimes known as the First Battle of Cold Harbor, took place on June 27, 1862. "We were here in 1862, under McClellan," Elisha Hunt Rhodes noted, "and some of the scenes are familiar."[8] The Army of the Potomac had faced Robert E. Lee for the first time on the previous day, at the Battle of Mechanicsville. At the time, the army was commanded by General George B. McClellan. Lee's aggressiveness at Mechanicsville not only unnerved McClellan but also convinced him to abandon his offensive against Richmond and begin withdrawing his entire army to the James River. While Grant's men were digging their trenches, some of them dug up the bones of those who had been killed back in 1862. This was not considered to be a good omen.

The name Cold Harbor is probably of British origin, from colonial days, meaning an inn or tavern that offered lodging for the night but did not provide hot meals. Some of Grant's men called the place "Cool Arbor." Another source thought that it was "probably named after the old home of some English settler."[9] None of the names made very much sense. There was nothing that was either cool or cold about the place—it was more like an oven than anything else—there was no grand Olde English house in the vicinity, and there was no harbor anywhere in sight. But by this time, everyone in the Army of the Potomac was thoroughly disgusted with Virginia and everything about it. Coming across a place called Cold Harbor in the middle of a dreary, hot wasteland did not come as any surprise.

Because so many of his men were too exhausted to make any sort of effort against the enemy, Grant decided to postpone his offensive until the following day. He ordered General Meade to prepare for an all-out attack for 4:30 on the following morning, June 3. Wright's and Baldy Smith's corps were to go in as the main force, reinforced by Winfield Scott Hancock. This would allow the army to get a night of desperately needed sleep, which was more important than any preparations that Mead and his staff might have in mind.

The only problem was that giving the army an extra day to rest also meant giving the Confederates an extra day to dig. If Grant's maximum effort had come at first light on June 2, it would have caught the enemy unprepared and off guard, with his earthworks only partially finished. But everyone had learned from unpleasant past experience that the rebels knew how to dig, and dig fast, and could turn the good Virginia soil into entrenchments and breastworks and rifle pits with amazing speed and dexterity. Grant knew all about this as well, and he also knew that he was allowing Lee precious time to prepare a formidable line of fortifications while his men were resting and recuperating.

But Grant was not all that concerned about the rebels or their well-known talent for digging trenches. By the beginning of June, he was convinced that Lee's army was all but finished. The Army of the Potomac may have been tired out and war weary, but it seemed to Grant that the Army of Northern Virginia was on the verge of collapse—low on morale and fighting spirit. If Lee did not attack him at the North Anna, when the army was at its most vulnerable and he might have inflicted serious damage, then something must be wrong. Lee's army must be on its last legs. Grant saw Lee's problem as an opportunity—he had Lee with his back up against another famous Virginia river, the Chickahominy, and he was not about to let the rebels get away. One more maximum effort and Lee's faltering army would be "whipped" once and for all.

Grant also had been informed that Lee was ailing and that his medical condition left him in no condition to command. A southern newspaper reported that that Lee was severely ill with an intestinal problem and was not able to carry on with his normal duties. A deserter from Lee's army and a runaway slave both confirmed the news that Lee had contracted some sort of disorder affecting his intestines, an ailment that was severe enough to take him out of action for several days. Some reports added that he had been taken to Richmond to recover.

This was very good news for Grant. With Lee out of the way, even for a few days, fighting the Army of Northern Virginia suddenly became a much less daunting proposition. Ulysses was too much his father's son, and had too much of the hardheaded tanner from Ohio in him, to let a chance like this pass him by.

On the night before Grant's big attack, Colonel Horace Porter walked through the camp of one of the regiments that would take part in the morning assault. As he made his way through the groups of men, Colonel Porter noticed that many of them had taken off their coats and were busy sewing up holes in them with needle and thread. This "exhibition of tailoring" struck him as odd, so he decided to stop and take a closer look. He discovered that the men were actually "calmly writing their names and home addresses on slips of paper and pinning them to the backs of their coats."[10] In case they were killed during the morning attack, they wanted to make certain that their bodies could be identified and "their fate made known to their families at home," instead of being dumped into some anonymous mass grave.

This is probably one of the best known and most affecting stories of the Civil War and has been repeated in just about every book and documentary that mentions Cold Harbor. It might also be one of the great myths connected with the battle. Colonel Porter's account is certainly moving and dramatic, but there is also a good possibility that it is not true.

A historian who has written extensively about the Virginia campaign states that Colonel Porter's "dramatic scenario" is "suspect." No other accounts of the battle, "nothing in letters, diaries, or contemporaneous newspaper accounts," support the story.[11] No one else who was at Cold Harbor mentions anything about soldiers pinning their names on the backs of their uniforms, or about anyone having a premonition of terrible casualties. "Judging from surviving letters and diaries, Union soldiers were no more concerned about the assault scheduled for the morning of June 3 than they had been before the campaign's other major attacks."

Colonel Porter's memoirs were published more than thirty years after the war ended. It is possible that his memory played tricks on him, or that he got his facts confused. It is also a possibility that he "embellished his accounts for dramatic effect." Whether the story is true or not, it is certainly dramatic and poignant, and is probably one of the best remembered stories about Cold Harbor.

"At 4:30 a.m., June 3, Hancock, Wright, and Smith moved forward promptly to the attack," as crisply reported by Colonel Porter.[12] As they advanced in the dawn light, the three corps could see the trenches in front of them were filled with thousands of Confederates. Every one of them held a rifled musket, and each musket was pointed directly at the Federal line. When they opened fire, muzzle flashes lit up the earthworks from end to end. The flash was followed by a deafening crash and a tremendous cloud of smoke that briefly hid the two sides from each other.

"From the works in front, and the works from our left, arose a musketry fire so heavy, it seemed almost like one continual crash of thunder, while heavy artillery on our left poured in the shells," is the way one officer in a New Hampshire regiment put it.[13] But there was not just one massive charge. There were many advances by individual brigades and regiments, all going forward at the same time. As they walked toward the trenches, the Confederates in them continued their murderous fire. It sounds like a cliché to say that the men were being "mowed down," but this was exactly what happened. "The men went down in rows, just as they marched in the ranks," a lieutenant remembered, and also said that they fell "half a platoon almost at a time." So many men were dropping to the ground that one man thought the order to lie down, to hit the dirt, had been given. He later recalled that he "dropped down myself among the dead" and did not realize what had actually taken place until "my living comrades" kept up their slow walk toward the entrenchments.[14]

General Meade urged his corps commanders to press forward with the attack. But by the time he sent his communiqué, which was at about 8:45, the offensive was all but over. All three corps, Warren's, Wright's, and Smith's, had been stopped by the overwhelming fire from the trenches. General Burnside's Ninth Corps had some small success, but Burnside was a couple of miles north of the main attack. The men who had survived the early morning killing found themselves pinned down in front of the Confederate position and did their best to dig trenches of their own. They used cups, bayonets, and anything they could find to scratch out a trench or a hole deep enough to protect themselves from the enemy's guns.

"The reports received by General Grant were at first favorable and encouraging," Colonel Porter wrote.[15] Grant may have been encouraged, but he must have suspected something. At seven a.m., he instructed General Meade, "The moment it becomes certain that an assault cannot succeed, suspend the offensive; but when one does succeed, push it vigorously and if necessary pile in troops at the successful point from wherever they can be taken."[16]

The general rode out to the front lines at around noon. He wanted see the situation for himself, but his main reason for going forward was to confer with his corps commanders. What he heard from Warren, Smith, and Wright must have come as a severe shock—a horror story of men being shot down by the thousands and of a full-scale assault being turned back in less than half an hour. Their on-the-spot reports were exactly what Grant did not expect to hear: the Confederate position could not be taken.

He sent a communiqué to General Meade: "The opinion of corps commanders not being sanguine of success in case an assault is ordered, you may direct a suspension of farther advance for the present. Hold our most advanced positions, and strengthen them."[17] The offensive was over. Fighting continued on and off—"there was a good deal of irregular fighting along the lines," is the way Horace Porter put it—but General Grant would order no more assaults on the Confederate trenches.[18]

A short while later, Grant sent a strange message to his chief of staff, Henry Halleck. "We assaulted at 4:30 o'clock this morning, driving the enemy within his entrenchments at all points, but without gaining any decisive advantage," he reported. "Our troops now occupy a position close to the enemy, some places within 50 yards, and are entrenching. Our loss was not severe, nor do I suppose the enemy to have lost heavily. We captured over 300 prisoners, mostly from Breckinridge's command" (Major General John Breckinridge's Division).[19]

By two o'clock, which was when Grant sent this message, he was fully aware that his losses had been much heavier than he had expected and that the situation was not nearly as encouraging as he had reported. Men *were* dug in only fifty yards away from the enemy trenches, but they remained in that position because they could not move without being killed. It is possible that he reported his losses as "not severe" because he knew that news reporters would pick up his message to Halleck and use it for their headlines in the morning editions—reporters had done this several times in the past. The press would find out the bad news soon enough, though.

One thing was now certain in Grant's mind—Lee's army was anything but "really whipped," as he had believed, and the morale of the enemy was far from broken. He was still absolutely certain that his army would prevail over Lee's—his combination of optimism and hardheadedness would not have allowed him to believe anything less. But after the attacks of June 3, he had to face the hard fact that any final success was going to take a lot longer than he had thought a few days earlier.

On June 4, General Grant ordered General Burnside to move his corps a few miles south, where it would be in a position to act as a reserve to Warren's and Smith's corps. He would also detach Phil Sheridan's cavalry to tear up as much of the Virginia Central Rail Road as they could, to interfere with the enemy's supply lines and communications. But he would not order any further attacks against the enemy's fortifications. Grant would now concentrate on withdrawing from Cold Harbor and moving on to the next phase of his unrelenting battle against Robert E. Lee.

But before he could leave Cold Harbor, Grant would have to do something about taking care of the hundreds of wounded who were lying between the Union and Confederate lines. Two days after the failed charge against the Confederate trenches, Grant wrote to General Lee suggesting that each side send out litter bearers to recover their wounded: "It is reported to me that there are wounded men, probably of both armies, now lying exposed and suffering between the lines occupied respectively by the two armies."[20]

What he had in mind was an informal ceasefire, as opposed to a formal truce carried out under a white flag. He proposed sending "unarmed men bearing litters to pick up their dead or wounded without being fired upon by the other party," but went on to advise Lee that this was only a suggestion. "Any other method equally fair to both parties you may propose for meeting the end desired, will be accepted by me," is the way Grant ended his note.[21]

It was a humane idea—many hundreds of men were lying out in no-man's land, bleeding and suffering in the intense heat, and Grant wanted to have them brought in for medical attention before it was too late. But few of the men out there were General Lee's, and Lee decided that he wanted a formal, written request from Grant before he would allow any Union wounded to be carried off the field. As far as Lee was concerned, an informal ceasefire was out of the question. He replied to Grant, "I fear that such an arrangement will lead to misunderstanding and difficulty. I propose, therefore, instead, that when either party desires to remove their dead or wounded, a flag of truce be sent, as is customary."[22]

It has been suggested that Grant's reluctance to ask for a flag of truce was based on the fear that this might be taken as an admission of defeat. This certainly sounds like Grant's way of thinking—keep on hammering the enemy, and never let him think that you are even thinking about showing a white flag. He was definitely Jesse Root Grant's son and did not want to show any sign of weakness, no matter how desperately he wanted to rescue his men. On the following day, June 6, he tried again. "Your communication of yesterday's date is received," he wrote to General Lee. "I will send immediately, as you propose, to collect the dead and wounded between the lines of the two armies, and will also instruct that you be allowed to do the same."[23]

But Lee was not satisfied. He still wanted his white flag and said so. Lee expressed his profound regret "to find that I did not make myself understood in my communication of yesterday" and proceeded to demand that Grant request a formal ceasefire "by flag of truce in the usual way."[24]

Grant finally saw that he would have to give in. "The knowledge that wounded men are now suffering from want of attention, between the two armies, compels me to ask a suspension of hostilities for sufficient time to collect them in, say two hours."[25]

Lee was satisfied by this request, and allowed the truce to proceed. But by this time, it was too dark to collect any wounded. The recovery details did not leave their lines until the next day. By that time it was much too late. It had been four days since the grand charge, and most of the men out in no-man's land were nothing but bloated corpses. Some of the wounded managed to crawl back to their own lines by themselves. Others were half dragged there by their friends, under cover of darkness. Only two were found still alive.

On June 7, General Grant sent a snippy note to General Lee that ended, "Regretting that all my efforts for alleviating the suffering of wounded men left upon the battlefield have been rendered nugatory, I remain &c, U. S. Grant." It was not like Grant to send such a sarcastic message. The stress and strain of the past week were beginning to affect him, as well.[26]

The number of dead and wounded at Cold Harbor made Grant a target for widespread criticism, to put it mildly. Newspaper editors accused Grant of being irresponsible and incompetent, called him a butcher, and wrote that he was a callous, unthinking general who thought nothing of slaughtering thousands of men to gain a worthless plot of Virginia ground. Even Mary Todd Lincoln, the president's wife, declared that Grant was not fit to lead an army.

Grant's aide Colonel Horace Porter gives the number of killed, wounded, and missing on June 3 alone as "nearly 7000."[27] The figure 7,000 has been quoted by most writers and historians in their accounts of the fighting on June 3, and has become the most widely accepted number for losses on this particular day since 1864. But later examinations have brought about some dramatic recalculations.

The same writer who questioned Horace Porter's story about troops pinning their names and addresses on the backs of their uniforms also downplays the number of Federal dead on June 3: "Union casualties have been grossly exaggerated and probably did not exceed 3,500."[28] He compares that attack with "Pickett's famous charge at Gettysburg" and points out that this was another frontal assault that lasted about as long as the Cold Harbor attack. Pickett's charge "cost the Confederates between 5,300 and 5,700 men, a number well in excess of the 3,500–4,000 that Grant lost during his main June 3 attack." The 3,500–4,000 figure for the June 3 losses is also 3,000–3,500 below the most widely quoted figure of 7,000 for the same attack.

Now that his attack had failed, General Grant's objective was to get his army out of their Cold Harbor entrenchments without letting General Lee know about it. He intended to move south again, just as he had done after the Wilderness and every other battle since the army had crossed the Rapidan just over a month before. But if Lee found out what Grant was up to and attacked the Union army as it moved south, the casualties he would be able to inflict would have been devastating.

Grant was well aware of the situation and took every precaution to make absolutely certain that no word of his projected movement reached Lee. His orders for the withdrawal were delivered only to his most senior and most trusted officers in the strictest secrecy. Planning the move, and arranging for all the logistics and mapping that went with it, took more than a week.

On the night of June 12, a Sunday, the army slipped out of Cold Harbor and started walking toward the James River under the cover of darkness. Baldy Smith's corps led the way, followed by Hancock, Wright, and Warren. Except for his corps commanders and a trustworthy few other officers, Grant did not let anyone else know anything about his plans—the fewer people who knew what was going on, the less chance there would be of Lee's spies finding out about his secret.

Grant's efforts to keep the withdrawal a secret certainly were effective. Shortly after the army left its trenches, a senior officer, "an officer of rank," approached General Grant with an idea for building another line of trenches at Cold Harbor. These would be dug some distance toward the rear of the trenches that were already there, the officer explained, and would probably prove useful in case the army had to fall back toward the James River anytime in the near future. Grant listened very politely to the suggestion, puffing away on an always present cigar, before quietly informing the well-meaning officer, "The army has already pulled out from the enemy's front and is now on its march to the James."[29] The officer was taken completely by surprise. Grant's reputation for being silent in several languages was never more evident than on June 12, 1864.

Grant's ironclad secrecy also managed to surprise Robert E. Lee. The night of June 12 was moonlit, and the thousands of men walking along the roads leading south churned up an alarming amount of dust that rose in high, dense clouds. But in spite of the fact that the army was giving its position away by sending up so much dust on a bright, moonlit night, General Lee would not discover that Grant had disappeared until the army was well on its way. General Grant had the satisfaction of knowing that he had managed to pull off one of his most successful maneuvers of the war. Everyone, including Grant, was very glad to get out of Cold Harbor, and they could not leave fast enough.

The men had just fought a grueling battle that had gone on for almost two weeks and had seen their friends and comrades shot down all around them. Now they had been pulled out of their positions and sent trudging off toward what was certain to be yet another grueling battle. Everyone knew that the odds of surviving the war decreased every time they went up against the enemy and that the next battle might very well be their last. But they kept on moving, walking slowly toward whatever was in front of them, knowing full well that whatever was up ahead was probably not going to be very pleasant.

Even though no one was looking forward to what was waiting for them at the end of their march, they had confidence in themselves.

By this time, they were convinced that they were every bit as good as Bobby Lee's boys, if not better. And just as important, the army also had confidence in their commanding general. Grant had shown many times during the past month that he was nothing at all like any of the generals that had commanded the army before him. So they left their Cold Harbor trenches and headed south. They were marching toward another battle, but they were certain that they were also moving closer toward the end of the war.

General Grant was just as confident that the end of the war was getting closer with each battle. In a letter written in February 1864 to his father, who was the source of his confidence and determination, Grant said, "All I want is to be left alone to fight this war out; fight all rebel opposition and restore a happy Union in the shortest possible time."[30] He never had any doubts in his mind that he would be able to do just that. Grant was also very sorry that so many men had been killed at Cold Harbor. He only had the number 7,000 to go by, the same as Colonel Porter. "I have always regretted that the last assault at Cold Harbor was ever made," he wrote toward the end of his life.[31] "At Cold Harbor, no advantage whatever was gained to compensate for the heavy loss we sustained." He went on to compare the third of June with his attack on Vicksburg in May 1863. "There was more justification for the assault at Vicksburg," he decided, because it led to the surrender of the city in July, about six weeks later.

General Meade joked that Cold Harbor finally convinced Grant that Virginia was not Tennessee and that Robert E. Lee was not General Braxton Bragg, who had been Grant's adversary at the Battle of Chattanooga in November 1863. This may have been a very clever remark—it was a variation of "but Grant never met Bobby Lee"—but General Grant was well aware of his opponent's identity, and had been aware of it long before Cold Harbor.

Grant did not let "the last assault at Cold Harbor" get him down, at least not for long. He treated it as a setback not a defeat. Lee and his army were still out there, and Grant was as determined as ever to get them. "The matter was seldom referred to in conversation," Colonel Porter noted, "for General Grant, with his usual habit of mind, bent all his energies toward consummating his plans for the future."[32]

There were those in the ranks who agreed with Grant that absolutely no advantage had been gained from the June 3 attack. An officer with a New Hampshire regiment wrote, "It was undoubtedly the greatest and most inexcusable slaughter of the whole war."[33] A soldier in the Sixth Corps thought that any first-year cadet at West Point would have been ashamed to order such a disastrous charge.

But any discouragement and demoralization was short lived. Grant himself observed, "When we reached the James River, however, all effects of the battle of Cold Harbor seemed to have disappeared."[34] Even before the army reached the James, the effects were already beginning to dissipate. In a diary entry dated Monday, June 6, a Massachusetts volunteer wrote that since May 4 the army had acquired "a well-established faith in General Grant." (He also noted that the army had been "under fire every day but two since May 4.")

The Massachusetts man remembered seeing the "Old Man" when Grant was having lunch one day. "In his old blouse and hat he appeared like the rest of us—ragged and dirty." His regiment spotted him sitting on a railway flatcar, "gnawing away on an old ham bone," and gave him a rousing cheer as they passed by. Grant acknowledged the cheer by casually waving the bone at them for a second, and then, just as casually, went back to eating his lunch. "It was wonderful how thoroughly this retiring, undemonstrative man had gained the confidence of the army," the soldier exuded, and concluded with, "the men are in good spirits, pleased that we were at last accomplishing something."[35]

Elisha Hunt Rhodes also seemed to be in an optimistic frame of mind regarding General Grant and the outcome of the war. On June 3, he noted that there was "a terrible battle" that day and also that "nothing seems to have been gained by the attack today."[36] But he did not seem at all discouraged by the day's events. "At any rate, General Grant means to hold on," he wrote, "and I know that he will win in the end."

A MERE QUESTION OF TIME

"We are confronting General Grant, and only waiting to have him located . . . before this army is let loose at its old opponent," Robert E. Lee's adjutant Walter H. Taylor noted on the morning of May 30, 1864.[37] But Colonel Taylor was as concerned over General Lee's health as he was about General Grant's whereabouts. Although he noted that the general was "now improving," Taylor also admitted that Lee's illness "was more serious than was generally supposed."

Although Lee was feeling a lot better and stronger than he had been a few days before, he was still not able to ride a horse or take on any physical activities. He was annoyed and frustrated by his ailment, mainly because it was not going away fast enough to suit him. But he was bothered even more by the fact that Grant and his army were still at large, which was just as bad as having his intestines in a constant uproar from some pigheaded illness.

At about seven p.m. on May 31, Fitzhugh Lee sent word that his cavalry had been attacked by an enemy cavalry unit at Cold Harbor. He was not absolutely certain, but he thought that Federal infantry was at his front as well.

Lee ordered other units to join forces with his nephew. It looked like there was going to be a battle on the following day, and he wanted to make certain that he had enough men at Cold Harbor to meet the enemy threat. Through his adjutant, Lee ordered General Richard Anderson to send every man he could to Cold Harbor:

> GENERAL: General Lee has received your note of 7 p. m. He also received a message from General Fitz. Lee through Major Mason, of his staff, that his command and a brigade of Hoke's had been driven from their position this evening by the enemy, and that they were of the opinion that infantry was in their front. General Hoke will, whilst occupying his present relative position to you, be under your control. He was directed to see you and arrange for co-opera-tion to-morrow. He has three brigades up, and the general wishes you to direct him to send back and try and get up the fourth.
> Very respectfully,
> W. H. TAYLOR,
> Assistant Adjutant-General.[38]

General Lee probably wished that he was strong enough to go to the front himself. He did move his headquarters to Shady Grove Church, a few miles behind the Confederate lines, which would at least put him closer to the fighting.

As Lee had guessed, fighting began on the following day, June 1. General Anderson's men were digging a line of trenches, running northwest to southeast, when they were attacked by Horatio Wright and Baldy Smith. That morning, Anderson had been outfought and outgunned by Phil Sheridan's cavalry and their magazine-loading Spencer repeating carbines. Wright's and Smith's late afternoon attack drove back two of Anderson's brigades; one regiment gave way in panic, which threatened to spread to other units. According to an artilleryman who saw what had happened, "the regiment went to pieces in abject rout and threatened to overwhelm the rest of the brigade."[39] He went on to say, "I have never seen any body of troops in such a condition of utter demoralization; they actually groveled upon the ground and attempted to burrow under each other in holes and depressions."

This day was an important anniversary for Robert E. Lee. Exactly two years before, on June 1, 1862, he had been given command of all Confederate forces in Virginia by President Jefferson Davis. He replaced General Joseph E. Johnston, who had been seriously injured in the Battle of Fair Oaks in May 1862, and he became the new commander of the Army of Northern Virginia.

During the Seven Days' Battles—as the battles between June 26 and July 1, 1862, have come to be known—Lee and General Stonewall Jackson outgeneraled Union commander George B. McClellan and pushed the Army of the Potomac right down the York/James Peninsula. McClellan had been threatening to break through the Confederate lines and attack Richmond itself, but Lee and his tactics of attack and maneuver—which were the equal of anything that Winfield Scott had accomplished during the Mexican War—relieved Richmond and made General Lee a hero in the South.

Two years later, Lee was still defending Richmond. But 1864 was not 1862, U. S. Grant was not George B. McClellan, and Grant's objective was not Richmond.

Lee was alarmed by the reports he was receiving from General Anderson's front, but he was also frustrated because there was nothing he could do to help the situation. He was still too sick to do anything but stay at headquarters and read the bad news that the messengers kept bringing at regular intervals.

But messengers were also keeping him advised of Grant's other activities, including the southward shift of Hancock's Second Corps. After reading these reports, General Lee concluded that Grant was strengthening the southern part of his line in preparation for another attack, which would probably come at first light on June 2. To counter Grant's move, Lee ordered A. P. Hill to move his corps south, which would strengthen Anderson's position. If all went well, Hill would be in place before Hancock arrived.

This movement had to be made quickly. Time was very much of the essence. General Lee tried his best to impress on Hill and all of his subordinates that it was vital for them to arrive in General Anderson's sector before Hancock reached his destination. If a reinforced enemy—four army corps instead of three—managed to break through the line, the result would be nothing short of disastrous. Not only would the battle be lost, but the way to Richmond would be wide open.

But there is always someone who never gets the word. On the night of June 1–2, that person was Major Henry B. McClellan.

Major McClellan had been a guide during the battle of the Wilderness and had impressed General Lee with his knowledge of the area and especially of the roads. Because McClellan had done such a good job at the Wilderness, Lee decided to send him out as a guide for Major General John C. Breckinridge's Division. Breckinridge was in the northwestern section of the Confederate line, and McClellan was given the assignment of leading the division to Cold Harbor. At around midnight, General Breckinridge began his slow march to join General Richard Anderson's First Corps, with Major McClellan leading the way.

McClellan might have been an expert on the roads in the vicinity of the Wilderness, but he did not know very much about Cold Harbor and environs. He had no idea that there were several country lanes that led directly to Cold Harbor, so he stayed on the main roads instead. This was a much more indirect route, which added several miles to the trip as well as several additional hours of travel time.

Also, McClellan did not know anything about the importance of arriving at Cold Harbor before Hancock. As far as he was concerned, it made no difference if Breckinridge arrived at six in the morning or at two in the afternoon. He took the exhaustion of the men into consideration as well, and allowed them to stop and rest at regular intervals throughout the night. The division shuffled into the village of Mechanicsville at about sunrise on June 2, still several miles away from their destination, where they proceeded to stop for breakfast.

General Lee had expected Breckinridge and his division to arrive before dawn. When they did not make their appearance by daybreak, he became worried and anxious. He became even more anxious when messengers informed him that the forward units of Hancock's corps were beginning to move into the Federal lines at Cold Harbor. The sky was beginning to brighten, which meant that Grant would probably be launching a full-scale attack within the hour. If Breckinridge did not arrive soon, the entire Confederate right flank would be undermanned and vulnerable.

But Grant's expected assault did not come, not at daybreak or at any other time that morning. When no Federal attack materialized, General Lee decided to go out and look for General Breckenridge himself. He mounted Traveller—it was the first time in ten days that he felt strong enough to ride a horse—and set out for Mechanicsville to begin his search. Lee had moved his headquarters again, this time to Gaines's Mill. Mechanicsville was the nearest village and seemed a good place to start looking.

When General Lee rode into the village, he found Major McClellan having a leisurely breakfast with Breckinridge and his men. McClellan explained exactly what had happened—he had no maps and decided to stay on the main roads instead of running the risk of getting lost, and he had allowed the exhausted men to take frequent breaks during the course of their march. Lee listened to what the major had to say and ordered Breckinridge to get back on the road to Cold Harbor with all possible speed. He also ordered more troops to reinforce Anderson's sector on the Confederate right, anticipating the attack that was to come.

When Breckinridge finally arrived in position at Cold Harbor, General Lee sent word for McClellan to come to his quarters. He went with "a sinking heart," and found the general sitting on a camp stool in front of his tent with an open map spread out on his lap. When McClellan approached him, Lee traced a road with his index finger and quietly said, "Major, this is the road to Cold Harbor."

"Yes, general, I know it now," McClellan replied.

Later on, McClellan reflected, "Not another word was spoken, but that quiet reproof sunk deeper and cut more keenly than words of violent vituperation would have done."[40]

The men of Anderson's corps were very glad to see Breckinridge's division. They did not know that the new arrivals were actually several hours late and would not have cared if they had known. They were happy and relieved to have more men on hand to face the attack that everyone knew was coming. Throughout the day on June 2, the troops worked at perfecting their entrenchments, making them deeper and wider and building barricades of earth in front. When the enemy came, which would probably be in the morning, they would be ready for them.

A heavy rain began at about four p.m., which made the air much cooler but also made digging more difficult. The newly deepened and widened trenches began to fill with water, which made life in general more uncomfortable—nobody enjoyed sleeping in several inches of water. The soldiers slept as best they could through the rain, tried unsuccessfully to keep dry, and waited for the morning.

General Lee was awake before sunrise on June 3, as he usually was. Along with everyone else on this particular morning, he anxiously waited for the enemy to make its attack. His wait ended at about 4:30 a.m., when the right side of the Confederate line literally exploded with musket fire. The noise very quickly spread all along the entire line. Lee listened intently to the sound of the firing, hoping that it would not come any closer. The awful noise would taper off occasionally and then would resume its full fury after a few minutes.

First reports began to come in at about five a.m. Breckinridge's line had been broken, the general was informed, but a counterattack recaptured the line of trenches before any real damage could be inflicted. Shortly afterward, a courier sent by A. P. Hill reported that Union dead covered the ground all along his front. Similar messages came in from other parts of the front, which said essentially the same thing.

The enemy charges continued throughout the morning, along with the almost continuous firing. Men compared the gunfire with a storm, with thunder, with a volcano. To a soldier from North Carolina, the musket fire up and down the line sounded like someone running their fingers up and down a piano keyboard. Artillery also joined in, adding to the general din. Cannon fire rattled windows in Richmond, alarming the city's residents and waking them out of a sound sleep. It was the loudest gunfire they had ever heard, even louder than during the Seven Days' Battles.

General Lee was busy reading reports from the front when Postmaster General John T. Reagan rode into his headquarters camp with two prominent friends, both of them judges. Reagan explained that they heard the artillery fire and rode out from Richmond to see how the battle was progressing. Was the artillery very active, he wanted to know?

"Yes," Lee patiently answered, "more than usual on both sides." He also gestured toward the sound of musket fire, which was close by but not moving any closer, and explained, "It is that that kills men."[41]

"General," Postmaster Reagan persisted, "if he breaks your line, what reserves have you?"

"Not a regiment and that has been my condition ever since the fighting commenced on the Rappahannock."

Actually, General Lee had quite a few regiments in reserve. Four full brigades had been moved south to back up the lower end of the trenches. But he went on to say, "If I shorten my lines to provide a reserve, he will turn me; if I weaken my lines to provide a reserve, he will break them." This was certainly true enough and was evidence that Lee was finally beginning to understand General Grant—Grant would do whatever it took, for as long as it took, to break Lee's army.

Since his uninvited guest was a government official with political connections and influence, General Lee decided to ask Postmaster Reagan for a favor. His army was undernourished and suffered from scurvy and other diseases resulting from an inadequate diet. They had been eating things like sassafras roots and wild grapes for added nourishment, but these were not enough to keep the men in good health, let alone in proper fighting condition. Would it be possible, the general asked, for the postmaster to talk to the commissary general and ask to send some potatoes and onions to the army? Postmaster Reagan promised to do his best. After urging the general to take care of himself—word had been circulating in Richmond that he had been taking too many risks—Reagan said goodbye and rode off.

By this time, which was early afternoon, the enemy offensive was over. It had become apparent that Grant had given up on trying to break through the Confederate line and had stopped making attacks. Lee's staff was feeling upbeat and optimistic about the results of the day's fighting. From the reports that were coming in to headquarters, it looked as though every one of the enemy's charges had been beaten back decisively. General Evander M. Law, who commanded an Alabama brigade at the southern end of the Confederate line, said that attacks were "a grand adventure, a desperate struggle, a bloody and crushing repulse."[42] He also said, "It was not war; it was murder."

General Lee sent a characteristically low-key report to Secretary of War James A. Seddon on the fighting of June 3. "Repeated attacks were made upon General Anderson's position, chiefly against his right under General Kershaw," he said. "These were met with great steadiness and repulsed in every instance."[43] He ended his message with, "Our loss today has been small, and our success, under the blessing of God, all that we could expect."

Most Confederate troops were not nearly as understated in their reactions. They considered the fighting of June 3 to be nothing less than a complete and overwhelming victory over Grant and his army. The general opinion of Grant was that he was an incompetent who would never take Richmond, was probably the worst commander that they had faced so far, and would probably lose the war if he kept on with his present tactics. Lee's adjutant, Colonel Taylor, thought that "Old U. S. Grant is pretty tired of us," and went on to say, "I fear our great danger is that we may become too self-reliant and boastful."[44] General Grant was no longer the army's major worry, at least not according to Taylor. The main problem was their own pride and lack of reverence— "We are apt to take too much credit to ourselves & to forget Him who is the giver of all victory & who has so signally favored us."

But through all the optimism and high spirits, one small detail seemed to have escaped everyone's attention—Old U. S. Grant was still there. His army was no longer making any attacks on the Confederate entrenchments, but it was not going away, either. The enemy had dug in, with some units only fifty yards from the Confederate lines, and showed no signs of retreating.

The Union dead and wounded were still there as well. Nothing could be done about the dead except to retrieve their bodies and give them a proper burial. The bodies rotted and decomposed in the hot sun throughout the fourth and fifth of June and turned the air foul and horrible—Confederates complained that Grant could not force them out of their trenches by full-scale attacks, so he was trying to stink them out instead. When Grant contacted Lee regarding the removal of the Union wounded, informally proposing that each side send out relief parties to collect the men, Colonel Taylor called these "disingenuous proposals."[45] Most Confederates, including General Lee, agreed with Taylor and were not overly concerned about the wounded. They were not Confederate wounded, so there was no need to worry about them.

After a truce had finally been worked out, and General Grant retrieved his two surviving wounded soldiers from no-man's land, General Lee spent the next several days keeping a close watch on the enemy. Artillery duels broke out between the two sides, along with sharp exchanges of musket fire from skirmishers, but there was nothing resembling the fighting of a few days earlier. On the evening of June 4, Lee informed Secretary of War Seddon, "Up to the time of writing nothing has occurred along the lines to-day except skirmishing, at various points. The position of the army is substantially unchanged."[46] He kept looking for some indication of movement that might help him to figure out exactly what Grant was going to do next. He kept hoping that Grant might tip his hand, in other words, but Grant was not about to give his opponent any help.

Lee was convinced that Grant would do one of two things: either he would make a drive for Richmond, which was only nine miles away, or he would cross the James River and make his way toward Petersburg, a vitally important rail center about twenty-three miles south of Richmond, a city that had to be defended. Whichever course Grant decided to take, he certainly was in command of the situation. A month earlier, Grant had complained that he was sick of hearing about what Lee was going to do. Now, Lee had to base his plans on what Grant was going to do. The state of affairs between the two generals had been completely reversed since Grant crossed the Rapidan, and Robert E. Lee was fully aware of it.

General Lee bombarded the Union lines with artillery fire every evening, just around sundown, to keep the enemy troops in

their trenches with their heads down. He wanted to make absolutely certain that Grant did not move out of Cold Harbor in secret
and unobserved. As soon as Grant gave any indication that he was
vacating his lines, Lee intended to go right after him. Whether Grant
was moving on Richmond or going south toward the James, he had
to be stopped. And Lee meant to stop him.

On the morning of June 13, patrols brought back word that
the general had been dreading: the enemy had abandoned their
trenches, all along the entire length of the Union line, and had vanished. During the night, Grant had simply disappeared. His army
of 100,000 men might just as well have been so many ghosts. All of
the newly dug emplacements, with their intricate fortifications, were
completely empty and unoccupied. He sent the bad news to Secretary of War Seddon: "At daybreak this morning it was discovered that
the army of General Grant had left our front."[47]

When he found out that the enemy's entire army had pulled out
right under his nose, without anyone taking any notice at all, and
in spite of all of his precautions, Lee was outraged. He always had
trouble controlling his temper, and on this particular occasion he
did not even try. Gentle, kindly, soft-spoken Robert E. Lee exploded.
"It was said that General Lee was in a furious passion—one of the few
times during the war," a Confederate officer remembered, almost
certainly understating the event. "When he did get mad, he was mad
all over."[48] And Lee *was* mad all over. He indulged himself in a mon-
umental temper tantrum, as everyone within earshot very quickly
discovered.

Not only had Grant disappeared, but, to make matters even
worse, Lee had no real idea where Grant had gone or where he was
headed. He wasted no time in trying to find out. Both cavalry and
infantry units were sent out to find the enemy. Lee also covered the
approaches to Richmond—he still thought this was Grant's ultimate
objective—along with roads heading south toward the James River.
Advance scouts sent back reports that contact had been made with
some of Grant's skirmishers, but no one had been able to locate
the main body of the army. Twenty-four hours after Lee had been
informed that Grant was gone, the Union army had still not been
located, much less stopped.

By June 14, when Grant's whereabouts were still a mystery to Lee and his staff, it had become obvious that Grant was not heading for Richmond—he would certainly have covered the distance between Cold Harbor and the city's outer defenses within twenty-four hours. "I think the enemy must be preparing to move south of the James River," Lee informed Jefferson Davis.[49] But there was still no definite information. Lee went on, "We ought therefore to be extremely watchful and guarded." After opposing Grant for a month, it was now Lee's turn to wonder if Grant was going to turn a double somersault and land on his rear and both his flanks at the same time.

Confederate patrols made contact with Federal cavalry and managed to drive them back without much resistance, but no one could tell Lee where the main body of Grant's army might be. Lee kept sending messages regarding Grant's whereabouts to General P. G. T. Beauregard, who was in Petersburg. "I do not know the position of Grant's army," and "Have not heard of Grant's crossing the James River," were two distress calls he sent on June 16. A few hours later, he asked, "Has Grant been seen crossing the James River?"[50] On the following day, Grant was still at large. "Can you ascertain anything of Grant's movements?" Lee telegraphed General Beauregard in Petersburg. "I am cut off now from all information."[51]

During the late afternoon of June 17, General Lee received his first communiqué indicating that Grant was now south of the James. General Beauregard sent a telegram at about five p.m., which ended, "They say Grant commanded on the field yesterday. All are positive they passed Grant on the road several miles from here."[52] Lee was well aware that a Federal force had been attacking Beauregard, but this was the first he had heard that Grant was at the head of the attacking force.

Early the next morning, the general received another message from Beauregard. The core of the message was, "Prisoners report Grant on the field with his whole army."[53] Later the same morning, Lee received another confirmation of Grant's movements, from a cavalry unit on the north bank of the James—the last of Grant's army had crossed the river via pontoon bridge: "The rear of their infantry column left this place last night."[54]

There could be no doubt about it now: Grant was across the James.

He had given Lee the slip, and he also had kept him guessing for five days. It was a move that would have made Winfield Scott proud. In his memoirs, General Scott described how he swung around "the strong eastern defenses" of Mexico City to get his army into position south of the capital. General Grant accomplished the same maneuver, except he went around Robert E. Lee and his army instead of fixed defenses.[55]

General Lee had been outmaneuvered, and he knew it. He ordered most of the army south to Petersburg, leaving one division of A. P. Hill's Third Corps north of the river in case it might be needed to defend Richmond. Lee himself rode into Petersburg at around eleven o'clock on the morning of June 18. But Grant had got the better of him, in spite of the fact that he had reacted so quickly to counter his maneuver.

Lee had a premonition of what lay ahead for him and his army. "We must destroy this army of Grant's before he gets to James River," he had told General Jubal Early.[56] "If he gets there, it will become a siege, and then it will be a mere question of time." Grant had not only reached the James but had crossed it. A biographer said, "It was the first time he had ever hinted at such an outcome."[57]

AN UNEXPECTED ALLY

But General Lee had an unexpected ally in his war against Grant, namely the population of the North. The horrible casualties of the past month were causing an increasing number of Northerners to lose faith in the war in general and in Grant in particular. Lee hoped that the ever-increasing number of killed and wounded would discourage the North from continuing with the war and that this war-weariness would lead to an outcry to stop the killing and end the war.

The Confederacy did not really have to win the war, which was something that Lee fully understood. All the South had to do was keep from losing it—keep on fighting, keep on killing the Yankee invaders in wholesale lots, and the North would eventually get tired of the slaughter. Kill enough of them, everyone hoped, and the survivors would give up and go back home. In the summer of 1864, Lee knew this was his best hope.

Newspapers throughout the North spread the word of the number of killed and wounded. An article on the fighting of June 3 reported, "The engagement which opened at gray dawn this morning and spent its fury in little over an hour" had cost "not less than five or six thousand killed or wounded."[58] Reporters always made prominent mention of very heavy losses. After the Battle of the Wilderness, the *New York Times* said, "We have no official reports from the front, but the Medical Director has notified the Surgeon General that our wounded were being sent to Washington from four to six thousand."[59]

The Medical Director of the US Army reported that the number of wounded for the first two and a half weeks of May totaled 21,578. This did not include the Ninth Corps, which added another 3,500. This also did not include the wounded of Cold Harbor.

HEADQUARTERS ARMY OF THE POTOMAC,
MEDICAL DIRECTOR'S OFFICE,
May 24, 1864.

Brigadier General S. WILLIAMS,
Assistant Adjutant-General, Army of the Potomac:

GENERAL: I have the honor to submit to you the following report of the number of wounded of the Army of the Potomac during the present campaign, May 5 to May 22, 1864:

Number of wounded sent to Washington via Belle Plain	15,148
Number of wounded remaining in Fredericksburg May 23 . .	5,830
Number of wounded in Wilderness (about)	600
Total	21,578
Number of officers	851
Number of enlisted men	20,727
Total	21,578
Number of wounded in-	
Second Corps	7,840
Fifth Corps	6,301
Sixth Corps	5,787
Cavalry Corps	650
Total	21,578

To the above total must be added the number of wounded of the Cavalry Corps during the recent expedition which number is not yet know at this office. The number of wounded in the Ninth Corps, so far as it can estimated from the reports received from the Fredericksburg hospitals, is about 3,500.

I am, general, very respectfully, your obedient servant,
THOS. A. McPARLIN,
Surgeon, U. S. Army, Medical Director.[60]

This was what the newspapers from Michigan to Maine were reporting to their readers—not necessarily the numbers verbatim, but the word that thousands of soldiers were bleeding to death in Virginia. And Thomas McParlin's numbers only concerned the wounded. It left out soldiers who had been killed during those two and a half weeks in May 1864, along with those who would die from their wounds in the days and weeks to come.

General Grant was absolutely certain that the war in Virginia was going his way, in spite of the casualties he was sustaining, and that Lee and his army would have to give up at some point. General Lee himself said that it was now just a matter of time. But readers of the *New York Times* could only go by what they read in the paper, and the things they were reading were not very encouraging. The Wilderness and Spotsylvania and Cold Harbor did not seem to have accomplished anything at all, except to produce thousands of dead and wounded. And the end of the war did not seem to be anywhere in sight. The optimism of early May, when Grant first crossed the Rapidan and began his campaign against Lee, had soured into gloom and depression.

General Lee was well aware of the discouragement and despair in the North—copies of the *New York Times* and other Northern newspapers managed to find their way to Lee's headquarters, where they were avidly read. He received a great deal of useful information from the Northern press about Grant and his activities. And from what he was reading, it seemed that Grant's war of attrition, of using his superior numbers to wear down the Army of Northern Virginia, was beginning to backfire.

In the summer of 1864, the weak point in the Northern war effort was public opinion. An increasing number of people were beginning to wonder if the war was really worth the cost. Forcing the South back into the Union at gunpoint was taking a lot longer, and costing a lot more lives, than anyone had dreamed back in 1861.

The qualities that had served Grant so well during the battles since May 4—his persistence, his aggressiveness, his flat refusal to back down or admit defeat—had been turned into liabilities. Lee realized that as long as he could keep fighting, and keep killing Grant's soldiers, he would be turning Grant's drive and determination against him. From what he was reading in the papers, and hearing from his spies, the North was tired of the never-ending battles and their endless casualties.

Another item that was making the North rethink its attitude toward the war was the Emancipation Proclamation. President Lincoln's decree became increasingly unpopular as the war, and its increasing number of killed and wounded, went on. Fighting to save the Union was one thing; fighting to free the slaves was something else again. Northerners simply refused to equate the lives of their husbands and sons and brothers and fathers with the lives of slaves.

The anti-war Democratic Party flatly opposed Lincoln's Proclamation. The Democrats advocated an end to the war and full independence for the Confederacy, which meant allowing the South to secede and to take their slaves with them. The official Democratic position on the war, which was announced at the party's convention in August 1864, was "that immediate efforts be made for a cessation of hostilities . . . to the end that at the earliest practicable moment peace may be restored on the basis of a Federal union of the United States."[61]

There were many who did not go along with the Democrats or share their point of view on Confederate independence. But there were also an increasing number who were beginning to agree with it and could not bring themselves to back the Emancipation Proclamation. "As a war measure it is unnecessary, unwise, ill-timed, impracticable, outside the Constitution, and full of mischief," said an editor at New York's the *Herald* about the Proclamation.[62] The Illinois Legislature even issued a resolution in opposition to it, which began, "Resolved: That the emancipation proclamation of the President of the United States is as unwarranted in military as in civil law; a gigantic usurpation, at once converting the war, professedly commenced by the administration for the vindication of the authority of the constitution, into the crusade for the sudden, unconditional, and violent liberation of 3,000,000 negro slaves."[63]

General Grant claimed that he did not care one way or another regarding the freeing of the slaves. In a letter to his father, he said, "I have no hobby of my own with regard to the negro, either to affect his freedom or to continue his bondage. If Congress pass any law and the President approves, I am willing to execute it."[64]

Grant intended to carry on with his current method of waging war against General Lee and his army, in spite of anything the public had to say. As he said in the same letter to his father, "I am sure that I have but one desire in this war, and that is to put down the rebellion."[65]

Chapter Seven

LAST CAMPAIGN

A SUITABLE MEETING PLACE

Nortone of the other members of his group could tell what was on General Lee's mind as they rode toward Appomattox—whether he was tense, angry, dejected, or just anxious to get the morning over with. Because General Grant had asked him to select the place where they would have their meeting, Lee assigned Colonel Charles Marshall to ride ahead with an orderly and find a suitable place for it. Colonel Marshall left the general and the other riders and went ahead into Appomattox to see what accommodations might be available. After Marshall rode off, Lee and the others continued toward the village in silence. The general did not say a word, preferring to be alone with his thoughts.

The first person Colonel Marshall came across was Wilmer McLean. Mr. McLean was a heavy-set and prosperous-looking resident of the village, a man who looked as though he might know someplace suitable for the meeting of two generals. "Can you show me a house where General Lee and General Grant can meet together?" Colonel Marshall asked him.

Colonel Marshall remembered, "He took me into a house that was all dilapidated and had no furniture in it. I told him it wouldn't do." McLean had another idea: "Maybe my house will do!" Colonel Marshall took a look at McLean's very imposing brick house, which was large and well-furnished, and decided that it would do very nicely. "He lived in a very comfortable house, and I told him I thought it would suit."[1]

Actually, Wilmer McLean had only lived in Appomattox for about two years. Before that time, he had lived near Manassas, about 120 miles away. He had come to Appomattox early in 1863, when he bought the house formerly owned by John Raine and his family. With time, and with the romance afforded by the passage of time, he would become famous as the man who moved to Appomattox as a sort of war refugee.

During the First Battle of Manassas, in July 1861, a Federal cannon ball destroyed his kitchen fireplace. To escape the war, and the destruction that went with it, McLean moved his family to the relative seclusion of Appomattox. It would later be said that the war began in his kitchen and ended in his front parlor. But in April 1865, he was still just Mr. Wilmer McLean of Appomattox and had not yet become part of a legend.

After instructing his orderly to ride back and escort General Lee and Colonel Babcock to McLean's house, Colonel Marshall went into the house and sat down. Lee and Colonel Babcock rode up "after a while."[2] The orderly took care of the horses, while Lee climbed the stairs and entered the house with Babcock. There was nothing to do now but sit and wait for General Grant. "So General Lee, Babcock and myself sat down in McLean's parlor and talked in the most friendly and affable way," Colonel Marshall remembered.

A GENERAL ASSAULT ALONG THE LINES

"When will wonders cease. Thirty six hours ago the Army of the Potomac was within nine miles of Richmond, and now we are forty miles distant," Elisha Hunt Rhodes wrote in his diary on June 14, 1864.[3] Grant's move out of his trenches at Cold Harbor, and his forced march south and across the James River, took his own men by surprise as much as Robert E. Lee. It had also left them in a state of almost total exhaustion.

"The men are used up by the intense heat and fatigue of the past week," Lieutenant Rhodes went on.[4] "As soon as my tent was pitched I lay down and slept for four hours." After he finished complaining about how hot and tired he was, Lieutenant Rhodes finally got to the crux of his diary entry: "It is said that we are to cross the James River and attack Richmond from the south side. Either way suits me if we can only win."

General Grant could not have agreed more. He intended to do everything in his considerable power to win, although his plans did not include attacking Richmond from any direction. His most immediate objective was the city of Petersburg, about twenty-three miles south of Richmond. Petersburg would have to be defended by General Lee—of all the rail lines that supplied Richmond from the south, all but one came up through Petersburg.

Both Grant and Lee were fully aware of Petersburg's strategic value. Grant's main objective was the surrender of the Army of Northern Virginia—something that Lee still did not realize—but he knew that Lee would have to defend Petersburg. If he lost Petersburg, he would lose Richmond, and if he lost Richmond he would lose the war. It was that simple.

On June 15, General William F. "Baldy" Smith's Eighteenth Corps started out for the trenches at Petersburg. The city's defenses certainly were intimidating—a network of rifle pits, breastworks, forts, ditches, and trenches, all designed and set up for maximum killing potential. General Smith had been fully briefed on Petersburg and its impressive series of trenches. But what he did not know was that there were hardly any Confederate soldiers in Petersburg to man them.

General Grant watched as Baldy Smith's men, masses of blue-uniformed troops, moved into position on the morning of June 15. Some of them actually marched—a band played a medley of marches, complete with beating drums, to help keep everybody in motion. Infantry columns, wagon trains, batteries of artillery, all kept going forward. The whole scene was so absorbing that Grant forgot all about lighting up his usual cigar.

Smith's men charged at the Petersburg trenches and drove the Confederates out of their works by early afternoon. But instead of following up this advantage by having his entire corps push through the enemy works and into Petersburg itself, Smith decided to hold his ground. He had no idea that the trenches were manned by only about 4,500 regulars, along with the old men and young boys of a local militia unit. After what had happened at Cold Harbor, he did not want to go up against another well-entrenched enemy. Winfield Scott Hancock's Second Corps was on its way, and was expected to arrive in the morning. Smith decided to wait until Hancock arrived with reinforcements before going up against any more dug-in Confederate troops.

The only problem was that the Second Corps was not moving with any kind of urgency. Nobody told Hancock that he was needed at once or that he would be reinforcing Smith's advance against the Petersburg trenches. He did not receive any kind of word that he should hurry until about five p.m., when a courier from Grant's headquarters relayed the message that he should move toward Petersburg with all possible speed. "This seems to be the first information that General Hancock had received of the fact that he was to go to Petersburg, or that anything in particular was expected of him," Grant explained. "Otherwise he would have been there by four o'clock in the afternoon."[5]

Now that he knew what he was supposed to do, General Hancock began driving his men, at least as hard as they could be driven in their exhausted condition. By the morning of June 16, the Second Corps had not only arrived at Petersburg but had also captured one of the redans in the Petersburg line. The line of defenses had thirteen of these redans, small forts, which were connected by a system of trenches and rifle pits that extended for miles. General Grant was of the opinion that if this line had been properly manned, it could have held out against any force that he sent against it.

General Hancock was relieved of command of the Second Corps on the afternoon of June 16—the severe wound he had received at Gettysburg had started acting up—and he was replaced by General David Bell Birney until he was fit again. With Birney in command, the Second Corps captured three more redans that afternoon. Even though the forts were not fully manned, their artillery batteries killed a good many Federal troops before they were overrun.

General Grant was encouraged by the attacks so far. Even though losses had been heavy, the attacks were having their effect on the Confederate defenses. But he was well aware that Lee was not just sitting idly by while his trenches were being overrun. Signalmen standing watch in lookout towers had been keeping Grant informed of Lee's movements ever since the Army of Northern Virginia started moving south from Cold Harbor.

The lookouts on these tall towers sent a steady stream of flag signals to advise Grant of exactly how many troop trains were heading his way, as well as when these trains could be expected in Petersburg. Scouts and Confederate prisoners also kept Grant informed of Lee's movements. And the advancing columns churned up so much dust that they gave away their position to anyone who cared to look. Lee was coming south, and he was coming fast.

Grant wanted the rest of the army to follow suit, to move south to Petersburg before Lee could get there. Grant telegraphed General Meade to order General Warren and his Fifth Corps to get to Petersburg. Warren's corps had not seen very much fighting since Spotsylvania, and had not suffered many casualties at Cold Harbor. But he had to fight his way through some Confederate skirmishers on his way to Petersburg and convinced himself that he had come up against a much larger force.

General Ambrose Burnside ordered units of his Ninth Corps to reinforce Warren by attacking an enemy position on his right flank. The leading division, commanded by General Robert B. Potter, charged the position, drove the rebels out of it, and dug in to wait for help to arrive. But the division that was supposed to back up Potter's men never got the word and was sound asleep when Potter made his attack.

Nothing seemed to be going right. Orders were bungled or sometimes missed altogether. A little bit of drive and determination by any of the corps commanders would have gone a long way. But the memory of Cold Harbor was still fresh in everyone's mind and had effectively curbed all thoughts of another frontal attack on the Confederate lines. The combined effects of Cold Harbor, the heat and exhaustion, and the almost continual marching and fighting since May 4, had stalled the offensive just as effectively as any Confederate counterattack could have done.

George Gordon Meade did his best to get the offensive moving forward. He was in a very bad mood—he was rarely in a good mood, but the "goddamned old goggle-eyed snapping turtle" was angrier and more foul-mouthed than usual on June 18. There was more than just a note of frustration in the telegraph he sent to his corps commanders that afternoon: "Finding it impossible to effect co-operation by appointing an hour for attack," he barked. "I have sent an order to each corps commander to attack at all hazards and without reference to each other."[6] In other words, if you cannot co-operate with each other, at least have the gumption to try to attack individually. At least do *something!*

But Lee had already won the race. By the time General Birney's Second Corps was ready to attack, Lee's veterans had arrived at Petersburg and were manning the trenches. Birney's men realized this, even though Birney himself did not seem to. When the order to attack was given, Birney's men simply ignored the order. They had been at Cold Harbor and knew exactly what would happen to them if they ran headlong at a line of enemy rifle pits. The first two lines of troops were made up of veterans; the last two were green troops who had never seen combat.

The veterans and one of the green regiments flopped down flat on the ground and refused to move, in spite of anything their officers said or did. Only one regiment, the nine hundred men of the First Maine, obeyed the order and started toward the enemy trenches. By the time the waiting Confederate infantry and artillery was finished with them, only three hundred were still unhurt and uninjured. The survivors ran back toward their own lines, leaving behind the remains of their friends and comrades. Some of the dead had been so badly mauled that they could hardly be recognized or identified.

It was the same story all along the line—officers waved their swords and shouted the order to advance, but the men just looked at them and stayed on the ground. These men were far from being cowards; they were from veteran units that had fought at Fredericksburg and Gettysburg and the Wilderness. But they were not about to throw their lives away. Rushing an enemy that was dug in behind well-designed fortifications was not fighting, it was suicide.

If luck had been with Grant, he might have been able to take the nearly empty trenches before the enemy arrived, which would have allowed him to enter Petersburg unopposed. "I do not think there is any doubt that Petersburg itself could have been carried without much loss," Grant would write many years after the war. If he had been able to accomplish this, it "would have given us greatly the advantage."[7] But too many things went wrong, and too many generals moved too slowly while Lee moved too quickly, and the opportunity was lost.

Colonel Horace Porter was of the opinion that the failure to take Petersburg came as the result of the almost incessant fighting of the past weeks. "It was apparent in the recent engagement that the men had not attacked with the same vigor that they had displayed in the Wilderness campaign," he noted.[8] This lack of drive and energy was due to the fact that the men "had been engaged in skirmishing or in giving battle from the 4th of May to the 18th of June." They did not have either the stamina or the spirit to carry out the plan to take Petersburg.

There were some who blamed Grant himself for the worn-down condition of the men and, indirectly, for their failure at Petersburg. "Why is the Army kept continually fighting until its heart has sickened within it?" one staff officer wondered.[9] "Grant has pushed his Army to the extreme limit of human endurance." The constant fighting since early May had blunted the army, the officer thought. It was beginning to look as though Grant's aggressiveness was not only backfiring on the home front, as General Lee had seen, but was also having a negative effect on his own army.

Grant did not have a temper tantrum when Lee's army won the race to Petersburg, the way Lee had done at Cold Harbor. Things had not gone the way he wanted, and he was certainly disappointed, but flying into a rage was just not part of his character. On the night of June 18, Grant sent a calmly worded telegram to General Meade that exactly expressed his point of view. "I am perfectly satisfied that all has been done that could be done, and that the assaults to-day were called for by all the appearances and information that could be obtained," he said. "Now we will rest the men and use the spade for their protection until a new vein can be struck."[10]

The general also did not want any recriminations or finger-pointing over the failure to capture Petersburg. When Winfield Scott Hancock suggested a full investigation of the matter, Grant immediately dismissed the idea. He wanted nothing to do with any investigation. He was determined to carry on with the war from Petersburg, and that was that. Calling names and delegating blame would not have served any useful purpose.

But regardless of who was to blame, and whether he liked it or not, Grant now had a siege on his hands. Not even the most optimistic general in the army thought that Petersburg could be taken by direct assault, especially not after Cold Harbor, and Grant was not about to retreat—and for that matter, neither was Lee. The only thing to do was for the Army of the Potomac to stay right where it was—to dig its own line of trenches that would run roughly parallel with the Confederate lines, keep extending its lines to the left in an attempt to outflank the enemy, and wait for some sort of opportunity to present itself. As Grant put it in his *Memoirs,* "The siege of Petersburg had begun."[11]

Although Grant was not very happy about the situation, he was not discouraged, either. In spite of the siege, he was still absolutely positive that he would win in the end. His letters to his father were as filled with confidence as ever, a confidence that carried over into conversations with members his staff. Adam Badeau, a former newspaperman who served on Grant's staff as a sort of secretary, was struck by the fact that General Grant seemed so certain of success.

"He believed all through the anxious days and weary nights," Badeau remembered, "that if he had not accomplished positive victory, he was not yet advancing, as all the world saw, toward Richmond, but towards the goal he had proposed for himself, the destruction of Lee and of the rebellion."[12] Just after Cold Harbor, Grant assured Badeau that "success was only a matter of time." Robert E. Lee had used almost the same exact phrase—a question of time, he said—but with a completely different meaning.

General Grant had no real reason to be anything but optimistic. He had conducted a siege against Vicksburg, Mississippi, in 1863, which had resulted in the outright surrender of the city. The surrender of Vicksburg was a turning point in the war, as essential at General Meade's victory at Gettysburg. Vicksburg had also made Grant a household name, in the South as well as the North.

Grant had pounded Vicksburg with his artillery, cut off the city's supplies, and finally compelled it to surrender. During the siege, which lasted from May 18 to July 4, 1863, the Federal lines extended for more than fifteen miles. These trenches were strengthened by engineers, who reinforced them with logs and sand bags, and siege guns were provided by US Navy gunboats on the Mississippi River.

Two "mines"—tunnels dug under the enemy positions and filled with explosives—were detonated, with some success. The second mine destroyed "an entire rebel redan," as noted by Grant himself, "killing and wounding considerable numbers of its occupants and leaving an immense chasm where it stood."[13]

The mine was touched off on July 1, 1863. "From that time forward," Grant would later write, "the work of mining and pushing our position nearer to the enemy was prosecuted with vigor."[14] And no one could prosecute with vigor the way U. S. Grant could. Two days after the second mine, on July 3, Vicksburg's commanding general, John C. Pemberton, agreed to surrender. General Pemberton was another of Grant's fellow Mexican War veterans—"Pemberton and I had served in the same division during part of the Mexican War," Grant remembered.[15] The actual surrender ceremony took place the following day, Independence Day. Grant sent a telegram to Washington to announce the event; the opening sentence was pure Grant, direct and straightforward: "The enemy surrendered this morning."[16]

Petersburg was going to be a tough nut to crack, General Grant could see that, but no tougher than Vicksburg. But Petersburg was not really under siege, not in the strictest sense, since it was not surrounded on all sides. Also, its main rail lines were still intact and in use, including the Richmond and Petersburg Railroad link into Richmond. And anyway, Grant's real objective was not Petersburg itself. He was after the city's rail lines and Lee's army, especially the latter.

On the morning of July 3, 1864, Grant sent a message to General Meade: "Do you think it possible, by a bold and decisive attack, to break through the enemy's center, say in General Warren's front somewhere?"[17] He just wanted Meade's opinion: "If it is not attempted we will have to give you an army sufficient to meet most of Lee's forces and march around Petersburg and come in from above." Grant wanted to get at Lee as soon as possible—via the center of his line, from the north, or any way at all. Meade thought it over and decided that neither of Grant's suggestions was feasible. This did not faze General Grant, though—he would keep on thinking about the problem, and would come up with another idea.

The following day was Independence Day—exactly one year after Pemberton surrendered to Grant and the siege of Vicksburg ended.

The war in Virginia was a different kind of war, against a completely different opponent, but a siege was a siege, whether it was in Virginia or in Mississippi. Elisha Hunt Rhodes, who had been recently promoted to captain, spent the Fourth of July in the Petersburg trenches reflecting on the events that were going on all around him. "The glorious fourth has come again," he wrote in his diary, "and we have had quite a celebration with guns firing shot and shell into Petersburg to remind them of the day."[18]

He went on to remember, "This day makes four 4th of Julys that I have passed in the army."[19] In July 1861, he was at Camp Clark, near Washington, DC; in 1862, he was at Harrisons Landing, Virginia; in 1863, Gettysburg; and now Petersburg. The men had a small celebration to commemorate the day, which included what Captain Rhodes called "a fine dinner." The menu consisted of:

Stewed oysters (canned)
Roast turkey (canned)
Bread pudding
Tapioca pudding
Apple pie (made in camp)
Lemonade
Cigars

"Tomorrow if we march," Captain Rhodes concluded, "hard tack and salt pork will be our fare."

The siege went on all throughout the month of July. A lieutenant colonel in a Pennsylvania regiment by the name of Henry Pleasants came up with an idea of ending the siege by destroying one of the fortresses in the Petersburg defenses. His idea was to dig a tunnel under the fort, load it full of explosives, and light the fuse. If all went well, the blast would not only destroy the fort, but would also blow a sizeable hole in the line of trenches. Attacking troops would be able to rush through the hole and charge into Petersburg before the rebels knew what had happened.

General Grant liked the idea and gave it his approval. The same sort of thing had worked at Vicksburg—a similar "mine" had destroyed a rebel fort, a redan on the Mississippi, just over a year before—and was worth trying again. It might just be a way to blow a hole in the Petersburg defenses and break the stalemate at the same time.

Colonel Pleasants's regiment was made up mainly of Pennsylvania coal miners, who were well-versed in digging trenches and ventilating mine shafts. From June 25 to July 30, the men dug, hauled explosives, and built the mine under the direction of Pleasants, who was a mining engineer. Army engineers did not think the idea was feasible and refused to help.

General Ambrose Burnside's Ninth Corps was given the assignment of carrying out the attack after the mine was detonated— Colonel Pleasants and the 48th Pennsylvania Regiment were part of the Ninth Corps. In fact, General Grant referred to the explosive-packed tunnel as "Burnside's mine." When the mine blew, at sixteen minutes before five o'clock on the morning of July 30, the explosion made a crater thirty feet deep and sixty feet wide.

The fort on top of the mine was totally demolished, and the three hundred men inside were either killed or badly wounded. A gap had been opened in the Petersburg defenses. "Burnside's mine" had worked, with a vengeance. It was as effective as Colonel Pleasants had said it would be. Now it was up to Burnside Ninth Corps to push its way through the gap and into Petersburg.

General Burnside was filled with good intentions and had plans for 15,000 infantrymen to charge into the gap in four separate waves. But his ambitions far outweighed his ability to carry them out, as he had shown on more than one occasion in the past. During his two and a half months as commander of the Army of the Potomac, from November 1862 until January 1863, General Burnside had demonstrated that he just did not have the stuff to make an effective combat commander. A month after taking command, he had presided over the disastrous Battle of Fredericksburg, which resulted in about 13,000 casualties. A little over a month later, in January 1863, Burnside ordered the embarrassing "mud march," an attempt at a winter campaign against Lee that had to be called off when the army bogged down in the rain and mud. On January 26, President Lincoln replaced Burnside with Fighting Joe Hooker. But it was at the Battle of the Crater, as it would come to be known, that General Burnside rose to the full level of his incompetence.

He appointed General James H. Ledlie's division to lead the charge into Petersburg, which was a serious mistake on Burnside's part. General Ledlie had a reputation for being a drunk and a coward, as well as an incompetent, and he certainly lived up to his reputation on July 30. When the men of his division left their trenches and ran toward the breach made by the explosion, Ledlie was safely behind the lines, taking shelter in a dugout and getting drunk on medicinal rum.

Ledlie's men ran directly into the crater instead of around it, as they should have done, and stayed there. Hundreds of men piled into the pit and did not move. They waited for someone to give them orders, to tell them what to do, but Ledlie was nowhere in sight. When Ledlie began receiving reports that his division was in trouble, that his men had jammed themselves into a crater in front of the rebel lines, he ordered them to move forward. Having done his duty, Ledlie turned his attention back to his medicinal rum.

General Burnside was not getting drunk, but he was not doing anything to help the situation, either. He had decided to visit an artillery battery behind the lines to observe the battle from a distance, but he was so far from the crater that he had no idea that the attack was going wrong. When he began receiving reports that his men were in trouble and were coming under attack by the enemy, he ordered still more troops to go in.

The men never had a chance, and by nine a.m., the Battle of the Crater was lost. Colonel Pleasants angrily informed General Burnside that he had nothing but fools and incompetents for division commanders. He had done his part; the mine had done exactly what he had said it would do. It was not his fault if Burnside's commanders were too stupid to take advantage of the opportunity he had created for them.

Word of the disaster spread fairly quickly throughout the army. "This has been a terrible day in more respects than one," wrote an officer with a New Hampshire regiment that had not taken part in the attack.[20] He had heard that a rebel fort had been blown up that morning and that an assaulting column "had charged into the breach" but had been driven back. The whole thing was a "sad failure," the captain concluded. "There has evidently been a blunder somewhere and a big one. Thousands slaughtered for nothing."

General Grant was angry and disappointed over what had happened at the crater, and he fully agreed that there had been a blunder. This was the second time he had been prevented from entering Petersburg in less than two months. Grant did not call names and point fingers, but he made it clear that if he had been either a division or a corps commander he would have been at the front giving personal directions on the spot. If the men had been properly led, he told an aide, they would have won the Battle of the Crater.

"The effort was a stupendous failure," Grant would write many years after the war, still angry about the failure. "It cost us about four thousand men, mostly, however, captured; and all due to inefficiency on the part of the corps commander and the incompetency of the division commander who was sent to lead the assault."[21]

As the result of their conduct on June 30, both the inefficient corps commander and the incompetent division commander left the army. Grant did not dress them down or humiliate them, as any one of his predecessors might have done. He did not even dismiss them from their commands. Instead, he arranged for both of them to disappear quietly. This was another example of Grant showing his other side: he would pound his enemies into submission, but showed every consideration for his fellow officers, even if they had let him down. On August 6, Brigadier General Ledlie went on sick leave for twenty days, a twenty days that lasted until December. When he reported for duty, he was instructed to go home and wait for further orders. Ledlie must have been able to read between the lines, because he did not sit and wait for orders he knew were never going to come. Instead, he resigned from the army a month later.

Something similar happened to Major General Burnside. He also left on a twenty-day furlough, which turned out to be a furlough that went on forever. Burnside was never recalled to active service. In spite of this—or maybe because of it—Grant and Burnside remained on friendly terms for the rest of their lives. Command of the Ninth Corps was taken over by Major General John G. Parke.

After the Crater, U. S. Grant and Robert E. Lee would not be the leading figures of the war, or at least not its most prominent generals, for the next several months. While Grant carried out his siege at Petersburg, the focus of the war shifted from the outskirts of Richmond to other places—to the Shenandoah Valley, and especially to Atlanta, Georgia, and vicinity. For a while, at least, Lee and Grant would not be in the headlines of the *New York Times* or any other newspaper, North or South.

Early in July, while Colonel Pleasants was digging his tunnel at Petersburg, General Lee sent about 14,000 men from the Shenandoah Valley to Maryland. This force, commanded by General Jubal A. Early, was sent north to burn houses, terrorize civilians, and create as much mischief and mayhem as possible. By July 11, Early reached Silver Springs, Maryland, a few miles northeast of Washington, DC. Residents of Washington thought the rebels were coming after them and were on the verge of panic.

General Grant was not panicked by Jubal Early's advance on Washington, not even slightly. But he did send both the Nineteenth Corps and the Sixth Corps to bolster Washington's defenses, which convinced Early that he should change his mind about attacking the city. After giving the citizens of Washington a very bad scare, Early turned around and went back to the Shenandoah.

When President Lincoln "suggested" that Grant go to Washington in person to oversee the city's defenses—a presidential suggestion usually amounts to a direct order—the general declined. His explanation was that leaving the army to go to Washington would have a bad effect on morale, or at least that was what he told the president. Grant told his staff something else: "One reason I do not wish to go to Washington to take personal direction of the movement against Early is that this is probably what Lee wants me to do."[22]

This was undoubtedly Grant's main reason for refusing the president's request. Grant never forgot, not for a second, that his main objective was Robert E. Lee and his army—not the capture of Richmond or even the defense of Washington, DC, in spite of anything that President Lincoln might "suggest."

With Jubal Early back in the Shenandoah, and the siege of Petersburg a hard fact, Grant was able to focus on other things. His next objective would be the Shenandoah Valley—not just Jubal Early and his army but the valley itself. The valley had been a threat to the Union since the beginning of the war—a sanctuary for Confederate armies, including Stonewall Jackson's and Jubal Early's. Now Grant intended to close the valley permanently.

There was already an army in the vicinity, about 30,000 men under General David Hunter. But Grant did not have enough confidence in General Hunter; he wanted a more able and aggressive general. He wanted Major General Philip H. Sheridan.

Phil Sheridan was short—five feet five inches tall—stocky, and aggressive. Grant had every confidence that Sheridan was the man for the job. On August 1, he issued orders that Sheridan should be put in command of all troops in the field. After some argument—Secretary of War Stanton thought that Sheridan was too young for such a command, but President Lincoln overruled him—Grant got what he wanted. He removed General Hunter from command of the army, which was actually just a collection of three army corps: the Sixth Corps, the Eighth Corps, and the Nineteenth Corps. Grant named this newly formed unit the Army of the Shenandoah and put Phil Sheridan in charge of it.

Grant wanted Sheridan to push Jubal Early out of the valley—either that or destroy his army. Just as important, he also wanted Sheridan to destroy the valley's role as the breadbasket of the Confederacy—the Shenandoah was "the principal storehouse they now had for feeding their armies around Richmond," was the way Grant phrased it.[23] The order issued by Sheridan's headquarters emphasized this: "You will seize all mules, horses, and cattle that may be useful to your army. . . . Officers in charge of this delicate but necessary duty must inform the people that the object is to make this Valley untenable for raiding parties of the rebel army."[24] General Sheridan probably thought it unnecessary to mention Jubal Early and his army.

Destroy the Shenandoah Valley's farms and you were well on your way to destroying Lee's army. This meant declaring war on civilian farmers, but Grant was not about to let this stand in the way of his determination to put down the rebellion. Grant was fully aware that Robert E. Lee and the Army of Northern Virginia *were* the rebellion.

Phil Sheridan took the first step in his Shenandoah campaign when he ordered a general advance on August 9. This persuaded Jubal Early to remove himself from the vicinity. "On the 10th of August Sheridan had advanced on Early up the Shenandoah Valley, Early falling back to Strasburg," General Grant noted.[25] Even though Early had about the same number of men as Sheridan—about 30,000, in round numbers—"The superior ability of the National commander [Sheridan] over the Confederate commander was so great that the latter's advantage of being on the defensive was more than counterbalanced by this circumstance," Grant would later reflect.[26]

With Early out of the way, Sheridan now could go ahead with his plan to burn out the farms of the Shenandoah. In fact, the valley's farmers would always remember what Sheridan did as "the burning." Grant ordered Sheridan to make everything in the Valley south of the Baltimore and Ohio railroad a fire-blackened desert. Sheridan did his best to carry out his orders to the fullest.

Sheridan's men burned hundreds of barns and destroyed anything else that might be useful to the enemy. The smoke from the fires could be seen for miles. The troops also stole horses, sheep, and cattle, and drove off all the livestock they could find. They turned the valley, which Elisha Hunt Rhodes called "a perfect garden," into a burnt-out wasteland, just as General Grant had ordered.[27] This deprived the Confederate army of a staging area for future raids, as well as a supply base for everything from food and provisions to horses. Unfortunately, it also destroyed a way of life. It would take many years for the Shenandoah to recover from Sheridan's campaign.

A month later, just outside the Shenandoah Valley town of Winchester, Sheridan caught up with Jubal Early. On September 19, he sent Grant this wordy report: "I have the honor to report that I attacked the forces of General Early on the Berryville pike at the crossing of Opequon Creek, and after a most stubborn and sanguinary engagement, which lasted from early in the morning until 5 o'clock in the evening, completely defeated him, and, driving him through Winchester, captured about 2,500 prisoners, 5 pieces of artillery, 9 army flags, and most of their wounded."[28] A news correspondent said that Sheridan and his army went "whirling through Winchester," a phrase that made headlines all throughout the North.

This was exactly what General Grant wanted to hear. He advised Sheridan, "If practicable, push your success and make all you can of it."[29] There was actually no need for Grant to send this message—Sheridan was cast in the same mold at Grant himself and would certainly do everything possible to push his success and to keep pushing Jubal Early until he was out of the Shenandoah permanently.

But by this time, the most important news of the war so far, even more important than "whirling through Winchester," had already hit the newsstands, "Five telegraphic words—Gen. SHERMAN has taken Atlanta, on Saturday, thrilled the nation," ran the headline of the *New York Times* on September 7, 1864.[30] General William Tecumseh Sherman had begun his campaign against Atlanta on the same day that Grant crossed the Rapidan, on May 4, and had steadily pushed his way south for four solid months—"Four months of constant and vigorous campaigning, a contested march of full two hundred miles, ten pitched battles, and two score of lesser engagements by night and day."

There were a good many people in the North—and the South—who had predicted that General Sherman's campaign to capture Atlanta would end in disaster and that it would be impossible for any Federal army to take any city by force that was so far inside the Confederacy. But on September 2, Sherman sent a message to General Henry Halleck in Washington that ended: "So Atlanta is ours, and fairly won."[31]

General Grant did not receive the news until September 4. As soon as he received Sherman's dispatch, he read it to his staff. He had been sitting in front of his tent discussing the Georgia campaign at the time. As the word spread, the entire army shouted and carried on and raised as much hell as their lungs would allow. Everybody realized this was the most significant war news since Gettysburg and Vicksburg, over a year before, and that the war was now a giant step closer to being won.

The news of Atlanta took the North by storm. Church bells were rung across the country, and patriotic speeches and orations were made to celebrate the occasion. President Lincoln ordered every naval base and military installation to fire a one-hundred gun salute. At Petersburg, General Grant also ordered a one-hundred-gun salute, but with a difference. Grant decided to use live ammunition for his one-hundred-gun celebration—why waste powder on firing blanks? It was another typical Grant move—keep pounding the enemy, even during a moment of triumph.

An even more significant piece of news came two months after Atlanta surrendered. On the morning of November 9, the front page of New York's *Herald* understated, "Abraham Lincoln Re-elected

President of the United States and Andrew Johnson of Tennessee Re-elected Vice President of the United States."[32] President Lincoln's reelection determined that the war would be fought to the finish, until one side or the other was beaten down to the point of surrender.

Until Atlanta was captured, it looked as though Lincoln was going to lose the election. Lincoln himself did not think that he would be voted back into office. "You think I don't know that I am going to be beaten," he told a friend, "*but I do*, and unless some great change takes place, *badly beaten*."[33] In the summer of 1864, it seemed to the North that winning the war was now impossible. Grant did not seem to be accomplishing anything in Virginia except running up a horrendous number of casualties; Robert E. Lee and his army seemed to be as dangerous as ever, in spite of the Wilderness, Spotsylvania, Cold Harbor, and thousands of dead. And Sherman did not seem to be doing any better in Georgia: he had fought several battles and was always getting closer to Atlanta, at least according to the newspapers, but he never seemed to get there.

The majority of voters in the North had become tired of the war and its endless casualties. They had lost faith not only in the war but also in the way Lincoln was running it. The Democrats were promising to end the fighting as quickly as they could arrange an armistice with the Confederate government. Their peace platform stated that "justice, humanity, liberty and the public welfare demand that immediate efforts be made for a cessation of hostilities."[34] Besides ending the war, they also intended to grant full independence to the seceded states and would also allow them to keep their slaves.

This position was becoming increasingly attractive to Northern voters. Stopping the war and the killing had become more important than winning the war, even if it meant letting the rebels have their independence. The Democratic candidate was George B. McClellan, the same George B. McClellan who had been dismissed as general-in-chief by President Lincoln for the rankest sort of incompetence. In August, it looked like McClellan would run away with the election in November, and that the Democrats would be calling for a peace conference a short time afterward.

General Sherman's capture of Atlanta completely changed all that, literally overnight. With Atlanta in Sherman's hands, the Democrats could no longer claim that the war was a failure. Only the capture of Richmond would have made more of an impression with Northern voters. Atlanta had completely reversed public opinion regarding the war—it now suddenly looked winnable. On November 8, 1864, voters not only sent Lincoln back to the White House for a second term but also gave their approval for the war to continue.

Soldiers in the field overwhelmingly voted for Lincoln as well, which came as something of a surprise. Many so-called political experts thought that the army would vote for McClellan, a fellow soldier and also the former commander of the Army of the Potomac. But they refused to vote for the party that would abandon the Union cause, not after they had spent the last three and a half years fighting for it.

General Grant was just as happy as everyone else about the election results. On November 10, he sent a telegram to the Secretary of War Edwin Stanton: "Congratulate the President for me for the double victory. The election having passed off quietly, no bloodshed or riot throughout the land, was a victory worth more to the country than a battle won."[35] As far as he was concerned, Lincoln's reelection was more essential than another Vicksburg or Gettysburg.

After the election had finally been settled, the most important war news still came from Georgia. In November, General Sherman began his march to the sea, from Atlanta to the Atlantic. After destroying what was left of the city, Sherman's army started walking toward the port of Savannah, 225 miles away. Along the way, they destroyed everything they came across: farms, railroads, houses, anything that might be of use to the enemy, and a good deal that was not. When Sherman entered Savannah on December 21, the North had an excuse for another celebration. And General Grant gave another one of his 100-gun live-ammunition salutes, fired into the Confederate works at Petersburg.

The last major battles of 1864 were not fought in either Georgia or Virginia, but in Tennessee. General Sherman's antagonist in northern Georgia, Confederate General John Bell Hood, tried to divert Sherman's army away from Savannah by moving his army north into Tennessee. But instead of following Hood, Sherman continued on his destructive way eastward. In Tennessee, General Hood fought two battles—at Franklin in November, against John M.

Schofield's Army of the Ohio, and at Nashville a month later, against a force commanded by George H. Thomas. Both ended in disaster for Hood. At Franklin, he lost a full quarter of his army, and after Nashville he was replaced as commanding general of his army by General Joseph E. Johnston. It was the second time that Joe Johnston had commanded the Army of Tennessee. He had been replaced by John Bell Hood outside of Atlanta in July 1864, after a two-month campaign in northern Georgia against William Tecumseh Sherman. Now he was back, and he would be seeing General Sherman again.

While fighting went on in other places, General Grant kept on extending his lines at Petersburg. Soldiers kept digging, adding on to the existing trenches, edging a bit further over to their left with each passing day—or at least on each day that the weather allowed the men to dig. Extending the lines accomplished two things. The most important accomplishment was that it forced General Lee to extend his own lines to keep pace with Grant, which actually meant that Lee was over-extending himself. Every additional foot of ground that Lee had to cover meant that he had to thin out his forces, putting his already-stretched-out army into trenches that were steadily growing longer.

Also, in moving his lines steadily to his left, Grant was always threatening to go around Lee's flank. If Lee did not keep pace with Grant's extending line of trenches, the Union army would be able to go right around the unprotected Confederate right flank. Grant realized that Lee was much too alert to let this happen, but there was always the outside possibility.

The ever-extending Union trenches were also getting closer to the rail lines into Petersburg, which General Lee had to keep intact. The Weldon and the South Side railroads kept both his army and Richmond supplied with everything from food and clothing and medicine to ammunition and all the basic necessities of life. General Lee already had enough problems. The North threatening the rail line meant he had something else to worry about.

In spite of the fact that the two armies had been going at each other for six months and more, or maybe because of it, a sort of camaraderie developed between the Northern troops and the Confederates. The men on both sides would sometimes come out of their trenches and socialize with each other, talking and joking as though they were fighting on the same side. They would trade newspapers, tobacco, whisky, coffee, and gossip, acting like long-lost friends instead of sworn enemies.

News reporters marveled at the way the two sides would think nothing of calling an informal truce. During the Wilderness campaign, a reporter with the *New York Times* took note of one such ceasefire:

"Yanks, ain't it about your time to cook coffee?" a Confederate would shout across the lines.

"Yes," a Yank would shout back.

"Then if you won't shoot while I make my johnny-cake, I won't shoot while you make your coffee."

The reporter reflected, "Whereupon the culinary truce was observed with scrupulous fidelity."[36]

A soldier with a Rhode Island regiment put it another way: "When we weren't killing each other, we were the best of friends."[37]

General Grant did not concern himself with culinary truces or informal ceasefires. His main concern was that Robert E. Lee would do to him what he had done to Lee at Cold Harbor: vanish without a trace. Grant was afraid that he would wake up one morning and find out that Lee had gone, "and that nothing was left but a picket line." Lee had the railroad at his disposal and just might decide to load all of his men, his artillery, and his stores on trains and disappear south: "I knew he could move much more lightly and more rapidly than I, and that, if he got the start, he would leave me behind so that we would have the same army to fight again further south and the war might be prolonged another year."[38]

General Grant never could figure out why Lee did not just leave Petersburg—and Richmond—far behind him. That is what he would have done—abandon his trenches, like he had done at Cold Harbor, move into North Carolina, join forces with Joseph E. Johnston, and make a concentrated attack against Sherman's army as it moved north toward Virginia.

The straightforward Midwestern mind of Ulysses S. Grant just could not comprehend why Lee simply refused to cut loose from Richmond. As far as Grant was concerned, Lee should have at least *tried* to join up with Joe Johnston. Even years after the war ended, this still puzzled him. "After I crossed the James, the holding of Richmond was a mistake," he told a reporter some years later, after he left the White House in 1877.[39] He then went on to reflect, "If [Lee] had left Richmond when Sherman invaded Georgia, it would have given us another year of war."

He could not possibly have understood that Robert E. Lee had been afflicted by a crippling sense of duty, or at least what Lee perceived to be duty. This sense of duty would not allow him to move away from Richmond for any reason, no matter how logical or practical. It certainly defied Grant's idea of logic, although it did not prevent him from taking advantage of the fact that Lee's sense of duty had become a liability for the Confederacy.

Grant was looking forward to renewing his campaign against Lee and his army, just as soon as spring arrived and the roads of northern Virginia dried up. The once proud Army of Northern Virginia was losing many able men by way of desertion. "They were losing at least a regiment a day," according to Grant's calculations, and the remaining troops "had lost hope and become despondent."[40] Grant was absolutely certain that the coming campaign would put an end to Lee's army, as well as the war.

Grant let his father know all about his enthusiasm. "We are now having fine weather, and I think will be able to wind up matters about Richmond soon," he said in a letter dated March 19, 1865.[41] "I am anxious to have Lee hold on where he is a short time longer so that I can get him in a position where he must lose a great portion of his army."

Grant was absolutely certain that the end of the war was almost at hand. "The rebellion has lost its vitality and if I am not much mistaken there will be no rebel army of any great dimensions in a few weeks hence," he went on. "Any great catastrophe to any one of our armies would of course revive the enemy for a short time. But I expect no such thing to happen."

He ended his letter, "My kindest regards to all at home. I shall expect to make you a visit the coming summer." The general-in-chief of the largest army in the world was as devoted to his father as ever.

But General Lee did not "hold on where he was," at least not for as long as Grant wanted or expected. On the morning of March 25, six days after Grant had written to his father, Lee attacked the Federal lines at Petersburg. Fort Stedman was his objective, an unimpressive little box of a fortress about two hundred yards from the Confederate trenches. The attack took everyone by surprise, including Grant, but Grant was not intimidated. He had not planned to start his spring offensive just yet, but if Lee wanted to start the war's final campaign at Fort Stedman, that was as good a place to start a fight as any.

The Fort Stedman section of the Petersburg line was manned by the Ninth Corps. General John G. Parke now commanded the Ninth Corps, replacing the departed Ambrose Burnside. General Parke was asleep when the attack began at four a.m., but he was soon wide awake and sending troops to beat back the predawn assault. He sent his Third Division to stop the enemy charge, which was exactly what they did. The Confederates managed to punch a hole in the Federal lines, but between Parke's counterattack and heavy artillery fire from forts close by, Lee's attack was stopped.

Fort Stedman was recaptured, along with all the ground that had been lost during the early morning hours. The artillery fire was hot and heavy enough to keep the Confederates from moving; they could not retreat or advance, and no reinforcements could reach them. "This effort cost [Lee] about four thousand men, and resulted in their killing, wounding and capturing about two thousand of ours," Grant summed up.[42] And nothing had changed: Lee was right back where he had been before the battle.

That afternoon, Abraham Lincoln paid Grant a visit. After the usual greetings and pleasantries, the two men walked across the scene of the morning's battle. There had not been time to clean up the battlefield before the president's visit, which meant that every-thing Lincoln saw that morning was graphic and explicit. Hundreds of dead and wounded were still on the ground, crumpled up and bleeding, waiting to be carted off to hospitals or mortuaries.

It was a sobering sight for Lincoln—and for Grant, as well, even though he had seen the same thing many times before. Reading about two thousand dead and wounded in the morning newspaper, or in the dispatches was one thing, but seeing them on the field, especially so soon after the battle had ended, was something else again.

Three days after Fort Stedman, Grant and President Lincoln had another meeting. This time they were accompanied by Grant's old friend, William Tecumseh Sherman, along with Admiral David Porter, who had known Grant since Vicksburg in 1863. They all met aboard the president's steamer *River Queen*, to talk about strategy and how to end the war. Everybody was dressed in their Sunday clothes and best uniforms—Mrs. Lincoln was also on board, so they all did their best to keep up appearances.

General Sherman noticed how tense and anxious the president seemed to be. As it turned out, the root cause of the president's anxieties concerned General Lee and General Johnston. But his worries relating to the two Confederate generals were just the opposite of Grant's—he was afraid that Joe Johnston might slip away from Sherman's army and come north, to join forces with Lee in Virginia. Both Grant and Sherman assured him that there was no chance of this, which seemed to put Lincoln's mind at ease.

But Lincoln was also worried about the ever-increasing lists of dead and wounded that the fighting had produced, and he expressed hope that the war would end without another major battle. Everyone else hoped for the same thing, but nobody could make any promises. The only thing that Grant and Sherman could guarantee was that they would continue to fight the enemy in the field until all the Confederate armies surrendered and the war was over.

Besides strategy and winding down the war, another topic was also discussed, one that was just as vital to the president: what would happen when the fighting was finally over. Lincoln wanted to implement a "soft peace"—bring Lee and Johnston to bay, and then allow every Confederate soldier to go home. There was to be no revenge or vindictiveness; the rebels would be Americans again. Lincoln was even inclined to look the other way if Jefferson Davis and other Confederate government officials escaped to Canada or the Caribbean. In fact, having Jeff Davis out of the country might be a very good idea—he would not be around to make any more trouble.

Admiral Porter thought that Lincoln was particularly anxious to end the war as soon as possible and was willing to accept peace on almost any terms. There were only two items that he absolutely insisted upon: the seceded states would be required to rejoin the

Union, and slavery would have to be abolished. Lincoln was not adamant about anything else. "Let them all go, officers and all. I want submission, and no more bloodshed. . . . I want no one punished; treat them liberally all around," he told the gathering of officers.[43] "We want those people to return to their allegiance to the Union and submit to the laws." He wanted a terrible war, but he also wanted a generous peace.

Grant saw what the president was driving at and agreed with him fully. When the war ended, he would do his best to see that all of Lincoln's wishes were carried out. But first the war had to be ended. He ordered Phil Sheridan to start moving against the enemy at Petersburg, to go right after him, to hit Lee's flank and rear. On the same day that Grant issued this order, Wednesday, March 29, Elisha Hunt Rhodes wrote in his diary, "Still on picket and very quiet, although every man is on the alert. Something is about to happen."[44]

Because of a steady downpour that had turned all the roads into quagmires, the fighting did not start until March 31. Sheridan was turned back at a hamlet called Dinwiddie Court House. But on the following day, at the crossroads of Five Forks, Sheridan personally led a charge against the Confederate flank, a position held by George E. Pickett's men. The rebel flank broke, Sheridan's men rushed in to complete the rout, and thousands of Confederates were taken prisoner. So many muskets were taken from Pickett's troops that they were used as part of the corduroy covering over the mud-soaked roads.

Colonel Horace Porter had been with Sheridan during the fighting and had seen everything. After it was all over, he rode over to General Grant's headquarters to give his report, as quickly as the mud would allow. Grant and his staff were sitting in front of a "blazing campfire" when Colonel Porter rode up. After he dismounted and everyone gathered around him, Colonel Porter was so excited that he began shouting out the news of what had happened that day: the rebels had been totally routed, Sheridan had given Bobby Lee a drubbing, the way to Lee's rear was now wide open, and thousands of prisoners had been taken. He became so carried away with himself, and with his news, that he rushed up to General Grant and gave him a slap on the back—much to Grant's surprise.

All of Grant's staff were as excited as Porter and began yelling and carrying on like schoolboys. This was no ordinary news. Everyone realized that Lee's defeat at Five Forks meant peace and home and the beginning of the end. The men had been hearing about "the last battle" and "the last campaign" since 1862, and the words had become a sort of ironic joke. But now, after nearly four years of countless battles and worm-infested rations and mud-marches, everyone could see that this really was the last campaign.

The general had been standing quietly in the middle of all the bedlam, with his usual cigar in his mouth, until he heard Porter mention prisoners. The number of prisoners taken during the course of a battle seemed to be his own personal yardstick for measuring the real extent of any victory, and he asked Porter, "How many prisoners were taken?" Colonel Porter estimated that the number exceeded five thousand, a number that actually changed Grant's expression from impassive to happy, or at least pleased.

After listening to the exchange between Colonel Porter and the other staff officers for a few minutes more, Grant disappeared into his tent to write some field dispatches, which he handed to an orderly to be sent via telegraph to all commands. He then rejoined the group and told everybody, "I have ordered a general assault along the lines." This was typical, brutally straightforward Grant—no nonsense, strictly business. Porter commented that Grant delivered his message "as coolly as if remarking upon the weather."[45]

Grant's general assault began at 4:45 on the following morning. An intensive artillery barrage of hundreds of guns was followed by an advance all along the lines. The men moved forward so quickly that some rebel units only had the chance to fire one round before they dropped their muskets and began running for the rear. Shortly after the attack began, Grant's headquarters received a communiqué from General Horatio Wright: his Sixth Corps had carried the enemy line and were pushing forward. A short time after that, General Parke reported that his Ninth Corps had captured the outer works in his section, along with twelve artillery pieces and eight hundred prisoners. Parke had lost over a thousand men in that attack, but he had broken the Confederate line, permanently and forever.

Less than two hours after the attack began, General Grant sent President Lincoln a telegram reporting the morning's success. "Both

Wright and Parke got through the enemy's lines. The battle now rages furiously," he said. "Sheridan with his cavalry, the Fifth Corps, and Miles's division of the Second Corps, which was sent to him since one this morning, is now sweeping down from the west. All now looks highly favorable."[46]

The fighting continued to look favorable throughout the morning. But the defenders kept on fighting, shooting and stabbing and clubbing and refusing to give up. General Grant watched from the top of a hill, which gave him a good view of what was going on. The Confederate artillery also had a good view of him, though, and began firing at him and his hilltop observation post.

In spite of the fact that rebel artillery shells were landing all around him, Grant kept on writing orders and receiving dispatches. Several staff officers advised him to move to a less conspicuous, and safer, position, but Grant carried on directing the battle from where he was sitting. When he had finished, he seemed to notice the artillery fire for the first time. At that point, he finally moved off the hill, out of range of the enemy's guns. Grant was famous for his one-track mind, for his ability to concentrate on any object or problem in spite of any distractions. He did not intend to be distracted by anything as trivial as enemy artillery fire.

By noon on April 2, almost the entire line of Confederate works had been captured. Some of Grant's staff officers advised the general to break through to Petersburg and capture the city, but Grant rejected that idea. He had the feeling that Petersburg would be evacuated that night, which would make another attack, and another round of casualties, unnecessary.

Grant guessed correctly. He was up at daylight on the morning of April 3, and the first report he received was that General Parke had gone through the lines at four a.m., and that Petersburg had surrendered at 4:38. The evacuation of the city had begun during the night, with most of its residents escaping with the army.

Grant rode into Petersburg later in the day and made temporary headquarters in the house of a man named Thomas Wallace. He had not been in Petersburg very long when President Lincoln came to visit, accompanied by his sons Tad and Robert and also by Admiral Porter. The president and General Grant talked for a while—about

General Sherman coming north to support Grant, about politics, and about showing leniency toward the Confederacy after the surrender had been signed. Clemency for the South was obviously a very urgent topic for the president. But Lee was now in full retreat at long last, heading westward along the Appomattox River and doing his best to get away from Grant and make contact with Joe Johnston in North Carolina. After about half an hour of pleasant conversation, Grant said his goodbyes to the president and rode off to get his troops in motion.

The army entered Petersburg with something of a flourish, with flags flying and bands playing, even though most of the city's inhabitants had already evacuated. But Grant was in no mood for a celebration. He knew that Lee was trying to escape, and he was determined to stop him. The drive that Grant inherited from his father, the determination to stop at nothing until he reached his objective, pushed him forward. Ever since he had crossed the Rapidan River, eleven months earlier and many battles ago, Grant had only one goal: stop Lee and destroy his army. Now that goal was in sight, and Grant was not about to let up.

Very shortly after taking his leave from President Lincoln, Grant received a dispatch that the entire population of the North had been waiting for since 1861, along with every soldier in the Army of the Potomac: Richmond had been captured at 8:15 that morning. The dispatch went on to report that the enemy left in great haste and that the city was on fire. The entire army shouted and carried on when they heard the news—the end of the war was another giant step closer.

General Grant, as usual, showed no emotion at all. He regretted that he did not receive word of Richmond before he left the president, and he ordered that the news be circulated among the troops as quickly as possible. Apart from that, he treated the Richmond dispatch like any routine message.

The news certainly did circulate. On April 3, Elisha Hunt Rhodes wrote, "We heard today that Richmond has been evacuated and is in flames. Well, let it burn, we do not want it. We are after Lee, and we are going to have him."[47]

Not everybody in the Army of the Potomac saw it that way. Most of the soldiers wanted Richmond very badly. Some had been in the army since George B. McClellan tried to get to Richmond in 1862, and it had been their goal for the past three years. They wanted to see what the enemy capital looked like, at least. The GIs of another war, eighty years later, would feel the same way about Berlin. But Richmond was not Grant's goal, and the army did not get to within twenty-five miles of it. Grant was going for Lee, just as Elisha Hunt Rhodes had said.

General Meade had the idea of trying to outmaneuver Lee, of following and then overtaking him, but Grant soon straightened him out on that point: "I explained to Meade that we did not want to follow the enemy; we wanted to get ahead of him."[48] His plan was to block Lee's route to North Carolina and to finish him off, once and for all.

But first, the army had to catch up with Lee, which meant several days of hard marching. The men realized that hard marching would be necessary if they were going to end this thing, and they were more than glad to do whatever it took; they had done more than their share of marching during the past eleven months, and it looked like this might just be the end of it. "Still following the demoralized army," Elisha Hunt Rhodes noted. "I do not know just where we are but do not care, for Grant was at the head and we shall come out all right."[49] On the following day, Rhodes made another telling entry in his diary: "Still plodding along following up Lee," he wrote. "He has often followed us, and we him, but this is the last time."

The two armies finally met on April 6, at Sayler's Creek. (Grant called the resulting battle "a heavy engagement;"[50] Elisha Hunt Rhodes said it was "a grand fight."[51] Whatever it was, it cost General Lee another seven thousand prisoners.) Grant later would write, "The enemy's loss was very heavy, as well in killed and wounded as in captures."[52] He went on to elaborate: "Some six general officers fell into our hands in the engagement, and several thousand men were made prisoners." The battle had begun in the middle of the afternoon, "and the retreat and pursuit were continued until nightfall," when it was too dark to see.

Grant knew that Lee could not afford to lose another seven thousand men. He kept the pressure on with a sharp skirmish at Farmville, a few miles west of Sayler's Creek, which stopped a Confederate column on April 7, and Phil Sheridan drove his cavalry to the west, never giving the retreating enemy any chance to stop and catch its breath. General Grant entered Farmville on the afternoon of April 7, wearing a dirty, mud-spattered uniform. All of his baggage had been left behind; taking it along would only slow him down. He wanted to be able to move fast and did not really care how he looked.

At Farmville, General Grant first had the idea of asking Lee to surrender. Grant did not know if Lee was ready to give up or not at that particular moment, but there was no harm in asking. He got out his pen and paper and wrote to General Lee:

HEADQUARTERS ARMIES OF THE UNITED STATES,
April 7, 1865—5 p.m.

General R. E. LEE,
Commanding C. S. Army:
GENERAL: The result of the last week must convince you of the hopelessness of further resistance on the part of the Army of Northern Virginia in this struggle. I feel that it is so, and regard it as my duty to shift from myself the responsibility of any further effusion of blood by asking of you the surrender of that portion of the C. S. Army known as the Army of Northern Virginia.
Very respectfully, your obedient servant,
U. S. GRANT,
Lieutenant-General,
Commanding Armies of the United States.[53]

The letter was given to an officer, who rode off toward the north bank of the Appomattox River with a flag of truce.

Grant decided to spend the night at a small hotel in town. While he was standing on the front porch, a unit of the Sixth Corps marched past, also on their way to the north bank of the Appomattox. Small bonfires had been lit all along the street, and the men took burning logs from the fires and held them up like torches. Some of them recognized General Grant as they passed the hotel and began cheering and shouting and waving their torches. Men who had no torch waved their hats instead. Grant watched them go past and disappear into the night. After the parade passed by, the general was shown a room in the hotel, which, he was told, General Lee had occupied the night before.

At around midnight, Grant was awakened by a messenger with a reply from General Lee:

APRIL 7, 1865

Lieutenant General U. S. GRANT,
Commanding Armies of the United States:
GENERAL: I have received your note of this date. Though not entertaining the opinion you express of the hopelessness of further resistance on the part of the Army of Northern Virginia, I reciprocate your desire to avoid useless effusion of blood, and therefore, before considering your proposition, ask the terms you will offer on condition of its surrender.
R. E. LEE,
General.[54]

Grant did not really expect Lee to surrender on the basis of his earlier letter. He would send another message in the morning, after he went back to sleep for a few more hours.

By morning, most of the army was north of the Appomattox. Everyone was pushing, everyone was driving, doing their best to get across Lee's front and block his escape. Grant rode north of the river as well, so that any messages for General Lee could get through the lines with as little delay as possible. Before he left Farmville, Grant decided to send another letter:

APRIL 8, 1865

General R. E. LEE,
Commanding C. S. Army:
GENERAL: Your note of last evening, in reply to mine of same date, asking the condition on which I will accept the surrender of the Army of Northern Virginia, is just received. In reply I would say that, peace being my great desire, there is but one condition I would insist upon, viz, that the men and officers surrender shall

be disqualified for taking up arms again against the Government of the United States until properly exchanged. I will meet you, or will designate officers to meet any officers you may name for the same purpose, at any point agreeable to you, for the purpose of arranging definitely the terms upon which the surrender of the Army of Northern Virginia will be received.

Very respectfully, your obedient servant,

U. S. GRANT,

Commanding Armies of the United States.[55]

These were very lenient terms. Grant wanted Lee to know that he would accept almost any conditions, and that he would be willing to meet Lee almost anywhere to discuss these conditions, as long as Lee agreed to surrender. "Lee's army was rapidly crumbling," Grant noted.[56] Soldiers were deserting and going home, "continually dropping out of the ranks." He met a Confederate colonel who introduced himself as Grant's host—he owned the hotel in which Grant had spent the night. The colonel went on to say that he was the last man in his regiment, so he dropped out and waited to surrender. Grant advised him to stay where he was and promised he "would not be molested."

Lee's army might have been crumbling, with his men deserting by the hundreds, but he gave no indication that he intended to surrender. His response to Grant's most recent letter was not very encouraging:

APRIL 8, 1865

Lieutenant-General GRANT,

Commanding Armies of the United States:

GENERAL: I received at a late hour your note of to-day. In mine of yesterday I did not intend to propose the surrender of the Army of Northern Virginia, but to ask the terms of your proposition. To be frank, I do not think the emergency has arisen to call for the surrender of this army; but as the restoration of peace should be the sole object of all, I desired to know whether your proposals would lead to that end. I cannot, therefore, meet you with a view to surrender the Army of Northern Virginia; but as far as your proposal may affect the C. S. forces under my command, and tend to the restoration of peace, I should be pleased to meet you at 10 a.m. to-morrow, on the old stage road to Richmond, between the picket-lines of the two armies.

Very respectfully, your obedient servant,
R. E. LEE,
General[57]

When he read what General Lee had to say, Grant was convinced that Lee would keep on fighting until somebody forced him to surrender. He did not know it at the time, but General Phil Sheridan was trying his best to do just that.

Sheridan had put his cavalry squarely in front of Lee's army, near Appomattox Court House, and he was certain that he would be able to finish Lee, once and for all, if enough infantry could be brought up by early morning. He had sent George Armstrong Custer's cavalry off to Appomattox Station, where he had been told that three Confederate trains, filled with food and provisions, were waiting to be unloaded. Custer got there before the rebels could unload the trains and had them moved out of range of Lee's troops before they could be recaptured. He moved past the station with the rest of his men and seized a wagon park and an artillery train. By this time, it was nearly dark. Custer's men could see the campfires of Lee's army just off to the west.

In the morning, everything seemed to happen very quickly. The infantry that Sheridan called for had been on the move since before sunrise, and they arrived during the morning hours. Sheridan ordered his cavalry up to the front and directed the infantry commanders to bring their troops up in support.

The last battle of the war began with the crackle of musket fire and the booming of artillery. But this was not like any other battle that the army had fought. As the men advanced, the Confederates began to withdraw. They still had their red battle flags flying, but they were not coming on the way they normally would have done, the way they always had done before.

Sheridan's men were in position, waiting for the moment to charge the enemy and break his line. But before it could happen, a young Confederate officer rode out of his lines at full speed, heading straight for the Union position with a white flag. He approached the first general officer he came across, General Joshua Lawrence Chamberlain. The officer dismounted, saluted, and told the startled general, "Sir, I am from General Gordon. General Lee desires a cessation of hostilities until he can hear from General Grant as to the proposed surrender."[58]

Until the young man spoke, General Chamberlain had been paying more attention to his flag of truce than to him—it was a white towel, fastened to a staff. Chamberlain wondered "where in either army was found a towel, and one so white." But the word "surrender" captured his full attention. After a moment, he told the messenger that he did not have the authority to discuss surrender terms and sent him off to the rear to speak with his superiors.

A short while afterward, Chamberlain met an officer from General Custer's staff, who was accompanied by another Confederate staff officer. Without bothering either to dismount or salute, the Union officer announced, "This is unconditional surrender! This is the end!" He quickly introduced the Confederate officer, and went on to say, "I am just from Gordon and Longstreet. Gordon says, 'For God's sake stop this infantry, or hell will be to pay! I'll go to Gordon!'" He then rode off, leaving the Confederate aide with Chamberlain."

General Grant received Lee's note requesting an interview to discuss surrender not long after General Chamberlain first heard the word "surrender." He was conducted to General Sheridan, who warned him that Lee's proposal was a trick. "But I had no doubt about the good faith of Lee, and pretty soon was conducted to where he was," Grant remembered. "I found him at the house of a Mr. Wilmer McLean, at Appomattox Court House, with Colonel Marshall, one of his staff officers, awaiting my arrival."[59]

A MEETING WITH GENERAL GRANT

In mid-June 1864, General Robert E. Lee wrote to General A. P. Hill that the army's primary goal was to prevent General Grant from "selecting such positions as he chooses"—to stop Grant's advance, now that he had already crossed the James River, and to "fight him in the field": "If he is allowed to continue that course we shall last be obliged to take refuge behind the works of Richmond and stand a siege, which would be but a work of time."[60] Lee was still defending the city from an attack that Grant never had any intention of making.

But General Lee's most immediate concern was Petersburg, and keeping the rail lines into Petersburg from being captured by the enemy. The railroad not only kept his own army fed but also kept Richmond fed and supplied. Lee was well aware that he had his work cut out for him. Even though he had managed to get to Petersburg before Grant, and despite the fact that his army now occupied the city's formidable line of defenses, he now had to keep Grant at bay with an army that was shrinking every day from sickness, starvation, and desertion.

General Lee realized that he had a siege on his hands at Petersburg and was no happier about the situation than Grant. He had done his best to keep the enemy from getting anywhere near Petersburg, but Grant had slipped out of Cold Harbor and across the James before he was even aware of it. Now Grant and his army were just south of the city, waiting for their chance to break through the defenses. Lee knew that he had to attach his army to the city as long as the enemy held its position. And Lee knew Grant well enough to know that he would hold until the end.

The general's son, Robert E. Lee Jr., blamed the Confederate government for not allowing his father to detach his army from Petersburg and Richmond and to fight the enemy in the field, as he had written to A. P. Hill. "If General Lee had been permitted to evacuate Petersburg and Richmond, to fall back on some interior point, nearer supplies for man and beast and within supporting distance of the remaining forces of the Confederacy," the general's son reflected, "the surrender certainly would have been put off—possibly never have taken place—and the result of the war changed."[61]

If General Lee had drawn up a formal plan for moving out of Petersburg—"to fall back on some interior point," as his son described it—and had explained that plan to the Confederate government, he would almost certainly have been given permission to carry it out. Everyone in the government, from President Jefferson

Davis on down, was willing to give General Lee anything he asked for, and would have allowed the general to carry out any plan he desired. Lee and Davis were both West Point graduates, and they spoke the same language. The president would have understood what Lee was driving at if he had explained that the most effective way of stopping Grant would be to confront him in the open countryside and not to tether the army to Richmond or Petersburg.

But Lee's sense of duty would never allow him to withdraw from Petersburg or from Richmond. He saw the defense of Richmond, the seat of the Confederate government, as his sworn obligation. And Robert E. Lee was not about to relinquish his duties or obligations, not with the load of baggage that his father, Light Horse Harry Lee, had left him. Colonel Charles Marshall, one of Lee's most trusted staff officers, recalled that the general "had been heard to say that Richmond was the millstone that was dragging down the army."[62] But Lee never did anything to divest himself of this millstone. He never even made the attempt.

The siege of Petersburg continued throughout June and July— or, rather, Grant's extension of his lines toward Petersburg's rail lines continued. This led to the occasional short but violent skirmish. One such scuffle took place on June 22, when the Federal army accidentally left a gap between two of its corps, the Sixth Corps and the Second Corps. As soon as the gap was discovered, three Confederate brigades charged into it and, by the end of the day, captured more than 1,600 prisoners.

This particular skirmish resulted in a Confederate success. But in spite of this setback, Grant's men kept on extending their trenches to the west. The odd skirmish was not going to prevent Grant from moving steadily westward until he overtook the rail lines into Petersburg, no matter how many Union prisoners were taken.

Toward the end of July, the army began receiving reports that the enemy was planning to explode some sort of mine to blow a hole in the Petersburg defenses. This information came from brief articles in the Northern press, as well as from prisoners and deserters. The idea seemed fantastic and far-fetched, and nobody was absolutely certain if it was true or not. General Lee and the rest of the army waited to see what would happen.

When the mine went off during the early morning hours of July

30, General Lee seemed more annoyed than frightened. "Yesterday morning the enemy sprung a mine under one of our batteries on the line and got possession of our intrenchments," he wrote very matter-of-factly. He went on to describe how two brigades of A. P. Hill's corps charged into the enemy "handsomely" when they tried to rush through the gap made by the explosion and also reported that 73 officers and 850 enlisted men were taken prisoner. "I do not know what he will attempt next," he said of Grant, making him sound like a chronically misbehaving schoolboy.[63]

Lee knew very well that his opponent would certainly try something else, although he had no idea where or when Grant's next attempt would take place. But after the failure of "Burnside's mine," Grant concentrated on digging new trenches, trying to out-dig the enemy instead of trying to out-fight him. One of General Lee's staff officers put it this way: "During the remainder of the summer and the autumn, the spade took the place of the musket, and both armies enjoyed themselves in constructing new and strengthening old works."[64] The men who did the digging would have been greatly surprised to find out that they were enjoying themselves, but they did keep on digging. Grant gradually extended the left of his line, "toward the railroads which he desired to capture," while Lee paralleled Grant's movement by lengthening his trenches to the right.

By August, the Federal line reached far enough to the left to come into contact with the Weldon Railroad. General Gouverneur K. Warren's Fifth Corps captured a section of track at a place called Globe Tavern, a few miles south of Petersburg. Warren had been ordered to rip up and demolish as much track as possible, but on August 19 these orders were changed—Warren was sent an additional six thousand men and instructed to hold the rail line, not destroy it. Confederate troops under A. P. Hill and P. G. T. Beauregard came at the Federals and did their best to dislodge Warren's men from the railroad for the next four days. The Confederates charged again and again, but the Federal divisions always managed to beat them back. On the morning of August 22, Warren sent word that the enemy had withdrawn to their Petersburg trenches. Lee decided to let the Union army have the segment of track at Globe Tavern—trying to recapture it was proving to be too grim and much too costly.

The capture of the Weldon Railroad at Globe Tavern was a major setback for General Lee. With the railroad in enemy hands so close to Petersburg, Lee now had to rely upon wagons to carry all goods and supplies into Petersburg, which was much slower and much more cumbersome. Also, he would now have to stretch his lines westward to Globe Tavern, which meant that he would also have to stretch his already overextended army—digging trenches was one thing; filling them with soldiers was something else again. As one of Lee's staff officers remarked, with a note of finality, "the Weldon road was lost to the Confederate cause."[65]

But the fighting over the Weldon was not over yet. Winfield Scott Hancock and his Second Corps arrived at Ream's Station, about five miles south of Globe Tavern, on August 24, and tore up about three miles of Weldon Railroad track by nightfall. General Lee sent about eight thousand men—infantry, cavalry, and artillery—to attack Hancock and push him out of Ream's Station. Not only had Hancock cut Lee's supply line, but he was also threatening to outmaneuver Lee and force him out of his trenches.

The Confederate brigades charged the Union position at about 5:30 p.m. on August 25, supported by artillery. It was all too much for Hancock's troops, who broke and ran in spite of the fact that Hancock himself had ridden to the front and tried to rally them. The Battle of Ream's Station was a one-sided victory for General Lee. Union casualties were three times the number of Confederate killed, wounded, and captured.

But Lee could see that it was also an empty, almost meaningless, victory. Grant still held the Weldon Railroad, as well as the ground they had captured at Globe Tavern. Even though his men had broken the Union line at Ream's Station, and had sent the Second Corps running from the field in panic, Grant was still there and was still as strong as before.

Maybe it was around this time that Lee came to the conclusion that defending Richmond—and possibly the future of the Confederate war effort—was now beyond hope. He might be able to win more battles—there were certainly more Ream's Stations in his future. But no matter how many battles he might win, it was beginning to dawn on him that he stood no chance of winning the war.

By this stage, he knew full well that he was not going to intimidate Grant the way he had been able to intimidate McClellan and Burnside and "Mr. F. J. Hooker," back when the war was still winnable. Grant would keep on advancing and would keep on hammering with his single-minded determination until one army or the other broke. And Lee was also well aware that his army was only a shadow of what it had been in 1862 and 1863 because of casualties and desertions, which meant that it was his army that would break, not Grant's.

Two messages that General Lee sent in August 1864 give a fairly vivid idea of his state of mind. The first was sent to Confederate Secretary of War James A. Seddon on August 23, concerning the army's deteriorating condition: "Unless some measures can be devised to replace our losses, the consequences may be disastrous . . . without some increase in our strength, I cannot see how we are to escape the natural military consequences of the enemy's numerical superiority."[66] A short time later, he wrote a letter in a similar vein to Jefferson Davis: "I beg leave to call your attention to the importance of immediate and vigorous measures to increase the strength of our armies. . . . It will be too late to do so after our armies meet with disaster."[67]

These two letters do not exactly brim with confidence or assurance. Grant was doing exactly what he had set out to do, which was to wear down Lee's army until it was no longer an effective fighting force, and Lee knew it. He told an acquaintance, "I have no ambition but to serve the Confederacy and do all I can to win our independence. I am willing to serve in any capacity to which the authorities may assign me."[68] Having said this, the general went on to make a telling comment: "I have done the best I could in the field, and have not succeeded as I should wish." The war was winding down, and General Lee could see that it was not turning out the way he had either expected or hoped for.

There was a grudging respect on the part of the Army of Northern Virginia, or at least some members of it, for the fighting abilities of the enemy. Despite everything that had happened since Grant crossed the Rapidan, some rebel soldiers held admiration for their adversaries. "It may justly be said of both armies that in this terrible thirty days' struggle that their courage and endurance was superb," one Confederate officer wrote. "Both met 'foemen worthy of their steel,' and battles were fought such as could only have occurred between men of kindred race, and nowhere else but in America."[69] The great tragedy was that men of kindred race had to fight so many battles against each other.

General Lee was showing the effects of the war. When General James Longstreet returned to the army after recovering from the wounds he had received at the Wilderness, he was struck by how weary Lee looked: "The general seemed worn by past labor, besides suffering at seasons from severe sciatica, while his work was accumulating and his troubles multiplying to proportions that should have employed half a dozen able men."[70] The general was very glad to have Longstreet back, an experienced corps commander and his trusted "old war horse." General Richard Anderson had done his best as commander of the First Corps while Longstreet was recuperating, but Lee realized that Anderson was no Longstreet.

General Lee also knew that he would be needing all the help he could get. Not only was Grant pushing his lines westward, forcing Lee to stretch his own lines or risk being outflanked, but word from the campaign in Georgia made the general fear the worst. In early September, he received word that Atlanta had been captured by William T. Sherman's army. Atlanta was the Confederacy's second city, next to Richmond. Anyone with any foresight could see that this brought the Confederacy one step closer to the end.

The general was under a great deal of strain, which frequently put him in a very unpleasant frame of mind. In a letter dated August 15, 1864, Lee's adjutant, Walter Taylor, gave a description of the general that goes against the calm, courtly, soft-spoken Robert E. Lee of myth and legend. "The general and I lost temper with each other yesterday, and of course, I was afterwards disgusted at my allowing myself to be placed in a position where I appear to such disadvantage," Colonel Taylor wrote. "I couldn't help, however; he is so unreasonable and provoking at times."[71]

General Grant's activities did not help to soften Lee's disposition or to cool his temper. On September 29, Grant captured Fort Harrison, which was north of the James River. Lee personally took charge of the drive to retake the fort, and his men did their best to comply with Lee's orders and his urgings. They charged the fort three times, but the defending Federals turned them back each time. On the following day, Lee tried again, with the same result. He did every-thing in his power to recapture Fort Harrison but could not dislodge Grant. It seemed that Grant could go anywhere and do anything he wanted, and there was not very much that Lee could do to stop him.

Lee did his best to keep up a brave front through all this, trying to conceal his worries from his staff. General A. L. Long said that Lee "continued in excellent health and bore his many cares with his usual equanimity."[72] He went on to say that that the general had aged somewhat since the beginning of the war, "but that his eyes were as clear and bright as ever," and also that he gave the appearance of being robust and confident, "capable of remaining in his saddle all day and at his desk half the night."

General Lee gave the impression of having absolute confidence, not only in his men and his army, but also in the future. But at the end of October, he advised his daughter not to go to Richmond. He could not guarantee that the city would not fall into Union hands while she was there.

As 1864 came to an end, it became more and more difficult for General Lee to keep up his confident appearance. He received almost nothing but bad news from all fronts. First came the word that Abraham Lincoln had been reelected, which resigned Lee to the fact that he had four more years of war in front of him—there would be no negotiated peace as long as Lincoln was in the White House. Next came news that John Bell Hood's Army of Tennessee had been humiliated in two battles, at Franklin and Nashville. After General Hood resigned his command following these two disasters, General Lee recommended that Joseph E. Johnston be reinstated as commander of the army to replace Hood.

President Davis had any number of misgivings about reap-pointing Joe Johnston—among other reasons, Davis held a grudge against Johnston that went back to their days at West Point—but Lee's recommendation made him change his mind. The president probably would not have listened to anyone except Robert E. Lee regarding this very touchy subject. After hearing what Lee had to say about Joseph E. Johnston and his competence, President Davis decided to reassign Johnston to command of the Army of Tennessee, much against his better judgment.

This could be used as evidence to support the idea that President Davis would also have listened if Lee had suggested withdrawing the army from Petersburg and Richmond. If Lee could persuade Davis to reinstate Joe Johnston to his old command, a person that he detested, then Lee would have had no trouble at all in convincing Davis of the military necessity of abandoning the Petersburg trenches. But Lee's terrible and crippling sense of duty would not even allow him to mention the subject.

On the same January day that the Confederate congress approved the reinstatement of Joseph E. Johnston as the Army of Tennessee's commanding general, it also approved the appointment of Robert E. Lee as general-in-chief of all Confederate armies. This meant that Lee finally had the same power and authority as Ulysses S. Grant, although he did not have anything even approaching the men or the resources that Grant had at his disposal.

There were many across the South, not just in the Army of Northern Virginia, who agreed that President Davis's appointment of Lee as general-in-chief was one of his better decisions, but they also protested that it was made much too late. "Had this appointment been made two years earlier," A. L. Long reflected, "it is probable that a different state of affairs would have existed; but at that late date it was merely an empty title."[73] Maybe President Davis thought, or at least hoped, that the very name of Robert E. Lee would inspire the Confederate armies to greater efforts. But by the beginning of 1865, it really was much too late.

By the time General Lee had been appointed general-in-chief, the Confederacy had suffered another irretrievable setback. In December, William Tecumseh Sherman had topped off his famous March to the Sea by capturing the port city of Savannah, Georgia. General Sherman entered the city himself on December 2, 1864, and sent President Lincoln a telegram presenting Savannah as a Christmas present. General Grant celebrated the occasion by ordering another one of his hundred-gun salutes to be fired into the Confederate works at Petersburg. Lee's adjutant, Colonel Taylor, was highly annoyed by these salutes and thought it was very unsporting of General Grant to indulge in this barbaric form of Yankee entertainment.

In February 1865, Sherman moved his army across the Savannah

River into South Carolina and then into North Carolina. Joseph E. Johnston was Sherman's antagonist in the Carolinas, just as he had been north of Atlanta in 1864. Only by this time, the Army of Tennessee had been wrecked by John Bell Hood, as Johnston was well aware. He was also aware that there was not very much he could do to stop Sherman as he moved north toward Virginia, and that his opponent could go anywhere he wanted in North Carolina, just as Grant was doing in Virginia. He complained to General Lee that the worst thing he could do to Sherman was annoy him.

Even Colonel Walter Taylor, who had always been an unfailing optimist concerning the Confederate army, was beginning to see that the war was already lost. "They are trying to corner this old army like a brave old lion brought to bay at last," he wrote on February 20, 1865.[74] "It is determined to resist to the death and if die it must, to die game." He also noted, "Our people must make up their minds to see Richmond go, to see all the cities go, but must not lose spirit." The tone of Taylor's letter was that the Confederacy should fight on until the end, but also that the end was not very far off. General Grant might have been looking forward to the coming of spring, and the offensive that went with it, but General Lee was dreading it. As soon as the weather allowed, and as soon as the roads dried up, Lee was certain that Grant would make his final drive for Richmond. "He expects to accumulate a force by which he can extend beyond our right and left," he had written five months before, "when I fear it will be too late to keep him out of Richmond."[75] Now that it was spring, there was no question in Lee's mind that Grant would be going for Richmond at any time.

But Lee intended to hit Grant first, to attack the Union army before it had the chance to mount its spring offensive. A writer thought that Lee might have had another reason for attacking Grant, as well: "If nothing else, Lee probably wanted to end this war with a bang instead of a whimper."[76] Lee certainly started the morning of March 25 with a bang, attacking Fort Stedman with a sizeable force before daylight.

The attack began well. Lee's troops not only captured Fort Stedman but also captured a section of the enemy's trenches, and even managed to turn the enemy's own artillery against them. But the Federal troops very quickly reacted to the early morning surprise and counterattacked. John B. Gordon's Second Corps had been given the job of capturing the fort and breaking through the enemy's lines in force. If everything went well, the attack might break the siege of Petersburg. But the support that General Gordon had been promised did not arrive, for a number of reasons, and the attack fell short of Gordon's—and Lee's—expectations.

"No good results followed Gordon's gallant attack," is how Lee's son, Robert E. Lee Jr., summed up the fighting at Fort Stedman.[77] "His supporters did not come up at the proper time, and our losses were very heavy, mostly prisoners." Young Robert met his father riding along the Confederate lines opposite the front and was struck by how sad and careworn he looked.

One week later, George E. Pickett met Phil Sheridan at Five Forks. Pickett had gotten the better of Sheridan the day before, at Dinwiddie Court House, but Sheridan turned the tables on Pickett at Five Forks. Lee had ordered Pickett to hold his position at all hazards, and to prevent the enemy from attacking the South Side Railroad. But General Pickett was taken completely by surprise and did not even know that his men were under attack until the fighting actually started. As General James Longstreet put it, "It was not until that period"—when his men realized that the battle was "irretrievable"— "that General Pickett knew, by the noise of the battle, that it was on."[78] By the time Pickett arrived at the scene of the fighting, thousands of his men had been taken prisoner and the battle was lost. Longstreet did not mention the fact that General Pickett was away from his troops at the time, joining several other officers at a fish bake a couple of miles away, which was why he missed the battle.

General Lee did not seem to understand what had happened at Five Forks. He received the first fragmented report of the fighting during the afternoon of April 1 and ordered reinforcements to go in and support Pickett. But by that time, Pickett was in no condition to be reinforced, the enemy was closing in on the South Side Railroad, and Lee was finally faced with the reality of having to abandon his Petersburg trenches. "Had Lee known early in the evening the full magnitude of the disaster that had befallen Pickett," a biographer wrote, "he might have ordered the evacuation of the Petersburg line before daylight."[79]

General Longstreet arrived at Lee's headquarters at about four o'clock in the morning. General Lee was still in bed when Longstreet arrived, but he was wide awake and asked Longstreet to sit next to his bed. He was not feeling very well—Longstreet supposed that he was feeling the effects of the rheumatic problem that had troubled him for years—but he was alert enough to issue orders. He instructed Longstreet to move his troops to Five Forks in support of Pickett.

While the two generals were talking, Colonel Charles Venable reached headquarters with very bad news: Federal skirmishers were coming their way and had already driven Confederate troops from their position on the line. If this was true, it meant that the enemy had broken Lee's defenses and was now in a position that would put them behind the Confederate right.

Lee and Longstreet walked to the front door of the house that Lee was using as his headquarters. They could see a line of skirmishers moving directly toward them, although it was still too dark to see if the men were wearing blue or gray. As the sun rose in the sky, the approaching troops gradually became more visible, along with the color of their uniforms. By the light of the early morning sun, the two generals could see that every man in the oncoming line wore blue.

Lee went back to his room to change into his full-dress uniform, complete with sword. A short time later, he left the house and walked outside to mount his horse. He had ridden only a little way before he was joined by several staff officers. One of the men was riding General A. P. Hill's horse, which is usually described as either gray or dappled gray. The rider, Sergeant G. W. Tucker, explained that General Hill and himself had come across two Federal soldiers earlier that morning and demanded that they surrender. Instead, they opened fire. The shot that was aimed at Sergeant Tucker went wide, but General Hill was hit and killed instantly. The sergeant took Hill's horse and rode off to report to General Lee what had happened.

The news of Hill's death brought an expression of grief and regret to General Lee's face. Since the beginning of the war, Hill had been one of his most reliable generals. It was Hill who had come to Lee's rescue at Antietam/Sharpsburg in 1862, when it looked as though the Union army under George B. McClellan would win the field. Hill's march from Harper's Ferry saved the day for General Lee. "He is at rest now," he was heard to say, "and we who are left are the ones to suffer."[80]

But Lee did not have either the time or the luxury to indulge in mourning. Grant had finally broken through his fortifications at Petersburg, which left him with no other feasible option except to give up his defense of the city. He sent a telegram to the Confederate Secretary of War to advise him of the situation and did not even try to soften the impact of his message.

The language he used was so blunt and to the point that it might have come from U. S. Grant. "I see no prospect of doing more than holding our position here till night," he said, pointblank. "I am not certain that I can do that."[81] At the end of his message, he went on to say, "I advise that all preparation be made for leaving Richmond to-night." Later in the day, he sent an equally blunt message to President Jefferson Davis, which began, "I think it absolutely necessary that we should abandon our position to-night."[82]

After advising Richmond of what he was about to do, General Lee issued orders for a withdrawal of all troops still at Petersburg, including instructions regarding which roads and bridges were to be used. The army was to move toward Amelia Court House, where supplies and rations would be waiting. As soon as the sun went down, the men began pulling out of Petersburg and heading west, along the north bank of the Appomattox River.

The evacuation was complete by about midnight. A Confederate officer wrote that "a death-like silence reigned in the breastworks which for nine months had been 'clothed in thunder.'"[83] General Lee was a good deal less poetic about the situation. "Well, colonel, it has happened as I told them in Richmond it would," he said to another officer, "the line has been stretched until it has broken."[84]

As the army moved out of its trenches, Richmond, or at least a major part of it, was burning to the ground. While the men walked silently through the night, they became aware of a dim but steady light off to the north, like a sunrise in the wrong place. A rearguard of troops from South Carolina had set fire to everything that might be of value to the enemy, including tobacco and munitions, before they evacuated Richmond. A south wind spread the flames throughout the city. The swelling fires set fire to the flour mills along the river, along with a great many other buildings that had absolutely no military value. This was what Lee's retreating army was seeing—the fires of Richmond after the army and the Confederate government had evacuated the city.

Now that General Lee was away from Petersburg, he would have the chance to take his army out into the open countryside "where he would have a wide field of maneuver," which some of his subordinates had been urging him to do for months.[85] His father would have approved of the evacuation of the Petersburg fortifications and the move westward. Many years before, Light-Horse Harry had advised "that in defending Virginia against an enemy who controlled the sea, an army might best withdraw inland from the navigable streams." Draw the enemy into the interior, Light-Horse Harry recommended, where his navy would not be of any help to him. The only trouble was that General Lee now had so few troops that moving inland did not really matter.

The army kept on moving west throughout the day on April 3, along the north bank of the Appomattox River, with Grant in close pursuit along the south bank. General Lee, along with every soldier in the army, expected to find a supply of stores and rations when he arrived at Amelia Court House on the morning of April 4. Instead, he found a trainload of harnesses and artillery ammunition. He had 30,000 men coming to the village, all of them expecting to be fed, and nothing to give them. It turned out that some anonymous railroad official had made a mistake, and the provision train had been sent on to Richmond without unloading its freight. The men would have to go without breakfast again.

It also meant that General Lee would have to stop his westward march for at least a day to collect the food his men so desperately needed. He ordered 200,000 rations to be sent to Amelia by rail as quickly as possible and also issued an appeal to the farmers and "the citizens of Amelia County, Va," to supply provisions "to the brave soldiers who have battled for your liberty for four years."[86] Specifically, he asked for "meat, beef, cattle, sheep, hogs, flour, meal, corn, and provender in any quantity that can be spared."

The delay was critical. Lee knew that Grant was right after him, on the other side of the Appomattox. His only chance of escaping was to reach the open hill country before Grant, and to keep moving into North Carolina. Stopping for a full day could very well prove to be fatal; Lee knew that his opponent was not about to let up in his pursuit, especially now that he was so close.

The foragers who went out to collect food for the army did not bring in very much, at least not as far as Lee's soldiers were concerned. But in spite of the fact that they were literally subsisting on starvation rations, the men kept moving westward, trying desperately to get away from the enemy. On April 5, two divisions of cavalry commanded by General Fitzhugh Lee attacked a Federal infantry brigade outside Amelia Springs. This battle is frequently overlooked, since it did not accomplish anything significant for either side—both sides suffered about one hundred casualties each, which did not have any effect at all on either army. Lee continued his determined push to the west, while Grant—just as determined—stayed right behind him.

General Lee received some much-needed good news on the morning of April 6: two regiments of Federal infantry, along with a cavalry unit, had been stopped from burning bridges over the Appomattox River. General Longstreet's corps had either killed or captured every one of the enemy before they could get anywhere near the bridges. It was the first bit of encouragement that Lee had received for quite some time.

But this was the last piece of cheerful information that General Lee would receive. It was good to know that General Longstreet had virtually wiped out an enemy raiding force, but he had lost contact with the rest of his army. Two-thirds of it had vanished into thin air, or at least it seemed that way to Lee. He could not get in touch with two of his senior commanders and had no idea where they might have gone. "Where is Anderson?" he asked Colonel Charles Venable. "Where is Ewell? It seems strange I can't hear from them."[87]

At that particular moment, Richard Anderson's and Richard S. Ewell's troops were separated by a two-mile gap near a stream called Sayler's Creek, a small tributary of the Appomattox River. As a result of this gap, Ewell's force was surrounded by Philip Sheridan's cavalry and all but wiped out. "My two divisions numbered about 3,000 each at the time of the evacuation," General Ewell would later write,

"2,800 were taken prisoner, about 150 killed and wounded" at Say-ler's Creek.[88]

The battle had been a disaster. General Lee watched from a high ridge overlooking the battlefield and saw what was left of his army running from the field in panic. Soldiers dropped their rifles and headed for the rear as fast as they could move. General Lee was almost physically stricken by the sight, as though someone had hit him. "My God," he said, "has the army been dissolved?"[89]

The army had not been dissolved, but it certainly had been deci-mated. Lee had lost between seven thousand and eight thousand men, about one quarter of his army, mostly as prisoners.[90] Among the prisoners was General Lee's son Custis Lee; General Richard S. "Baldy" Ewell, who had been captured with the rest of his men; along with several other generals. After April 6, Lee only had about 12,000 infantrymen left, along with about 3,000 cavalry.

Desertion also continued to be a major problem for General Lee, a constant drain on his already desperately depleted forces. In an order to his men, dated March 27, 1865, Lee pronounced, "The penalty for advising or persuading a soldier to desert is death."[91] He had been reliably informed "that the evil habit prevails with some in this army of proposing to their comrades in jest to desert and go home." Even *suggesting* that a fellow soldier should give up and go home was now a capital offense, and even if that suggestion was meant as a joke. But the men were not intimidated by this warning and continued to slip away from their units in ever increasing numbers every day.

In spite of everything, General Lee would not even consider the possibility of surrendering what was left of his army. On the same day as the disaster at Sayler's Creek, he asked one of his generals, General Henry A. Wise, what he thought of "the situation."[92]

"The situation?" General Wise shouted. "There is no situation! Nothing remains, General Lee, but to put your poor men on your poor mules and send them home in time for spring ploughing." He went on to say that the army was "hopelessly whipped" and that "to prolong this struggle is murder, and the blood of every man who is killed from this time forth is on your head."

The general was completely taken aback by this response. "What would the country think of me if I did what you suggest?"

General Wise told Lee that it made no difference what "the country" thought. As far as the Army of Northern Virginia was concerned, *he* was the country. "They have fought for you," General Wise said. "They have shivered through a long winter for you. Without pay or clothes, or care of any sort, their devotion to you and faith in you have been the only things which have held this army together. If you demand the sacrifice, there are still left thousands of us who will die for you." He went on to repeat, "the blood of any man killed hereafter is upon your head."

What General Wise said was absolutely true. At that point in the war, General Lee was both the country and the government to his men, as well as to much of the South. There was not much else to fight for, or to have faith in. Richmond had been abandoned. President Jefferson Davis and his cabinet and all of his ministers had boarded trains and were on the run. Only General Lee remained. He was leading a greatly weakened army, it was true, but he was still there. As long as General Lee remained, the army would go on fighting. Lee listened to General Wise in silence, staring out of an open window and making no response.

The general still had his mind set on evading capture. His plan was to move to Danville, down near the North Carolina border, by a roundabout route. The enemy held most of the railroad in the immediate vicinity of Petersburg, which ruled out a direct route to Danville. He also had to have rations for the troops. But after meeting the supply train at Appomattox Station, and giving his men the first meal in five days, he would begin his march—west, then south to Danville, then to North Carolina and Joseph E. Johnston's army.

His plans received a major setback later in the day on April 7, when Federal infantry was spotted on the north side of the Appomattox River. The enemy columns were steadily making their way toward Lee's left flank. The general had ordered two bridges across the Appomattox to be burned to stop the enemy from crossing the river, but his retreating men had only set fire to one of them. As a result, an entire Federal division had crossed the remaining bridge, and also had managed to beat back a Confederate attempt to retake the bridge.

As soon as he heard the news, General Lee once again lost

his famous temper. Because some damn fool of an officer had not destroyed both bridges, as ordered, the escape of the Army of Northern Virginia was now in jeopardy. General A. L. Long said that Lee "spoke of the blunder with warmth and impatience," which was a polite way of saying that he indulged in another temper tantrum.[93] After venting his considerable anger over this possibly fatal mistake, Lee ordered artillery up to defend against a Federal attack.

Much later in the day, sometime after 9:30 p.m., a dispatch rider arrived with a message from General Grant, which began, "The result of the last week must convince you of the hopelessness of further resistance on the part of the Army of Northern Virginia in this struggle."[94] General Longstreet was sitting at Lee's side when the note was delivered. Lee silently read the note and handed it to Longstreet without saying anything about its contents; the message did not seem to come as any surprise. After Longstreet finished reading the letter, he handed it back to Lee with a terse, two-word comment: "Not yet."[95]

General Lee's reply to Grant reflected Longstreet's reaction. He did not think the Army of Northern Virginia's resistance was hopeless, he said in his letter, but he would like to ask what terms Grant was prepared to offer on condition of surrender. It was a good, diplomatic answer: it allowed his army to keep moving westward without making any sort of commitment on his part, and it also gave Grant something to think about.

Most of the following day, April 8, was fairly quiet, although General Longstreet noted that "the troops of our columns were troubled and faint of heart."[96] Some artillery commanders reported that their horses were now too weak from hunger to pull their guns. Longstreet gave orders to bury the guns and to cover them up with leaves and underbrush.

Later in the day, General Lee received another note from Grant on the subject of surrender. His terms were straightforward enough—"there is but one condition I would insist upon, viz, that the men and officers surrendered shall be disqualified for taking up arms again against the Government of the United States until properly exchanged."[97] But Lee was still not ready to give up. "To be frank, I do not think the emergency has arisen to call for the surrender of this army," he replied to Grant.[98] He did not even want to talk about the possibility of surrender until there was no hope left at all of escaping Grant and his damned tenacity.[99]

General Lee received more bad news that afternoon, information that certainly lowered his hopes. The desperately needed rations at Appomattox Station had been captured by the enemy. This almost certainly meant that the army would be too weak to make anything even resembling a forced march, to Danville or anywhere else.

Lee met with three of his generals that night: John B. Gordon, his nephew Fitz Lee, and Longstreet. Fitz Lee and Gordon sat on blankets, Longstreet sat on a log, while Lee stood by the campfire. Lee asked for advice: what should he do now? The four of them decided that they should make every effort to break through the enemy's forces when morning came. If the breakthrough happened to succeed, and Fitz Lee and Gordon were able to clear the road of enemy troops, the army would keep fighting. But if the Federals could not be dislodged, then there would be only one realistic option—surrender.

The necessary orders were issued, and the advance began during the morning hours of April 9, which was Palm Sunday. General Lee could hear the firing and sent Colonel Charles Venable to ask Gordon if he could fight his way through the enemy. Colonel Venable returned with Gordon's reply: he could not hope to accomplish anything without support from Longstreet's corps. But Longstreet was doing his best to hold off two Federal corps at the Confederate rear and could not give Gordon any support. General Lee had no choice but to face the fact that his army was now surrounded, and the end had finally come. It had taken nearly a full year, but General Grant and his hammering and resolve had prevailed.

General Lee dictated a letter to his aide, Colonel Charles Marshall, which would be delivered to General Grant. The note was short and to the point: Lee acknowledged Grant's note of earlier that morning, which stated that "the terms upon which peace can be had are well established" and asked "definitely what terms" Grant had in mind "with reference to the surrender of this army." Even writing the word "surrender" must have caused the general something very close to physical pain.[100]

After signing the letter, General Lee handed it to Colonel Marshall. Marshall, in turn, gave it to a member of General Grant's staff, Lieutenant Colonel Charles Whittier, who rode off with it toward Grant's camp. Lee and Grant exchanged three more notes regarding the pending surrender "interview"—the word was used in all of the notes, two from Lee and one from Grant—before the general and Colonel Marshall were escorted by Colonel Orville Babcock into Appomattox Court House. As General Lee passed through the rear-guard of the Confederate lines, Marshall said that the men cheered him "as of old."[101]

Chapter Eight

A FEW VITAL HOURS ON A SUNDAY AFTERNOON

THE BEST POSSIBLE EFFECT

"**I**n about half an hour we heard horses, and the first thing I knew General Grant walked into the room," Colonel Charles Marshall recalled. General Grant's entry into Wilmer McLean's sitting room promptly ended the conversation between Colonel Marshall, Lieutenant Colonel Orville Babcock, and General Lee. "General Lee was standing at the end of the room opposite the door when General Grant walked in," Colonel Marshall would later write.[1]

When Colonel Horace Porter entered the room a few minutes later, at about 1:30 on the afternoon of April 9, 1865, he saw General Grant sitting in "an old office armchair in the middle of the room."[2] General Lee sat "in a plain armchair beside a square marble-topped table" facing General Grant. Colonel Marshall stood next to Lee. Several Union officers, including General Philip Sheridan, either found seats or stood around the sides of the room.

It was the first time that Lee and Grant had met since the Mexican War, when Captain Lee of the Engineers gave Lieutenant Sam Grant a severe ticking-off for looking dirty and disheveled. Seventeen years later, Grant was still as dirty and disheveled as ever. "He had on his single-breasted blouse of dark blue flannel, unbuttoned in front and showing a waistcoat underneath," Colonel Porter noticed.[3] His boots and his uniform were dirty and muddy, he did not carry any kind of sword or sidearm, and a pair of three-star shoulder straps were all that indicated his standing as general-in-chief.

General Lee, on the other hand, looked like an illustration out of the army manual, just as he had in Mexico all those years ago. "General Lee was dressed in a full uniform which was entirely new, and was wearing a sword of considerable value," Grant himself pointed out. "In my rough travelling suit, the uniform of a private with the straps of a lieutenant general, I must have contrasted very strangely with a man so handsomely dressed, six feet high and of faultless form."[4]

The two generals certainly did contrast very strangely, strangely enough that everyone in the room could not help but notice. "The contrast between the two commanders was singularly striking, and could not fail to attract marked attention as they sat, six or eight feet apart," Colonel Porter remarked.[5] Colonel Marshall, the only other Confederate officer in the room besides Lee, seemed to have been slightly taken aback by Grant's scruffy appearance. "He looked as though he had had a pretty hard time," he said, as though he expected the Union army's general-in-chief to have at least cleaned himself up a bit for the occasion.[6]

It was Winfield Scott, Old Fuss and Feathers, meeting up with Zachery Taylor, Old Rough and Ready. It was also the son of Light-Horse Harry Lee, trying to retain some trace of honor and respectability in the face of failure, meeting the son of Jesse Root Grant, confident enough not to care how he looked and not at all surprised that he should be sitting exactly where he was at that particular moment.

According to Jefferson Davis, who was not there, Lee opened the proceedings by saying, "General, I deem it due to proper candor and frankness to say at the very beginning of this interview that I am not willing even to discuss any terms of surrender inconsistent with the honor of my army, which I am determined to maintain to the last."[7]

Doing his best to be genial, General Grant replied, "I have no idea of proposing dishonorable terms, General, but I would be glad if you would state what you consider honorable terms." General Lee's concern with Grant's terms and the honor of the army certainly fits in with what he said to General Longstreet that morning, when Longstreet advised him to break off the interview if Grant demanded any unreasonable terms. But Horace Porter does not mention this conversation and neither does Colonel Marshall, and they *were* there.

General Grant made an effort toward putting General Lee at ease, only he did not know exactly where to start. "What General Lee's feelings were I do not know," he would recall many years later.[8] "As he was a man of much dignity with an impassable face, it was impossible to say whether he felt inwardly glad that the end of the war had finally come, or felt sad over the result and was too manly to show it." Grant could not decipher Lee's silence any more than Lee's staff officers could.

In an attempt to get some sort of conversation started, General Grant mentioned Mexico and the "old army" days he had in common with Lee. "I met you once before, General Lee, while you were serving in Mexico, when you came over from General Scott's headquarters to visit Garland's brigade, to which I then belonged," he said in his very best conversational manner.[9] "I have always remembered your appearance, and I think I should have recognized you anywhere."

"Yes," Lee replied, "I know I met you on that occasion, and have often thought of it and tried to recall how you looked, but I have never been able to recall a single feature." It was not a very gracious reply, but Grant did not notice, or at least he pretended not to. Grant certainly understood. After all, General Lee was surrendering his army to a Union officer who had been his subordinate in Mexico, who was fifteen years his junior, and who was also his social inferior. He was a Virginia aristocrat forced to talk peace terms with a tanner's son from Ohio.

It was to Lee's disadvantage that he did not remember U. S. Grant. His recollection of George B. McClellan, the overcautious artillery officer he knew in Mexico, allowed him to intimidate McClellan all the way down the York/James Peninsula in 1862. But Lee never remembered Grant, never knew Grant, and never fathomed that *he* was Grant's objective and not Richmond.

After this rocky beginning, the two generals began a fairly pleasant conversation. According to Colonel Marshall, they "talked about the weather and other things in a very friendly way."[10] Grant himself said, "We soon fell into a conversation about old army times. Our conversation grew so pleasant that I almost forgot the object of our meeting."[11] But the conversation did not distract General Lee. "I suppose, General Grant, that the object of our present meeting is fully understood," he said. "I asked to see you to ascertain upon what terms you would receive the surrender terms of my army."[12]

There was probably a hint of ice in Lee's voice, especially when he mentioned "my army," but Grant chose to ignore it. "The terms I propose are those stated substantially in my letter of yesterday," he responded, without changing his composure, "that is, the officers and men surrendered to be paroled and disqualified from taking up arms again until properly exchanged, and all arms, ammunition, and supplies to be delivered up as captured property."[13]

Colonel Porter noted that "Lee nodded an assent."[14] A biographer remarked that Lee's assent "meant more than his adversary realized."[15] It amounted to a sigh of relief. Grant's terms meant that there would not be any imprisonment for his men: "The phantom of a proud army being marched away to prison disappeared as Grant spoke." These were the terms that General Longstreet had said that Lee could expect from Grant.

Grant said that he hoped that a general suspension of hostilities would result from this meeting and went on to give his views on the prospects of peace. Lee was anxious to get the proceedings over with and suggested that Grant put his proposed surrender terms in writing. General Grant, ever the hardheaded Midwesterner, very quickly agreed to write them out.

"When I put my pen to the paper I did not know the first word that I should make use of in writing the terms," Grant later wrote.[16] Colonel Porter, who was standing nearby, saw that the general wrote very quickly once he got started and did not pause until he came to the phrase "the officer appointed by me to receive them," which dealt with property being turned over to the US forces. At that point he looked over at Lee, and at the impressive-looking sword that he wore. Later on, he would explain that he did not want to humiliate Lee or any of his officers by requiring them to give up their swords or personal belongings. After thinking it over for a minute, Grant wrote, "This will not embrace the side-arms of the officers, nor their private horses or baggage."[17]

When he had finished, Grant went over the draft with Colonel

Ely Parker. Together, they made a few minor alterations. As soon as this had been done, he took the document and began to rise to hand it to General Lee for his inspection. Colonel Porter quietly stepped forward, took it from Grant, and handed it to Lee.

General Lee made quite a little show of preparing to read Grant's terms. First, he pushed a few books and two brass candlesticks aside to make room. Then he put the document on the table, took his steel-rimmed glasses out of his pocket, wiped them with his handkerchief, made himself comfortable in his chair, and adjusted his glasses. All of this was done with the deliberation of an orator preparing to deliver a longwinded speech; he did everything but clear his throat. After a minute or so, he finally started to read the document, which consisted of two pages.

He came across a minor error at the top of the second page and called it to Grant's attention: Grant had accidentally omitted the word "exchanged" after "until properly." Grant immediately gave his permission for General Lee to insert the word. When Lee could not find a pencil in any of his pockets, Colonel Porter loaned Lee his own pencil. Throughout the rest of the meeting, Lee nervously twirled it with his fingers and occasionally tapped the table with it. When the general gave it back, Colonel Porter kept the pencil as a souvenir, a memento of the occasion.

When Lee read Grant's sentence about the officers being allowed to keep their sidearms, horses, and personal effects, his nervousness seemed to leave him, at least temporarily. Colonel Porter noticed that "he showed for the first time during the reading of the letter a slight change of countenance, and was evidently touched by this act of generosity."[18] He said to Grant, "with some degree of warmth" in his voice, "This will have a very happy effect upon my army."

General Lee was very happy with Grant's terms overall, but there was one item he wanted to mention. He informed Grant that "their army" was arranged a little differently than the United States Army—"still maintaining by implication that we were two countries," Grant would grumble many years later—namely that the members of the Confederate cavalry and artillery owned their own horses, not the army.[19] Lee wanted to ask if Grant would allow the soldiers, the enlisted men, to retain their horses.

Grant answered that the terms did not allow for that and that only officers would be allowed to retain their private property. Lee reread the terms and said that he could see that was the case. But Grant was not the "Unconditional Surrender Grant" of earlier in the war. He said that he hoped this would be the last battle of the war. Because most of the men in the ranks were small farmers, he would instruct his officers to let every man that claimed to own a horse or a mule to take the animal home. The United States Government did not want them, and the soldiers would need them to plant the crops that would see their families through the next winter.

General Lee seemed to be greatly relieved by Grant's concession. "This will have the best possible effect on the men," he said. "It will be very gratifying, and will do much toward conciliating our people."[20] This was exactly what Grant wanted to hear—Grant the Hammerer had become Grant the Reconciler.

"This was the greatest day in the career of General Grant," Winston Churchill would pronounce, "and stands high in the story of the United States."[21] Even Lee's principal biographer, who did not have many good things to say about U. S. Grant or any other Union officer, said, "It could not have been put more understandingly or more generously."[22]

Now that the terms had finally been ironed out, Grant asked Colonel Ely S. Parker to make a formal copy in ink of the rough pencil draft. Another staff officer had started making the copy, but his hand shook so badly that he finally gave up and turned the job over to Colonel Parker. At the same time, Lee asked Colonel Marshall to draft a reply to Grant's agreement.

While Parker and Marshall were busy writing, General Grant introduced the other men in the room to General Lee. If an officer extended his hand, Lee shook hands. If the officer simply bowed, Lee bowed slightly. The only person he spoke with was General Seth Williams; the two had known each other when Lee was superintendent at West Point in the 1850s. Their conversation was pleasant enough, but when General Williams made a joke about something that had happened at West Point years ago, Lee did not even smile.

When it was Colonel Parker's turn to be introduced, Lee gave Parker a startled look "and his eyes rested on him for several seconds."[23] Ely S. Parker was a full-blooded Seneca Indian, with a very dark complexion. It seemed to Colonel Porter, who was standing close to Lee, that the general "at first mistook Parker for a negro" and was surprised that "the commander of the Union armies had one of that race on his personal staff."

When the formal copy was ready, both General Lee and General signed the agreement.

Appomattox C. H., Va.
Apr. 9th, 1865

Gen. R. E. Lee,
Comd. C.S.A.

Gen.
 In accordance with the substance of my letter to you of the 8th instant I propose to receive the surrender of the Army of N. Va. on the following terms, to-wit:
 Rolls of all the officers and men to be made in duplicate, one copy to be given to an officer designated by me, the other to be retained by such officer or officers as you may designate. The officers to give their individual paroles not to take up arms against the Government of the United States until properly exchanged and each company or regimental commander sign a like parole for the men of their command.
 The arms, artillery and public property to be parked and stacked and turned over to the officer appointed by me to receive them.
 This will not embrace the sidearms of the officers, nor their private horses or baggage. This done each officer and man will be allowed to return to their homes not to be disturbed by United States authority so long as they observe their paroles and the laws in force where they may reside.
 Very respectfully,
 U. S. Grant, Lt Gl.[24]

Colonel Marshall then handed Grant the reply he had written for General Lee:

HEADQUARTERS OF THE ARMY OF NORTHERN VIRGINIA
April 9, 1865

I received your letter of this date containing the terms of the surrender of the Army of Northern Virginia proposed by you. As
they are substantially the same as those expressed in your letter of
the 8th instant, they are accepted. I will proceed to designate the
proper officers to carry the stipulations into effect.

R. E. Lee, General[25]

With the signing of the surrender terms by the two generals, the
ceremony was over. Colonel Marshall was astonished by the simplicity
and unpretentiousness of the proceedings. There had been no pomp
and no theatrical display at all. Everything that had happened in
Wilmer McLean's parlor had been plain and simple and straightforward, totally lacking in pretentiousness—much like General Grant
himself. Grant probably did not know how to be anything but unpre-
tentious and low-key, even on such a momentous occasion.

Although the surrender terms had been signed, General Lee still
had something on his mind. He told Grant that "his army was in a
very bad condition for want of food."[26] His men had been living on
handfuls of parched corn, he explained, and asked Grant for rations
for his men as well as for a thousand or so Union prisoners. He also
requested forage for his horses.

Grant instantly replied "certainly," and asked how many rations
he would need. According to Colonel Parker, Lee said that he did
not really know. Grant himself recalled that Lee said that he needed
about 25,000 rations. Both Grant and Porter agree that the general
allowed 25,000 rations to be sent over to the Confederate commissary. There was no forage for the horses, Grant explained; the Union
forces had depended upon the countryside for that, allowing their
horses to graze in the fields.

The rations that Grant promised were actually the provisions
that had been captured by General Custer's cavalry that morning. In
other words, Grant was actually giving Lee his own rations. Lee was
not aware of this, but Grant certainly was. It was a gesture that would
have brought a smile to the face of Grant's father. According to his

reputation, Jesse Root Grant "could pinch a penny as well as any man alive."[27]

All the business of the meeting had now been taken care of, and the two generals had only a few things to say to one another before going their separate ways. General Grant apologized for not having his sword with him. He had not seen his personal baggage for several days, he explained, and rarely wore a sword, anyway. Lee replied that he was in the habit of wearing a sword most of the time—he could not resist issuing a mild rebuke to Grant for being unmilitary, even though he claimed that he did not remember Sam Grant from Mexico.

Lee also asked General Grant to notify General Meade of the surrender. Now that the armistice had been signed, the last thing he wanted was for accidental skirmishing to break out between the two sides. Grant agreed and sent two of his officers through the Confederate lines to bring the news to Meade. A few Confederate officers accompanied them, so that there would be no misunderstanding.

A little before four o'clock, General Lee shook hands with General Grant, bowed to the other Union officers in the room, and stepped out onto the front porch with Colonel Marshall. The general called for his orderly, Sergeant Tucker, to bring his horse. While the sergeant replaced Traveller's bridle, General Lee stood on the bottom step of the porch and stared off into the distance, in the general direction of his army. He put his gloves on, absentmindedly punched the palm of his left hand with his right, and mounted his horse.

General Grant stepped out of the house, walked down the steps, and raised his hat to General Lee in the way of a salute. All the other Union officers also raised their hats. Lee returned the salute by raising his own hat and rode off to break the news of the surrender to the men of his army.

General Lee did not write anything in the way of memoirs and never gave any indication of what was going through his mind as he rode toward his army to tell his soldiers that he had surrendered. The men did not take the news very well—some cried, some cursed, and some threatened to go on fighting just the same. Lee told everyone that they should all go home and that he had done the best he could for them.

Robert E. Lee had surrendered, but he had not disgraced himself or let down his men. He had not copied Light-Horse Harry's example—one writer called it "his father's shameful example"—and he had done the best he could for his soldiers and for Virginia.[28]

When news of the surrender spread throughout the Union camp, the reaction was predictable: everyone went crazy with joy and relief. "The Batteries began to fire blank cartridges, while the Infantry fired their muskets in the air," Elisha Hunt Rhodes recalled.[29] "The men threw their knapsacks and canteens in the air and howled like mad."

Even General Meade himself joined in the mayhem. He "rode like mad down the road shouting 'The war is over, and we are going home!'" Colonel Rhodes himself was more reflective: "I cried and laughed by turns. I never was so happy in my life," he wrote in his diary. "I thank God for all His blessings to me, and that my life has been spared to see this glorious day."

General Grant did not join in the celebration. As soon as he heard the commotion, in fact, he ordered all the celebrating and saluting to be stopped at once. "The Confederates were now our prisoners," he explained, "and we did not want to exult over their downfall."[30]

At Spotsylvania, nearly a year before, he had shown the same consideration toward Confederate General Edward Johnson, his friend and a fellow Mexican War veteran. General Johnson had been taken prisoner during the battle, and Grant went out of his way to be courteous and considerate to him. He was now showing the same consideration for General Lee and the Army of Northern Virginia—the Confederates were no longer the enemy, they were fellow Americans once again.

After General Lee departed to rejoin his army, Grant and his staff headed back toward their own headquarters camp. They had not ridden very far before Colonel Porter came up with a very pertinent suggestion for the general: would it not be a very good idea to inform the War Department that General Lee had just surrendered his army?

General Grant admitted that he had not even thought of informing Washington of the surrender. He stopped, dismounted by the roadside, sat down on a large stone, and wrote this message to Secretary of War Stanton, dated 4:30 p.m.:

Honorable E. M. Stanton, Secretary of War, Washington

General Lee surrendered the Army of Northern Virginia this afternoon on terms proposed by myself. The accompanying additional
correspondence will show the conditions fully.
    U. S. Grant, Lieutenant-General[31]

That was all. General Grant had just written one of the most
important communiques in American history, certainly the most
important of his military career, and he made it sound as though he
sent this sort of message every day. He was certainly a man who would
be silent in several languages. Even on this truly historic occasion, he
would not allow his feelings to show.

General Lee was a good deal more effusive in his farewell to the
Army of Northern Virginia, officially known as General Order No.
9, which was dated April 10, 1865. In the first line of his farewell,
Lee informed his men, "After four years of arduous service, marked
by unsurpassed courage and fortitude, the Army of Northern Virginia has been compelled to yield to overwhelming numbers and
resources."[32]

He did not say anything about an equally important factor, probably the most important factor, that had compelled him to yield: the
grit and determination of his opponent, U. S. Grant. Every Union
general before Grant who had opposed him—Burnside, Hooker,
McClellan, and even John Pope—had the same "overwhelming
numbers and resources." But none of them had Grant's drive and
resolve. None of them would have driven Lee and his army relentlessly south through the Wilderness and Spotsylvania and Cold
Harbor to Petersburg, or would have kept the Confederates bottled
up in its trenches all winter long. None of them would have sent a
communiqué even remotely resembling, "I intend to fight it out on
this line if it takes all summer," and meant it. Even though Grant's
predecessors also had overwhelming numbers of men and materiel
at their disposal, none of them had Jesse Root Grant for a father.

CHANGING ATTITUDES

After Appomattox, both Ulysses S. Grant and Robert E. Lee became national heroes, as well as national icons. Grant became infected with the presidential bug, just as Lincoln suspected would happen, and succeeded the luckless Andrew Johnson as president in 1868. But his two terms in the White House will always be overshadowed by his military career, especially by his eleven months in Virginia in 1864 and 1865.

Historians have called U. S. Grant a great general, the first of the great modern generals. Some Union officers compared him with Napoleon. William Tecumseh Sherman, who was a friend of Grant's and understandably prejudiced, said that Grant was the greatest soldier of his time, and possibly of all time. Confederates, including General John B. Gordon, praised Grant for being magnanimous in victory and for showing sympathy for all paroled Confederate soldiers at Appomattox.

The terms that Grant set down at Appomattox were not just noble-sounding-but-meaningless words, as President Andrew Johnson found out a few months after the war ended. In June 1865, a Federal grand jury in Norfolk, Virginia, indicted Robert E. Lee, James Longstreet, Joseph E. Johnston, and other Confederate officers for treason. After Lincoln's assassination, many Northerners wanted vengeance against the former Confederate states, and General Lee was an obvious symbol of the Confederacy.

General Lee was naturally upset by the news of his indictment. He wrote to General Grant about the issue, asking if the terms he had signed at Appomattox did not take precedence over any grand jury's actions. Grant was also upset by the news, and wrote to Secretary of War Edwin M. Stanton to remind him that President Lincoln himself had approved the surrender terms. He went on to say that, according to these terms, Lee could not be tried for treason as long as he observed the conditions of his parole.

But Grant was not satisfied just to leave the matter with Secretary Stanton. After writing to Stanton, he went to the White House to discuss the situation with President Johnson in person and very quickly found out that the president stood squarely behind the indictment. As far as Johnson was concerned, Lee deserved to be put on trial for treason.

Quite a little heated discussion between Grant and Johnson broke out concerning Lee's indictment. Grant immediately objected to the grand jury's action and informed the president that the terms of Appomattox were bound to be upheld. Johnson was not at all happy to hear this and demanded to know by what right a general in the United States Army defended a traitor from the laws of the land. Now it was Grant's turn to be unhappy. He informed the president, in no uncertain terms, that the surrender terms had been executed according to military law and that he would never consent to the arrest of General Lee as long as he observed the terms of his parole.

If he had not agreed to parole Lee and his army, Grant went on, and had insisted that Lee and his senior officers be tried for treason, General Lee would not have surrendered and the war would have continued, with many more killed and wounded as a result. To emphasize his objections to the indictment, and to Johnson's support of the indictment, Grant told the president that he would resign his command rather than arrest Lee or any of his officers. He would not stay in the army if the pledges he made at Appomattox were broken.

Andrew Johnson believed Grant, who had a reputation for meaning what he said. He could not afford to lose his general-in-chief, especially so soon after the end of the war, and especially over such a sensitive issue. The grand jury in Norfolk was instructed to drop all proceedings against Lee and his fellow officers. Grant wrote to General Lee to let him know that the United States Government would not prosecute him for treason.

U. S. Grant had fought for General Lee with as much determination as he had fought against him in Virginia. He had stood his ground against both the secretary of war and President Johnson. No one else in the entire country had the rank, the reputation, or the gumption to make such a stand, especially on behalf of Robert E. Lee. The United States Government did not renege on the conditions Grant had set down at Appomattox, but only because Grant himself had the courage of his convictions.[33]

There were many throughout the North who did not share

General Grant's magnanimity. Not very many Northerners would have objected if Robert E. Lee had been put on trial for high treason. Henry Adams, the son of the American ambassador to Great Britain, thought that General Lee should have been hanged. But Grant's benevolence was not widely held against him. He was the man of the hour, at least in the North: the hero of Donelson, Shiloh, Vicksburg, and now Appomattox, and also the savior of the Union. In just over three years, he would be elected president of the United States.

In the South, Robert E. Lee was the Savior. For generations, he has been regarded not only as a military genius but also as a good and great man, whose greatness and goodness sometimes bordered on holiness. A story used to circulate about a boy who came home from Sunday school to ask his father a question about the Bible: was General Lee in the Old Testament or the New Testament?

The image of a saintly General Lee was furthered by the four-volume biography of Lee by Douglas Southall Freeman, which was published in the 1930s. Freeman's Lee is just about faultless and perfect, or at least as faultless and perfect as anyone on earth can be, and might very well be a character from the Bible. "Simple and spiritual—the two qualities which constitute the man cannot be separated," is only one of Freeman's pronouncements regarding R. E. Lee. He also referred to the general as "the Southern Arthur."[34] Another biographer said, "This same Lee has been the patron saint of the American South."[35]

Robert E. Lee was looked upon as an American hero for more than a hundred years, sometimes as a tragic hero—the defender of the Lost Cause. His birthday, January 19, was listed on calendars, North and South, along with George Washington's and Abraham Lincoln's birthday. In 1907, on the one hundredth anniversary of Lee's birth, President Theodore Roosevelt paid a tribute to the general, not only for his military leadership but because of his poise and his bearing. Lee was revered for his honor, his courage, and his dignity, as well as for his generalship. An encyclopedia entry from the 1940s summed up the point of view of mainstream America at the time: "General Lee was an able military commander, a man of noble character, and much revered and beloved."[36]

Beginning in the late 1960s, the image of Robert E. Lee began to change, just as the national attitude toward the Civil War itself began to change. Lee's family owned slaves, which, in the opinion of the American public, meant that Lee was a defender of slavery. Even some Southerners conceded that the issue of slavery cast a shadow over Lee and his reputation as a good and honorable man, as well as over his achievements on the battlefield. One Southern writer said, "For many contemporary Americans, Lee is at best the moral equivalent of Hitler's brilliant field marshal Erwin Rommel."[37]

Robert E. Lee was no longer the paragon of honor. His life had not changed, but the country's outlook had. The two hundredth anniversary of his birth, in 2007, went unmentioned and unobserved—any national figure who made a speech in praise of Lee would have risked being called politically insensitive, at best. Saying anything even mildly complimentary about him had become tantamount to praising one of Hitler's generals from the Second World War.

While General Lee's reputation was diminishing, U. S. Grant was gaining stature in the public eye. In the years following his death in 1885, Grant's status deteriorated from national hero to a figure of public scorn. His presidency was seen as an eight-year disaster of corruption, dishonesty, and cronyism. After leaving the White House, he invested $100,000 in a Wall Street brokerage firm, but the business went bankrupt and left Grant penniless. Shortly afterward, he was diagnosed as having inoperable throat cancer—all those cigars had finally taken their toll. In a last desperate attempt to provide an income for his wife and children, he wrote his memoirs, which he managed to finish just shortly before his death in July 1885.

Grant was considered a failure in politics and in business, and in civilian life generally. Even his reputation as a general was discredited. During the early part of the twentieth century, he was widely criticized as a drunkard and an incompetent, a general who slaughtered his men in obscene numbers. He had become "Grant the butcher," who won battles only by sheer brute force. By the 1950s, he was reduced to the subject of a Groucho Marx joke: "Who is buried in Grant's Tomb?"

But at about the same time that Lee's reputation began to disintegrate, Grant's stock began to rise. Writers and historians reassessed his standing as a general and decided that his battlefield tactics were direct and effective instead of brutal and murderous. He was no longer "Grant the butcher." In fact, one historian wrote, "if any general deserved the label 'butcher,' it was Lee."[38] Even though Lee fought on the defensive most of the time, "For the war as a whole Lee's army had a higher casualty rate than the armies commanded by Grant."

The attitude regarding his decision to write his memoirs has also been transformed, from a failure's last desperate attempt to atone for another financial disaster to a gallant effort to leave his family a legacy. It is also sometimes pointed out that Grant's *Personal Memoirs* went on to become one of the best-selling books of the nineteenth century. Grant's drinking problem has also been reconsidered. Recent biographers have reached the conclusion that his reputation as a drunkard was based largely upon gossip and hearsay and myth. But the image of Grant as a heavy drinker refuses to go away—the myth has been around far too long to be driven off by facts or reassessments. His presidency has been reevaluated as well—the Grant administration may not have been the most renowned in American history, historians argue, but at least it was not as corrupt and dishonest as had been reported in years gone by.

An exhibition by the New York Historical Society in 2008, called "Grant and Lee in War and Peace"—which was called "Lee and Grant" when the same exhibit was given by the Virginia Historical Society—explored a comparison of the two generals. Photos of Grant and Lee in their younger days were included, which showed that young Robert was better looking than Sam Grant. According to one observer, Lee "looks like a Byronic hero, while Grant appears to be squirming under a pair of epaulets the size of scrub mops."[39] The uniforms of the two generals were also on display: Lee's was "trimly tailored and festooned with gold braid," while Grant's was "made of shapeless sackcloth and is devoid of decoration." The point being made by the reporter was that good looks and fancy uniforms do not necessarily translate into success on the battlefield.

A sample of the drawings and sketches of both men while they were West Point cadets was also included in the Historical Society's show, which prompted this response: "Grant, though otherwise a dismal, demerit-ridden student, turns out to have been a better artist than Lee, just as he proved to be by far the better writer." At the time of the exhibition, many historians would have acknowledged that Grant was also the better general.

But regardless of their reputations and how they changed over the years, both men should be remembered most of all for how they behaved during a few vital hours on a Sunday afternoon in April 1865. After Appomattox, General Lee's primary goal was "to save useless effusion of blood," as he put it. He would not allow the war to degenerate into a guerrilla campaign, which probably would have gone on for years and would have made any sort of reconciliation between North and South impossible. "A partisan war may be continued, and hostilities protracted, causing individual suffering and destruction to the country," Lee wrote to Jefferson Davis on April 20, "but I see no prospect by that means of achieving a separate independence."[40]

When he was convinced that the cause of Confederate independence was finally lost beyond all hope of recovery, Robert E. Lee wanted nothing more than for the entire South to come back into the Union peacefully and honorably. After becoming president of Washington College in August 1865—which was renamed Washington and Lee almost immediately after his death in October 1870—he declared that his aim was to educate young men to be good Americans. The war was over. It was time to stop fighting and start looking forward to the reunification of the country.

Ulysses S. Grant underwent a transformation of his own after Appomattox. He had accomplished what he had set out to do; he had pounded the Army of Northern Virginia until it could not fight any longer. Now the war was over, and Grant had his own idea for bringing the rebel states back into the Union: offer them the most generous surrender terms he could. General Lee was no longer the enemy, so Grant did not treat him like one.

"I felt like anything rather than rejoicing at the downfall of a foe who had fought so long and valiantly, and had suffered so much for a cause," he recalled toward the end of his life, "though that cause was, I believe, one of the worst for which a people ever fought, and one for which there was the least excuse."[41] Grant rose above his feelings regarding the Confederates and their cause, overlooked the deaths of all the friends and colleagues he had lost during the war, and let 'em up easy.

U. S. Grant and Robert E. Lee came from completely different backgrounds, had totally different upbringings, and looked at the world from completely different points of view. But what they did at Appomattox was not only the climax of the Civil War, and of both men's military careers, but is also one of the defining moments in American history.

ACKNOWLEDGMENTS

I received a great deal of assistance from librarians and historians in gathering all the material needed to put this book together and would like to single out a few individuals who went out of their way to help me out.

I would like to thank Jeffrey Bridgers at the Library of Congress for his assistance with photos.

Dr. James Cornelius of the Abraham Lincoln Presidential Library and Museum was also a great help. Among other things, Dr. Cornelius informed me that one dollar in 1860s currency was worth forty dollars in current US currency. He also gave me a bit of insight regarding the story about Lincoln's comments on U. S. Grant's fondness for the bottle, which turned out to be more intriguing than the original story.

Also, many sincere thanks go out to the staff of the Union, NJ, public library. Thank you to Laura, Eileen, Denise, Susan, and all of their colleagues for their assistance.

And last, but certainly not least, many thanks to Laura Libby for all of her help and understanding, and for putting up with me while I was refighting all those battles in Virginia.

NOTES

INTRODUCTION

    1. Ulysses S. Grant, *The Personal Memoirs of Ulysses S. Grant* (Old Saybrook, CT: Konecky & Konecky, 1992), p. 116.

    2. Winston Churchill, *A History of the English Speaking Peoples*, vol. 4, *The Great Democracies* (New York: Dodd, Meade, 1958), p. 262.

CHAPTER ONE: ROADS BEGINNING

    1. Horace Porter, *Campaigning with Grant* (Secaucus, NJ: Blue and Grey, 1984), p. 464.

    2. Any number of Northern newspapers, most notably New York's *The World*, had been strong advocates of Confederate independence prior to Lincoln's re-election in November 1864.

    3. A. L. Long, *Memoirs of Robert E. Lee* (Secaucus, NJ: Blue and Grey, 1983), p. 419.

    4. Ibid., p. 459.

    5. Porter, *Campaigning with Grant*, p. 463.

    6. Ulysses S. Grant, *Personal Memoirs* (Old Saybrook, CT: Konecky & Konecky, 1992), p. 626.

    7. Ibid., p. 626.

    8. Ibid., pp. 626–27.

    9. Porter, *Campaigning with Grant*, p. 468.

    10. Grant, *Personal Memoirs*, p. 627.

    11. Geoffrey Ward, *The Civil War* (New York: Vintage Books, 1990), p. 309.

    12. Porter, *Campaigning with Grant*, p. 489.

    13. Grant, *Personal Memoirs*, p. 72.

    14. Geoffrey Perret, *Ulysses S. Grant: Soldier and President* (New York: Random House, 1997), p. 65.

15. The story of Grant's ride through Monterrey is in Grant, *Personal Memoirs*, pp. 72–73.

16. Jean Fritz, *Stonewall* (New York: G. P. Putnam, 1979), p. 30.

17. Colonel Red Reeder, *The Story of the Mexican War* (New York: Meredith, 1967), p. 37.

18. Ibid.

19. Martin Dugard, *The Training Ground: Grant, Lee, Sherman, and Davis in the Mexican War, 1846–1848* (New York: Little, Brown, 2008), p. 173.

20. Grant, *Personal Memoirs*, p. 63.

21. Ibid.

22. Ibid., p. 68.

23. Perret, *Ulysses S. Grant*, p. 60.

24. Ibid.

25. Grant, *Personal Memoirs*, p. 96.

26. Ibid.

27. Ibid.

28. Perret, *Ulysses S. Grant*, p. 71.

29. Grant, *Personal Memoirs*, p. 90.

30. Ibid., p. 115.

31. Perrett, *Ulysses S. Grant*, p. 140.

32. Grant, *Personal Memoirs*, p. 115.

33. Ibid., p. 116.

34. Perrett, *Ulysses S. Grant*, p. 65.

35. Douglas Southall Freeman, *Robert E. Lee*, vol. 1 (New York: Scribner's, 1934), p. 298.

36. Dugard, *Training Ground*, p. 337.

37. Grant, *Personal Memoirs*, p. 116.

38. Long, *Memoirs of Robert E. Lee*, p. 691.

39. Freeman, *Robert E. Lee*, vol. 1, p. 294.

40. The two writers are, respectively, Emory M. Thomas, *Robert E. Lee* (New York: W. W. Norton, 1995), p. 215, and Roy Blount Jr., *Robert E. Lee* (New York: Viking/Penguin, 2003), p. 24. Two biographies specifically about Harry Lee are: Charles Royster, *Light-Horse Harry Lee and the Legacy of the American Revolution* (New York: Alfred A. Knopf, 1981), and, Thomas Boyd, *Light-Horse Harry Lee* (New York: Charles Scribner's Sons, 1931). The papers of George Washington in the Library of Congress also give insights into Harry Lee's life.

41. Boyd, *Light-Horse Harry Lee*, p. 142.

42. Thomas, *Robert E. Lee*, p. 17.

43. John Edward Weems, *To Conquer a Peace: The War Between the United States and Mexico* (Garden City, NY: Doubleday, 1974), p. 375.

44. Thomas, *Robert E. Lee*, pp. 126–127.

45. Freeman, *Robert E. Lee*, vol. 1, pp. 245–246.

46. Weems, *To Conquer a Peace*, p. 378.

47. Freeman, *Robert E. Lee*, vol. 1, p. 247.

48. Long, *Memoirs of Robert E. Lee*, p. 53.

49. Grant, *Personal Memoirs*, p. 81.

50. Ibid.

51. Freeman, *Robert E. Lee*, vol. 1, p. 248.

52. Long, *Memoirs of Robert E. Lee*, p. 56.

53. Freeman, *Robert E. Lee*, vol. 1, p. 251.

54. Bruce Catton, *U. S. Grant and the American Military Tradition* (Boston: Little, Brown, 1954), p. 40.

55. Ibid., p. 269.

56. Ibid.

57. Long, *Memoirs of Robert E. Lee*, p. 59.

58. Freeman, *Robert E. Lee*, vol. 1, p. 271.

59. Ibid.

60. Reeder, *Story of the Mexican War*, p. 160.

61. Long, *Memoirs of Robert E. Lee*, p. 60.

62. Blount, *Robert E. Lee*, p. 47.

63. Freeman, *Robert E. Lee*, vol. 1, p. 297.

64. Ibid.

65. Ibid., p. 299.

66. Freeman, *Robert E. Lee*, vol. 1, p. 298. After Second Manassas, the entire Army of Virginia was merged into the Army of the Potomac. The Army of Virginia ceased to exist.

67. Bruce Catton, *The Civil War*, 4th ed., American Heritage (New York: Tess, 2009), p. 206.

68. "History of the Aztec Club: Overview," *Aztec Club of 1847*, www.aztecclub.com/LeadPg.htm.

69. J. F. C. Fuller, *Grant and Lee: A Study in Personality and Generalship* (Bloomington, IN: University of Indiana Press, 1957), p. 245.

70. Ward, *Civil War*, p. 231.

CHAPTER TWO: PREPARATIONS

1. Ulysses S. Grant, *The Personal Memoirs of Ulysses S. Grant* (Old Saybrook, CT: Konecky & Konecky, 1992), p. 624.

2. Ibid.

3. Douglas Southall Freeman, *Robert E. Lee*, vol. 4 (New York: Scribner's, 1935), p. 109.

4. Ibid., p. 115.

5. Ibid., p. 118.

6. A. L. Long, *Memoirs of Robert E. Lee* (Secaucus, NJ: Blue and Grey, 1983), p. 421.

7. William Marvel, *A Place Called Appomattox* (Carbondale, IL: Southern Illinois University Press, 2008), p. 235.

8. Morris Schaft, *The Sunset of the Confederacy* (Boston: John W. Luce, 1912), p. 215.

9. Jay Winik, *April 1865: The Month That Saved America* (New York: Harper Perennial, 2001), p. 145.

10. Long, *Memoirs of Robert E. Lee*, p. 421.

11. Freeman, *Robert E. Lee*, vol. 4, p. 120.

12. Long, *Memoirs of Robert E. Lee*, p. 422.

13. Freeman, *Robert E. Lee*, vol. 4, p. 121.

14. Ibid.

15. James Longstreet, *From Manassas to Appomattox: Memoirs of the Civil War in America* (New York: Konecky & Konecky, 1992), p. 624.

16. Ibid.

17. Ibid., p. 619.

18. Ibid., p. 625.

19. Freeman, *Robert E. Lee*, vol. 4, p. 122.

20. Ibid., p.123.

21. Ibid.

22. Ibid., p. 124.

23. Ibid., p. 125. There are minor differences in the greeting and the signature between this letter and the version given in U. S. Grant's memoirs.

24. Ibid., p. 127.

25. Longstreet, *From Manassas*, p. 332.

26. Freeman, *Robert E. Lee*, vol. 3, p. 161.

27. Ibid.

28. Ibid., p. 161n127.

29. Winston Churchill, *A History of the English Speaking Peoples*, vol. 4, *The Great Democracies* (New York: Dodd, Meade, 1958), p. 241.

30. Bernard A. Olsen, ed., *Upon the Tented Field* (Red Bank, NJ: Historic Projects, 1993), p. 232.

31. Bruce Catton, *A Stillness at Appomattox* (Garden City, NY: Doubleday, 1953), p. 37.

32. Elisha Hunt Rhodes, *All for the Union: The Civil War Diary and Letters of Elisha Hunt Rhodes* (New York: Vintage Civil War Library, 1985), p. 134.

33. Edward G. Longacre, *General Ulysses S. Grant: The Soldier and the Man* (Cambridge, MA: Perseus Books, 2006), p. 189.

34. Ibid., pp. 188–89.

35. James Cornelius, curator at the Abraham Lincoln Presidential Library and Museum in Springfield, Illinois, says that this "old chestnut" is not true, or at least "is not recorded anywhere at the time." Dr. Cornelius thinks this story is based upon another joke, allegedly told by George III about General Wolfe. When someone complained that General Wolfe was insane, the king is supposed to have said, "Have him bite my other generals."

36. Stanton P. Allen, *Down in Dixie: Life in a Cavalry Regiment in the War Days, From the Wilderness to Appomattox* (Boston: D. Lothrop, 1893), p. 182.

37. Bruce Catton, *Glory Road* (Garden City, NY: Doubleday, 1952), p. 306.

38. James Harrison Wilson, *The Life of John A. Rawlins: Lawyer, Assistant Adjutant-General, Chief of Staff, Major General of Volunteers, and Secretary of War* (New York: Neale, 1916), p. 427.

39. *New York Times*, March 17, 1864.

40. Freeman, *Robert E. Lee*, vol. 3, p. 264.

41. R. Lockwood Tower, ed., *Lee's Adjutant: The Wartime Letters of Colonel Walter Herron Taylor, 1862–1865* (Columbia, SC: University of South Carolina Press, 1995), p. 148.

42. Ibid., p. 139.

43. Ibid., p. 61. In his book *Battle Cry of Freedom: The Civil War Era* (New York: Oxford University Press, 1988), James McPherson states that "Pickett's charge represented the Confederate war effort in microcosm: matchless valor, apparent initial success, and ultimate disaster." (p. 662).

44. Horace Porter, *Campaigning with Grant* (Secaucus, NJ: Blue and Grey, 1984), p. 47.

45. Robert E. Lee Jr., comp., *Recollections and Letters of General Robert E. Lee* (New York: Barnes and Noble, 2004), p. 108.

46. Ibid., pp. 107–108.

47. Ibid., p. 109.

48. Ibid., p. 108.

49. William Tecumseh Sherman, *The Memoirs of William T. Sherman* (Bloomington, IN: University of Indiana Press, 1977), p. 271.

50. Lee, *Recollections and Letters*, p. 108.

CHAPTER THREE: NO TURNING BACK

1. Adam Badeau, *Military History of Ulysses S. Grant*, vol. 3 (New York: D. Appleton, 1895), pp. 599–601.

2. Ulysses S. Grant, *The Personal Memoirs of Ulysses S. Grant* (Old Saybrook, CT: Konecky & Konecky, 1992), p. 627.

3. Frank Wilkeson, *Recollections of a Private Soldier in the Army of the Potomac* (New York: G. P. Putnam's Sons, 1886), p. 48.

4. Oliver Carelson, *The Man Who Made News: James Gordon Bennett* (New York: Duell, Sloan and Pierce, 1942), p. 364.

5. Ida M. Tarbell, *Life of Abraham Lincoln*, vol. 2 (New York: Doubleday & McClure, 1900), p. 187.

6. Ibid., p. 188.

7. *New York Times*, January 15, 1864.

8. W. E. Woodward, *Meet General Grant* (New York: Liveright, 1928), pp. 308–309.

9. Ibid., p. 309.

10. Bruce Catton, *Grant Takes Command* (Boston: Little, Brown, 1969), p. 125.

11. Horace Porter, *Campaigning with Grant* (Secaucus, NJ: Blue and Grey, 1984), p. 19.

12. Ibid., p. 21.

13. Ibid.

14. Frederick Dent Grant, "Reminiscences of General U. S. Grant, Read Before Illinois Commandery Loyal Legion of the United States, January 27, 1910,"*Journal of the Illinois State Historical Society* 7, no. 1 (April 1914): 72–76.

15. Ibid.

16. Ibid.

17. Carl Sandburg, *Abraham Lincoln: The Prairie Years and the War Years, One Volume Edition* (New York: Harcourt, Brace & World, 1958), p. 463.

18. Ibid.

19. Clifford Dowdey, ed., *The Wartime Papers of Robert E. Lee* (Boston: Little, Brown, 1961), p. 718.

20. Douglas Southall Freeman, *Robert E. Lee*, vol. 3 (New York: Scribner's, 1935), p. 268.

21. Ibid., p. 270.

22. James Longstreet, *From Manassas to Appomattox: Memoirs of the Civil War in America* (New York: Konecky & Konecky, 1992), p. 555.

23. Wilkeson, *Recollections*, p. 48.

24. Ibid., pp. 50–51.

25. A. L. Long, *Memoirs of Robert E. Lee* (Secaucus, NJ: Blue and Grey, 1983), p. 327.

26. Freeman, *Robert E. Lee*, vol. 3, pp. 278–79.

27. Wilkeson, *Recollections*, p. 63.

28. Long, *Memoirs of Robert E. Lee*, p. 328.

29. Wilkeson, *Recollections*, p. 79.

30. Freeman, *Robert E. Lee*, vol. 3, p. 286.

31. Ibid., p. 287.

32. Robert K. Krick, "'Lee to the Rear,' the Texans Cried," in *The Wilderness Campaign*, ed. Gary W. Gallagher (Chapel Hill, NC: University of North Carolina Press, 1997), p. 177.

33. Ibid., p. 181.

34. Ibid.

35. Ibid., p. 182.

36. Longstreet, *From Manassas*, p. 564.

37. Freeman, *Robert E. Lee*, vol. 3, p. 297.

38. General John B. Gordon, *Reminiscences of the Civil War* (New York: Charles Scribner's Sons, 1903), p. 261.

39. Freeman, *Robert E. Lee*, vol. 3, p. 303.

40. Ibid., p. 298.

41. Earl Schenck Miers, *The Last Campaign: Grant Saves the Union* (Philadelphia: Lippincott, 1972), p. 62.

42. Freeman, *Robert E. Lee*, vol. 3, p. 298.

43. Clifford Dowdey, *Lee's Last Campaign* (New York: Bonanza Books, 1960), p. 176.

44. R. E. Lee to Secretary of War [James A. Seddon], 6 May 1864, in *The War of the Rebellion: A Compilation of the Official Records of the Union and Confederate Armies*, ed. US War Department, series 1, vol. 36, part 2 (Washington, DC: Government Printing Office, 1891), p. 960.

45. Grant, *Personal Memoirs*, p. 423.

46. Porter, *Campaigning with Grant*, p. 41.

47. Ibid., pp. 41–42. The Battle of Austerlitz, which took place in December 1805, was one of Napoleon's greatest triumphs. When the sun broke through the fog on the morning of the battle, Napoleon predicted that the sun of Austerlitz was a sign that his army would win a great victory that day. At least this is the legend.

48. Elisha Hunt Rhodes, *All for the Union: The Civil War Diary and Letters of Elisha Hunt Rhodes* (New York: Vintage Civil War Library, 1985), p. 135.

49. Porter, *Campaigning with Grant*, p. 44.

50. Ibid.

51. Ibid., p. 48.

52. Rhodes, *All for the Union*, p. 136.

53. Porter, *Campaigning with Grant*, p. 64.

54. Rhodes, *All for the Union*, p. 136.

55. Stanton P. Allen, *Down in Dixie: Life in a Cavalry Regiment in the War Days, From the Wilderness to Appomattox* (Boston: D. Lothrop, 1893), p. 259.

56. Bruce Catton, *A Stillness at Appomattox* (Garden City, NY: Doubleday, 1953), p. 74.

57. Henry Steele Commager, ed., *The Civil War Archive: The History of the Civil War in Documents* (New York: Black Dog & Leventhal, 2000), p. 980.

58. Woodward, *Meet General Grant*, p. 322.

59. Geoffrey Ward, *The Civil War* (New York: Vintage Books, 1990), p. 232.

60. Porter, *Campaigning with Grant*, p. 56.

61. Ibid., p. 61.

62. Ibid.

63. Ibid., p. 69.

64. Grant, *Personal Memoirs*, p. 116.

65. Rhodes, *All for the Union*, p. 132.

66. Grant, *Personal Memoirs*, p. 458.

67. "Wilderness," The American Battlefield Protection Program: CWSAC Battle Summaries, www.nps.gov/abpp/battles/va046.htm.

68. Rhodes, *All for the Union*, p. 138.

69. Charles Bracelen Flood, *Grant and Sherman: The Friendship That Won the Civil War* (New York: Farrar, Straus, Giroux, 2005), p. 244.

70. Porter, *Campaigning with Grant*, p. 79.

71. Wilkeson, *Recollections*, p. 79.

72. Porter, *Campaigning with Grant*, p. 79.

73. Rhodes, *All for the Union*, p. 138.

74. Commager, *Civil War Archive*, pp. 384–85.

75. Bernard A. Olsen, ed., *Upon the Tented Field* (Red Bank, NJ: Historic Projects, 1993), p. 234.

76. J. F. C. Fuller, *Grant and Lee: A Study in Personality and Generalship* (Bloomington, IN: Indiana University Press, 1957), p. 215.

77. Bruce Catton, *This Hallowed Ground* (Edison, NJ: Castle Books, 2002), p. 326.

78. Harry Wing, *When Lincoln Kissed Me: A Story of the Wilderness Campaign* (New York: Eaton & Mains, 1913), p. 13.

79. Ibid., pp. 37–38.

CHAPTER FOUR: ADVANTAGES AND DISADVANTAGES

1. Theodore Lyman, *Meade's Headquarters, 1863–1865: Letters of Colonel Theodore Lyman from the Wilderness to Appomattox* (Boston: Atlantic Monthly, 1922), p. 357.

2. Geoffrey Perret, *Ulysses S. Grant: Soldier and President* (New York: Random House, 1997); H. W. Brands, *The Man Who Saved the Union* (New York: Doubleday, 2012).

3. Ulysses S. Grant, *The Personal Memoirs of Ulysses S. Grant* (Old Saybrook, CT: Konecky & Konecky, 1992), p. 20.

4. The title of chapter 22 in volume 3 of Douglas Southall Freeman's biography, *Robert E. Lee*, is "And Still Grant Pounds."

5. Perret, *Ulysses S. Grant*; Brands, *Man Who Saved the Union*.

6. Grant, *Personal Memoirs*, p. 27.

7. Ibid., p. 28.

8. John Y. Simon, ed., *The Papers of Ulysses S. Grant*, vol. 14, *February 21–April 30, 1865* (Carbondale, IL: Southern Illinois University Press, 1985), vol. 14, pp. 186–87.

9. Grant, *Personal Memoirs*, p. 460.

10. Bruce Catton, *A Stillness At Appomattox* (Garden City, NY: Doubleday, 1953), p. 93.

11. Grant, *Personal Memoirs*, p 460.

12. Gordon C. Rhea, *The Battles for Spotsylvania Court House and the Road to Yellow Tavern, May 7–12, 1864* (Baton Rouge, LA: Louisiana State University Press, 1997), p. 64.

13. The exchange between George Gordon Meade and Philip Sheridan is from Horace Porter, *Campaigning with Grant* (Secaucus, NJ: Blue and Grey, 1984), p. 84.

14. Ibid.

15. Philip H. Sheridan, *Personal Memoirs* (New York: Charles L. Webster, 1888), pp. 370–71.

16. James M. McPherson, *Battle Cry of Freedom: The Civil War Era* (New York: Oxford University Press, 1988).

17. Bernard A. Olsen, ed., *Upon the Tented Field* (Red Bank, NJ: Historic Projects, 1993), p. 236.

18. Porter, *Campaigning with Grant*, p. 90.

19. Ibid., p. 85.

20. Grant, *Personal Memoirs*, p. 472.

21. Ibid., p. 472.

22. Elisha Hunt Rhodes, *All for the Union: The Civil War Diary and Letters of Elisha Hunt Rhodes* (New York: Vintage Civil War Library, 1985), p. 142.

23. Rhea, *Battles for Spotsylvania*, p. 209.

24. Grant's letter of May 11 to General Henry Halleck is in Grant, *Personal Memoirs*, p. 473.

25. "Wilderness," The American Battlefield Protection Program: CWSAC Battle Summaries, www.nps.gov/abpp/battles/va046.htm. Other sources give slightly different figures, on both sides. Colonel Horace Porter gives the total known losses at 17,666.

26. Grant, *Personal Memoirs*, p. 473.

27. *New York Times*, June 1, 1864.

28. "Jesse Root Grant and Hannah Simpson Grant," *American Experience*, www.pbs.org/wgbh/americanexperience/features/biography/grant-parents.

29. Grant, *Personal Memoirs*, p. 126.

30. Porter, *Campaigning with Grant*, p. 101.

31. Ibid.

32. Ibid., p. 102.

33. Ibid., p. 103.

34. Ibid.

35. Ibid., p. 104.

36. Ibid.

37. Ibid., p. 105.

38. Ibid.

39. G. Norton Galloway, "Hand-to-Hand Fighting at Spotsylvania," in *Battles and Leaders of the Civil War*, ed. Robert Underwood Johnson and Clarence Clough Buel (New York: Century, 1887), pp. 171–72.

40. Ibid., pp. 171–72.

41. Rhea, *Battles for Spotsylvania*, p. 293.

42. Rhodes, *All for the Union*, p. 145.

43. Grant, *Personal Memoirs*, p. 477.

44. Ibid., p. 477.

45. Ibid., p. 477.

46. Edward Bonekemper, in his *A Victor Not a Butcher* (Washington, DC: Regnery, 2004), gives the number of Confederate prisoners taken at Spotsylvania at 5,719 (pp. 308–309).

47. "Spotsylvania and the Bloody Angle," in *Elson's New History* (Springfield, MA: Patriot, 1912).

48. Rhea, *Battles for Spotsylvania*, p. 307.

49. Rhodes, *All for the Union*, p. 142.

50. *Times* (London), May 25, 1864.

51. Grant, *Personal Memoirs*, p. 477.

52. Rhodes, *All for the Union*, p. 145.

53. Grant, *Personal Memoirs*, p. 480.

54. Clifford Dowdey, ed., *The Wartime Papers of Robert E. Lee* (Boston: Little, Brown, 1961), p. 792.

55. Porter, *Campaigning with Grant*, p. 86.

56. Rhea, *Battles for Spotsylvania*, p. 307.

57. Freeman, *Robert E. Lee*, vol. 3, p. 313.

58. A. L. Long, *Memoirs of Robert E. Lee* (Secaucus, NJ: Blue and Grey, 1983), p. 313.

59. General John B. Gordon, *Reminiscences of the Civil War* (New York: Charles Scribner's Sons, 1903), p. 279. General Gordon remembers this incident as having happened on May 12, not May 10. He also says that Jeb Stuart died on May 10.

60. Freeman, *Robert E. Lee*, vol. 3, p. 313.

61. Ibid., p. 313.

62. Rhea, *Battles for Spotsylvania*, p. 210.

63. Robert E. Lee Jr., comp., *Recollections and Letters of General Robert E. Lee* (New York: Barnes and Noble, 2004), p. 110.

64. Long, *Memoirs of Robert E. Lee*, p. 339.

65. Emory M. Thomas, *Robert E. Lee* (New York: W. W. Norton, 1995), p. 328.

66. Freeman, *Robert E. Lee*, vol. 3, p. 317. Some sources, including General Gordon's memoirs, put the Spotsylvania "Lee to the rear!" episode at the point, on May 12. A. L. Long says that it happened on May 10. I am inclined to believe A. L. Long, who seems to have a more reliable memory than General Gordon.

67. E. M. Law, "A Half-Dozen Take the Place of Every One We Kill," in *Battles and Leaders of the Civil War*, ed. Ned Bradford (New York: Gramercy Books, 2001), p. 482.

68. Ibid., p. 483.

69. R. Lockwood Tower, ed., *Lee's Adjutant: The Wartime Letters of Colonel Walter Herron Taylor, 1862–1865* (Columbia, SC: University of South Carolina Press, 1995), p. 160.

70. Dowdey, *Wartime Papers*, p. 728.

CHAPTER FIVE: HOLDING ON LONGER

1. Charles Marshall, "The Story of Appomattox," speech, Society of the Army and Navy of the Confederate States, Baltimore, MD, January 9, 1894, leefamilyarchive.org/reference/essays/marshall/.

2. R. E. Lee to U. S. Grant, 9 April 1865, in *The War of the Rebellion: A Compilation of the Official Records of the Union and Confederate Armies*, ed. US War Department, series 1, vol. 46, part 3 (Washington, DC: Government Printing Office, 1891), p. 665.

3. James Longstreet, *From Manassas to Appomattox: Memoirs of the Civil War in America* (New York: Konecky & Konecky, 1992), p. 667.

4. Douglas Southall Freeman, *Robert E. Lee*, vol. 4 (New York: Scribner's, 1935), p. 132.

5. Excerpt from Henry Lee's *Memoirs* in Marshall, "Story of Appomattox."

6. Freeman, *Robert E. Lee*, vol. 4, p. 133. Freeman states that General Lee was "impelled to this personal surrender" because his father had made an "unfavorable reference" to Lord Cornwallis's absence at Yorktown.

7. Ibid.

8. Ibid.

9. A. L. Long, *Memoirs of Robert E. Lee* (Secaucus, NJ: Blue and Grey, 1983), p. 91.

10. Ibid., p. 92.

11. Ibid., pp. 92–93.

12. Ibid., p. 94.

13. Robert E. Lee Jr., comp., *Recollections and Letters of General Robert E. Lee* (New York: Barnes and Noble, 2004), pp. 19–20.

14. Ibid.

Following are the three letters reproduced in their entirety:

Arlington, Washington City, P.O.

20 Apr 1861

Lt. Genl Winfield Scott,
Commd U.S. Army

Genl,

Since my interview with you on the 18th Inst: I have felt that I ought not longer to retain any Commission in the Army. I therefore tender my resignation which I request you will recommend for acceptance. It would have been presented at once but for the struggle it has Cost me to separate myself from a Service to which I have devoted all the best years of my life, & all the ability I possessed. During the whole of that time, more than a quarter of a century, I have experienced nothing but kindness from my superiors & the most Cordial friendships from any Comrades. To no one Genl have I been as much indebted as to yourself for kindness & Consideration & it has always been my ardent desire to merit your approbation. I shall carry with me, to the grave the most grateful recollections of your kind Consideration, & your name & fame will always be dear to me. Save in the defense of my native state shall I never desire again to draw my sword. Be pleased to accept my most earnest wishes for the Continuance of your happiness & prosperity & believe me.

Most truly yours,
R. E. Lee

Arlington, Virginia, April 20, 1861

My Dear Brother Smith: The question which was the subject of my earnest consultation with you on the 18th inst. has in my own mind been decided. After the most anxious inquiry as to the correct course for me to pursue, I concluded to resign, and sent in my resignation this morning. I wished to wait till the Ordinance of secession should be acted on by the people of Virginia; but war seems to have commenced, and I am liable at any time to be ordered on duty which I could not conscientiously perform. To save me from such a position, and to prevent the necessity of resigning under orders, I had to act at once, and before I could see you again on the subject, as I had wished. I am now a private citizen, and have no other ambition than to remain at home. Save in defense of my native State, I have no desire ever again to draw my sword. I send you my warmest love.

Your affectionate brother,

R. E. Lee

Arlington, Virginia, April 20, 1861

My Dear Sister: I am grieved at my inability to see you. . . . I have been waiting for a "more convenient season," which has brought to many before me deep and lasting regret. Now we are in a state of war which will yield to nothing. The whole South is in a state of revolution, into which Virginia, after a long struggle, has been drawn; and though I recognise no necessity for this state of things, and would have forborne and pleaded to the end for redress of grievances, real or supposed, yet in my own person I had to meet the question whether I should take part against my native State.

With all my devotion to the Union and the feeling of loyalty and duty of an American citizen, I have not been able to make up my mind to raise my hand against my relatives, my children, my home. I have therefore resigned my commission in the Army, and save in defense of my native State, with the sincere hope that my poor services may never be needed, I hope I may never be called on to draw my sword. I know you will blame me; but you must think as kindly of me as you can, and believe that I have endeavoured to do what I thought right.

To show you the feeling and struggle it has cost me, I send you a copy of my letter of resignation. I have no time for more. May God guard and protect you and yours, and shower upon you everlasting blessings, is the prayer of your devoted brother,

R. E. Lee

16. Lee, *Recollections and Letters*, p. 22.

17. Freeman, *Robert E. Lee*, vol. 1, p. 169.

18. Ibid.

19. Gordon C. Rhea, *To the North Anna: Grant and Lee, May 13–25, 1864* (Baton Rouge, LA: Louisiana State University Press, 2000), p. 220.

20. Ibid.

21. Clifford Dowdey, ed., *The Wartime Papers of Robert E. Lee* (Boston: Little, Brown, 1961), pp. 744–45.

22. Freeman, *Robert E. Lee*, vol. 3, p. 347.

23. Dowdey, *Wartime Papers*, p. 747.

24. Walter H. Taylor, *Four Years with General Lee* (Bloomington, IN: Indiana University Press, 1962), p. 132.

25. George Michael Neese, *Three Years in the Confederate Horse Artillery* (New York: Neale, 1911), p. 275.

26. R. D. Mainwaring and C. G. Tribble, "The Cardiac Illness of General Robert E. Lee," *Surgery, Genecology, and Obstetrics* 174, no. 3 (March 1992): 237–44.

27. Freeman, *Robert E. Lee*, vol. 3, p. 357n30.

28. R. Lockwood Tower, ed., *Lee's Adjutant: The Wartime Papers of Walter Herron Taylor, 1862–1865* (Columbia, SC: University of South Carolina Press, 1995), p. 164.

29. Lee, *Recollections and Letters*, p. 112.

30. Colonel C. S. Venable, *The Campaign from the Wilderness to Petersburg* (Richmond, VA: Geo. W. Gary, Printer, 1879), p. 13.

31. Ibid.

32. Dowdey, *Wartime Papers*, p. 750–51.

33. R. E. Lee to Secretary of War [James A. Seddon], 26 May 1864, in *The War of the Rebellion: A Compilation of the Official Records of the Union and Confederate Armies*, ed. US War Department, series 1, vol. 36, part 3 (Washington, DC: Government Printing Office, 1891), p. 834.

34. The National Park Service says that each side suffered approximately 2,000 casualties. Several other authors and websites besides the NPS give Union casualties between 2,000 and 2,600 and Confederate casualties between 1,500 and 2,000. Shelby Foote states that Grant "has suffered only 1,976 casualties, and Lee less than half that number" (Shelby Foote, *The Civil War: A Narrative*, vol. 3, *Red River to Appomattox* [New York: Vintage Books, 1974], p. 276).

35. Tower, *Lee's Adjutant*, p. 162.

36. Ulysses S. Grant, *Personal Memoirs of Ulysses S. Grant* (Old Saybrook, CT: Konecky & Konecky, 1992), p. 483.

37. Elisha Hunt Rhodes, *All for the Union: The Civil War Diary and Letters of Elisha Hunt Rhodes* (New York: Vintage Civil War Library, 1985), p. 146.

38. Horace Porter, *Campaigning with Grant* (Secaucus, NJ: Blue and Grey, 1984), p. 128.

39. Ibid.

40. Ibid., p. 129.

41. G. K. Warren to Major-General Humphreys, 22 May 1864, in *War of the Rebellion*, series 1, vol. 36, part 3, p. 92.

42 Grant, *Personal Memoirs*, p. 484.

43. Porter, *Campaigning with Grant*, p. 142.

44. U. S. Grant to H. W. Halleck, 23 May 1864, in *War of the Rebellion*, series 1, vol. 36, part 3, pp. 113–14.

45. H. W. Halleck to U. S. Grant, 23 May 1864, in *War of the Rebellion*, series 1, vol. 36, part 3, p. 114.

46. Charles A. Dana, *Recollections of the Civil War* (New York: D. Appleton, 1898), p, 203.

47. U. S. Grant to H. W. Halleck, 24 May 1864, in *War of the Rebellion*, series 1, vol. 36, part 3, p. 145.

48. G. K. Warren to S. W. Crawford, 24 May 1864, in *War of the Rebellion*, series 1, vol. 36, part 3, p. 162.

49 U. S. Grant to H. W. Halleck, 25 May 1864, in *War of the Rebellion*, series 1, vol. 36, part 3, p. 183.

50. Grant, *Personal Memoirs*, p. 487.

51. U. S. Grant to G. G. Meade, 25 May 1864, in *War of the Rebellion*, series 1, vol. 36, part 3, p. 183.

52. Porter, *Campaigning with Grant*, p. 152.

52. Grant, *Personal Memoirs*, p. 487.

53. Ibid., p. 490.

CHAPTER SIX: STRIKING AND MANEUVERING

1. Horace Porter, *Campaigning with Grant* (Secaucus, NJ: Blue and Grey, 1984), p. 468.

2. Ibid., p. 469.

3. A. W. Bartlett, *History of the Twelfth Regiment New Hampshire Volunteers in the War of the Rebellion* (Concord, NH: Ira C Evans, 1897), p. 198.

4. John H. Brinton, *Personal Memoirs of John H. Brinton* (New York: Neale, 1914), p. 239.

5. Ulysses S. Grant, *The Personal Memoirs of Ulysses S. Grant* (Old Saybrook, CT: Konecky & Konecky, 1992), pp. 493–94.

6. Ibid., p. 494.

7. John Y. Simon, ed., *The Papers of Ulysses S. Grant*, vol. 11 (Carbondale, IL: Southern Illinois University Press, 1982), p. 5.

8. Elisha Hunt Rhodes, *All for the Union: The Civil War Diary and Letters of Elisha Hunt Rhodes* (New York: Vintage Civil War Library, 1992), p. 148.

9. Porter, *Campaigning with Grant*, p. 174.

10. Ibid.

11. The historian in question is Gordon C. Rhea, in *Cold Harbor: Grant and Lee, May 26–June 3, 1864* (Baton Rouge, LA: Louisiana State University Press, 2002), p. 312, and footnote no. 73, pp. 458–59.

12. Porter, *Campaigning with Grant*, p. 175.

13. Bartlett, *History of the Twelfth Regiment*, p. 203.

14. Ibid., p. 203.

15. Porter, *Campaigning with Grant*, p. 176.

16. Grant, *Personal Memoirs*, p. 499.

17. U. S. Grant to George G. Meade, 3 June 1864, in *The War of the Rebellion: A Compilation of the Official Records of the Union and Confederate Armies*, ed. US War Department, series 1, vol. 36, part 3 (Washington, DC: Government Printing Office, 1891), p. 526.

18. Porter, *Campaigning with Grant*, p. 178.

19. U. S. Grant to H. W. Halleck, 3 June 1864, in *War of the Rebellion*, series 1, vol. 36, part 3, p. 524.

20. U. S. Grant to R. E. Lee, 5 June 1864, in *War of the Rebellion*, series 1, vol. 36, part 3, p. 600.

21. Ibid.

22. R. E. Lee to U. S. Grant, 5 June 1864, in *War of the Rebellion*, series 1, vol. 36, part 3, p. 600.

23. U. S. Grant to R. E. Lee, 6 June 1864, in *War of the Rebellion*, series 1, vol. 36, part 3, p. 638.

24. R. E. Lee to U. S. Grant, 6 June 1864, in *War of the Rebellion*, series 1, vol. 36, part 3, p. 638.

25. U. S. Grant to R. E. Lee, 6 June 1864 (II), in *War of the Rebellion*, series 1, vol. 36, part 3, p. 638.

26. U. S. Grant to R. E. Lee, 7 June 1864, in *War of the Rebellion*, series 1, vol. 36, part 3, p. 666.

27. Porter, *Campaigning with Grant*, p. 178.

28. Rhea, *Cold Harbor*, pp. 359, 386. In his *Regimental Losses in the American Civil War, 1861–1865* (Albany, NY: Albany, 1889), p. 547, William L. Fox gives the Union losses between June 2 and 4 at 1,844 killed, 9,077 wounded and mortally wounded, and 1,816 captured and missing, for a total of 12,737.

29. Porter, *Campaigning with Grant*, pp. 195–96.

30. Jesse Grant Cramer, *Letters of Ulysses S. Grant to His Father and His Youngest Sister, 1857–78* (New York: G. P. Putnam's Sons, 1912), p. 100.

31. Grant, *Personal Memoirs*, p. 503.

32. Porter, *Campaigning with Grant*, p. 179.

33. Bartlett, *History of the Twelfth Regiment*, p. 202.

34. Grant, *Personal Memoirs*.

35. Charles E. Davis Jr., *Three Years in the Army: The Story of the Thirteenth Massachusetts Volunteers* (Boston: Estes and Lauriat, 1894), p. 364.

36. Rhodes, *All for the Union*, p. 150.

37. Walter H. Taylor, *Four Years with General Lee* (Bloomington, IN: Indiana University Press, 1962), p. 134.

38. W. H. Taylor to Richard Anderson, 31 May 1864, in *War of the Rebellion*, series 1, vol. 36, part 3, p. 858.

39. Robert Stiles, *Four Years under Marse Robert* (New York: Neale, 1904), p. 274.

40. Douglas Southall Freeman, *Robert E. Lee*, vol. 3 (New York: Scribner's, 1935), p. 383.

41. Freeman, *Robert E. Lee* p. 389, and Rhea, *Cold Harbor*, p. 363.

42. E. M. Law, "From the Wilderness to Cold Harbor," in *Battles and Leaders of the Civil War*, ed. Robert Underwood Johnson and Clarence Clough Buel, vol. 4 (New York: Thomas Yoseloff, 1956), pp. 142, 141.

43. Clifford Dowdey, ed., *The Wartime Papers of Robert E. Lee* (Boston: Little, Brown, 1961), p 764.

44. R. Lockwood Tower, ed., *Lee's Adjutant: The Wartime Papers of Walter Herron Taylor, 1862–1865* (Columbia, SC: University of South Carolina Press, 1995), p. 167.

45. Taylor, *Four Years*, p. 135.

46. R. E. Lee to James A. Seddon, 4 June 1864, in *War of the Rebellion*, series 1, vol. 36, part 1, p. 1033.

47. R. E. Lee to James A. Seddon, 13 June 1864, in *War of the Rebellion*, series 1, vol. 36, part 1, p. 1035.

48. Eppa Hunton, *The Autobiography of Eppa Hunton* (Richmond, VA: William Byrd, 1933), p. 113.

49. Douglas Southall Freeman, ed., *Lee's Dispatches: Unpublished Letters of General Robert E. Lee* (Baton Rouge, LA: Louisiana State University Press, 1994), p. 227.

50. R. E. Lee to P. G. T. Beauregard, 16 June 1864, in *War of the Rebellion*, series 1, vol. 40. part 2, p. 659.

51. Ibid., p. 664.

52. P. G. T. Beauregard to R. E. Lee, 17 June 1864, in *War of the Rebellion*, series 1, vol. 51, part 2, p. 1080.

53. P. G. T. Beauregard to R. E. Lee, 17 June 1864, in *War of the Rebellion*, series 1, vol. 40, part 2, p. 666.

54. W. H. F. Lee to Walter H. Taylor, 17 June 1864, in *War of the Rebellion*, series 1, vol. 51, part 2, p. 1080.

55. Winfield Scott, *Memoirs of Lieut.-General Scott, LL. D.*, vol. 2 (Freeport, NY: Books for Libraries, 1970), p. 469.

56. J. William Jones, *Personal Reminiscences, Anecdotes, and Letters of General Robert E. Lee* (New York: D. Appleton, 1875), p. 40.

57. Freeman, *Robert E. Lee*, vol. 3, p. 398.

58. *New York Times*, June 7, 1864.

59. *New York Times*, May 9, 1864.

60. Thomas A. McParlin to S. Williams, 24 May 1864, in *War of the Rebellion*, series 1, vol. 36, part 3, p. 146.

61. *Official Proceedings of the Democratic National Convention, Held in 1864 at Chicago* (Chicago, IL: Times Steam Book and Job Printing House, 1864), p. 27.

62. Charles A. Dana to William H. Seward, September 23, 1862, Abraham Lincoln Papers, Library of Congress, transcribed and annotated by the Lincoln Studies Center, Knox College, Galesburg, IL.

63. *Illinois State Register*, January 7, 1863. The full text of the Resolution:

Resolution of the Illinois Legislature in Opposition to the Emancipation Proclamation, 1863

Resolved: That the emancipation proclamation of the President of the United States is as unwarranted in military as in civil law; a gigantic usurpation, at once converting the war, professedly commenced by the administration for the vindication of the authority of the constitution, into the crusade for the sudden, unconditional, and violent liberation of 3,000,000 negro slaves; a result which would not only be a total subversion of the Federal Union, but a revolution in the social organization of the Southern States, the immediate and remote, the present and far-reaching consequences of which to both races cannot be contemplated without the most dismal foreboding of horror and dismay. The proclamation invites servile insurrection as an element in this emancipation crusade—a means of warfare, the inhumanity and diabolism of which are without example in civilized warfare, and which we denounce, and which the civilized world will denounce, as an ineffaceable disgrace to the American people.

64. Cramer, *Letters of Ulysses S. Grant*, p. 85.

65. Ibid.

CHAPTER SEVEN: LAST CAMPAIGN

1. Charles Marshall, *An Aide de Camp of Lee* (Boston: Little, Brown, 1920), pp. 268–69.

2. Ibid., p. 269.

3. Elisha Hunt Rhodes, *All for the Union: The Civil War Diary and Letters of Elisha Hunt Rhodes* (New York: Vintage Civil War Library, 1992), pp. 153–54.

4. Ibid., p. 154.

5. Ulysses S. Grant, *The Personal Memoirs of Ulysses S. Grant* (Old Saybrook, CT: Konecky & Konecky, 1992), p. 516.

6. George G. Meade to John H. Martindale, 18 June 1864, in *The War of the Rebellion: A Compilation of the Official Records of the Union and Confederate Armies*, ed. US War Department, series 1, vol. 40, part 2 (Washington, DC: Government Printing Office, 1891), p. 205.

7. Grant, *Personal Memoirs*, p. 518.

8. Horace Porter, *Campaigning with Grant* (Secaucus, NJ: Blue and Grey, 1984), pp. 210–11.

9. Noah Andre Trudeau, *The Last Citadel: Petersburg, Virginia, June 1864–April 1865* (Baton Rouge, LA: Louisiana State University Press, 1991), p. 417.

10. U. S. Grant to George G. Meade, 18 June 1864, in *War of the Rebellion*, series 1, vol. 40, part 2, p. 157.

11. Grant, *Personal Memoirs*, p. 518.

12. Adam Badeau, *Military History of Ulysses S. Grant*, vol. 2 (New York: D. Appleton, 1881), p. 318.

13. Grant, *Personal Memoirs*, p. 325.

14. Ibid.

15. Ibid., p. 329.

16. Ibid., p. 344.

17. U. S. Grant to George G. Meade, 3 July 1864, in *War of the Rebellion*, series 1, vol. 40, part 2, p. 599.

18. Rhodes, *All for the Union*, p. 158.

19. Ibid., p. 159.

20. A. W. Bartlett, *History of the Twelfth Regiment New Hampshire Volunteers in the War of the Rebellion* (Concord, NH: Ira C. Evans, 1897), p. 224.

21. Grant, *Personal Memoirs*, p. 527.

22. Porter, *Campaigning with Grant*, p. 238.

23. Grant, *Personal Memoirs*, p. 528.

24. S. L. Gracey, *Annals of the Sixth Pennsylvania Cavalry* (Philadelphia: E. H. Butler, 1868), p. 286.

25. Grant, *Personal Memoirs*, p. 533.

26. Ibid., p. 531.

27. Rhodes, *All for the Union*, p. 170.

28. P. H. Sheridan to U. S. Grant, 19 September 1864, in *War of the Rebellion*, series 1, vol. 43, part 2, p. 110.

29. U. S. Grant to P. H. Sheridan, 20 September 1864, in *War of the Rebellion*, series 1, vol. 43, part 2, p. 118.

30. "The Fall of Atlanta," *New York Times*, September 7, 1864.

31. William Tecumseh Sherman, *The Capture of Atlanta and the March to the Sea* (Mineola, NY: Dover, 2007), p. 105.

32. Harry J. Maihafer, *War of Words: Abraham Lincoln and the Civil War Press* (Washington, DC: Brassey's, 2001), p. 222.

33. David Herbert Donald, *Lincoln* (New York: Simon & Schuster, 1995), p. 529.

34. *Official Proceedings of the Democratic National Convention, Held in 1864 at Chicago* (Chicago, IL: Times Stream Book and Job Printing House, 1864), p. 27.

35. U. S. Grant to E. M. Stanton, 10 November 1864, in *War of the Rebellion*, series 1, vol. 42, part 3, p. 581.

36. *New York Times*, June 7, 1864.

37. Trudeau, *Last Citadel*, p. 292.

38. Grant, *Personal Memoirs*, p. 592.

39. John Russell Young, *Around the World with General Grant*, vol. 2 (New York: American News, 1879), p. 627.

40. Grant, *Personal Memoirs*, p. 593.

41. Jesse Grant Cramer, ed., *Letters of Ulysses S. Grant to his Father and his Youngest Sister, 1857–78* (New York: G. P. Putnam's Sons, 1912), pp. 106–107.

42. Grant, *Personal Memoirs*, p. 597.

43. Donald, *Lincoln*, p. 574.

44. Rhodes, *All for the Union*, p. 215.

45. Porter, *Campaigning with Grant*, pp. 442–43.

46. U. S. Grant to T. S. Bowers, 2 April 1865, in *War of the Rebellion*, series 1, vol. 46, part 3, p. 448.

47. Rhodes, *All for the Union*, p. 219.

48. Grant, *Personal Memoirs*, p. 618.

49. Rhodes, *All for the Union*, p. 219.

50. Grant *Personal Memoirs*, p. 620.

51. Rhodes, *All for the Union*, p. 219.

52. Grant, *Personal Memoirs*, p. 620.

53. U. S. Grant to R. E. Lee, 7 April 1865, in *War of the Rebellion*, series 1, vol. 46, part 3, p. 619.

54. R. E. Lee to U. S. Grant, 7 April 1865, in *War of the Rebellion*, series 1, vol. 46, part 3, p. 619.

55. U. S. Grant to R. E. Lee, 8 April 1865, in *War of the Rebellion*, series 1, vol. 46, part 3, p. 641.

56. Grant, *Personal Memoirs*, p. 624.

57. R. E. Lee to U. S. Grant, 8 April 1865, in *War of the Rebellion*, series 1, vol. 46, part 3, p. 641.

58. Joshua Lawrence Chamberlain, *The Passing of the Armies* (Gettysburg, PA: Stan Clark Military Books, 1994), pp. 240–41.

59. Grant, *Personal Memoirs*, p. 627.

60. R. E. Lee to A. P. Hill, June 1865, in *War of the Rebellion*, series 1, vol. 40, part 2, p. 703.

61. Robert E. Lee Jr., comp., *Recollections and Letters of General Robert E. Lee* (New York: Barnes and Noble, 2004), pp. 115–16.

62. Douglas Southall Freeman, *Robert E. Lee*, vol. 3. (New York: Scribner's, 1935), p. 496.

63. Lee, *Recollections and Letters*, p. 497.

64. A. L. Long, *Memoirs of Robert E. Lee* (Secaucus, NJ: Blue and Grey, 1983), p. 391.

65. Ibid., p. 395.

66. Clifford Dowdey, ed., *The Wartime Papers of Robert E. Lee* (Boston: Little, Brown, 1961), pp. 843–44.

67. Ibid., pp. 847–50.

68. Long, *Memoirs of Robert E. Lee*, p. 401.

69. E. M. Law, "From the Wilderness to Cold Harbor," in *Battles and Leaders of the Civil War*, ed. Robert Underwood Johnson and Clarence Clough Buel, vol. 4 (New York: Thomas Yoseloff, 1956), p. 144.

70. James Longstreet, *From Manassas to Appomattox: Memoirs of the Civil War in America* (New York: Konecky & Konecky, 1992), p. 573.

71. R. Lockwood Tower, ed., *Lee's Adjutant: The Wartime Letters of Colonel Walter Herron Taylor, 1862–1865* (Columbia, SC: University of South Carolina Press, 1995), p. 182.

72. Long, *Memoirs of Robert E. Lee*, pp. 396–97.

73. Ibid., p. 401.

74. Tower, *Lee's Adjutant,* p.225.

75. R. E. Lee to S. Cooper, 10 October 1864, in *War of the Rebellion,* series 1, vol. 42, part 3, p. 1144.

76. Emory M. Thomas, *Robert E. Lee* (New York: W. W. Norton, 1995), p. 353.

77. Lee, *Recollections and Letters,* p. 132.

78. Longstreet, *From Manassas,* p. 599.

79. Freeman, *Robert E. Lee,* vol. 4, p. 43.

80. Ibid., p. 48.

81. R. E. Lee to J. C. Breckinridge, 2 April 1865, in *War of the Rebellion,* series 1, vol. 46, part 3, p. 1378.

82. R. E. Lee to Jefferson Davis, 2 April 1865, in *War of the Rebellion,* series 1, vol. 46, part 3, p. 1378.

83. Long, *Memoirs of Robert E. Lee,* p. 410.

84. Ibid.

85. Freeman, *Robert E. Lee,* vol. 3, p. 496.

86. Ibid., vol. 4, p. 67.

87. Ibid., vol. 4, p. 84.

88. R. S. Ewell to R. E. Lee, report, 20 December 1865, in *War of the Rebellion,* series 1, vol. 46, part 1, p. 1295.

89. Freeman, *Robert E. Lee,* vol. 4, p. 84.

90. U. S. Grant to E. M. Stanton, report 22 July 1865, in *War of the Rebellion,* series 1, vol. 46, part 1, p. 55; Freeman, *Robert E. Lee,* vol. 4, p. 93.

91. Dowdey, *Wartime Papers,* p. 850.

92. John S. Wise, *The End of an Era* (Boston: Houghton, Mifflin, 1899), pp. 434–35.

93. Long, *Memoirs of Robert E. Lee,* p. 412.

94. U. S. Grant to R. E. Lee, 7 April 1865, in *War of the Rebellion,* series 1, vol. 46, part 3, p. 619.

95. Longstreet, *From Manassas,* p. 619.

96. Ibid., p. 620.

97. U. S. Grant to R. E. Lee, 8 April 1865, in *War of the Rebellion,* series 1, vol. 46, part 3, p. 641.

98. R. E. Lee to U. S. Grant, 8 April 1865, in *War of the Rebellion,* series 1, vol. 46, part 3, p. 641.

99. Porter, *Campaigning with Grant,* p. 463.

100. Freeman, *Robert E. Lee,* vol. 4, p. 125, 127.

101. Marshall, *Aide de Camp of Lee,* p. 260.

CHAPTER EIGHT: A FEW VITAL HOURS ON A SUNDAY AFTERNOON

1. Charles Marshall, *An Aide de Camp of Lee* (Boston: Little, Brown, 1920), p. 270.

2. Horace Porter, *Campaigning with Grant* (Secaucus, NJ: Blue and Grey, 1984), p. 473.

3. Ibid.

4. Ulysses S. Grant, *The Personal Memoirs of Ulysses S. Grant* (Old Saybrook, CT: Konecky & Konecky, 1992), p. 630.

5. Porter, *Campaigning with Grant*, p. 473.

6. Marshall, *Aide de Camp of Lee*, p. 270.

7. Jefferson Davis, *The Rise and Fall of the Confederate Government*, vol. 2 (Richmond, VA: Garrett and Massie, 1938), p. 559.

8. Grant, *Personal Memoirs*, p. 629.

9. Porter, *Campaigning with Grant*, p. 475.

10. Marshall, *Aide de Camp of Lee*, p. 270.

11. Grant, *Personal Memoirs*, p. 630.

12. Porter, *Campaigning with Grant*, p. 475.

13. Ibid.

14. Ibid.

15. Douglas Southall Freeman, *Robert E. Lee*, vol. 4 (New York: Scribner's, 1935), p. 136.

16. Grant, *Personal Memoirs*, p. 631.

17. Porter, *Campaigning with Grant*, p. 476.

18. Ibid., p. 478.

19. Grant, *Personal Memoirs*, p. 631.

20. Porter, *Campaigning with Grant*, pp. 479–80.

21. Winston S. Churchill, *A History of the English Speaking Peoples*, vol. 4, *The Great Democracies* (New York: Dodd, Meade, 1958), p. 262.

22. Freeman, *Robert E. Lee*, vol. 4, p. 139.

23. Porter, *Campaigning with Grant*, p. 481.

24. Grant, *Personal Memoirs*, p. 632.

25. Marshall, *Aide de Camp of Lee*, p. 272.

26. Grant, *Personal Memoirs*, p. 633.

27. "Jesse Root Grant and Hannah Simpson Grant," *American Experience* www.pbs.org/wgbh/americanexperience/features/biography/grant-parents. In his *Personal Memoirs*, Grant recalled, "I authorized him [General Lee] to send his own commissary and quartermaster to Appomattox Station, two or three miles away, where he could have, out of the trains we had stopped, all the provisions wanted" (p. 633).

28. Roy Blount Jr. *Robert E. Lee* (New York: Viking/Penguin, 2003), p. 73.

29. Elisha Hunt Rhodes, *All for the Union: The Civil War Diary and Letters of Elisha Hunt Rhodes* (New York: Vintage Civil War Library, 1985), p. 222.

30. Grant, *Personal Memoirs*, p. 636.

31. Porter, *Campaigning with Grant*, p. 488.

32. Clifford Dowdey, ed., *The Wartime Papers of Robert E. Lee* (Boston: Little, Brown, 1961), pp. 934–35. The full text of the message:

> Head-Quarters, Army of Northern Virginia
> April 10, 1865

> After four years of arduous service, marked by unsurpassed courage and fortitude, the Army of Northern Virginia has been compelled to yield to overwhelming numbers and resources. I need not tell the survivors of so many hard-fought battles, who have remained steadfast to the last, that I have consented to this result from no distrust of them: but, feeling that valour and devotion could accomplish nothing that could compensate for the loss that would have attended the continuation of the contest, I have determined to avoid the useless sacrifice of those whose past services have endeared them to their countrymen. By the terms of the agreement, the officers and men can return to their homes and remain there until exchanged. You will take with you the satisfaction that proceeds from the consciousness of duty faithfully performed; and I earnestly pray that a merciful God will extend to you His blessing and protection. With an increasing admiration of your constancy and devotion to your country, and a grateful remembrance of your kind and generous consideration of myself, I bid you an affectionate farewell.

> R. E. Lee, General

33. Adam Badeau, *Grant in Peace* (Hartford, CT: S. S. Scranton, 1887), pp. 25–26; and John Russell Young, *Around the World with General Grant*, vol. 2 (New York: American News, 1879), pp. 460–61.

34. Freeman, *Robert E. Lee*, vol. 4, p. 501, 505.

35. Emory M. Thomas, *Robert E. Lee* (New York: W. W. Norton, 1995), p. 13.

36. "Lee, Robert Edward," *World Scope Encyclopedia*, vol. 9 (New York: Readers League, 1945).

37. Roy Blount Jr., "Making Sense of Robert E. Lee," *Smithsonian Magazine*, July 2003, http://www.smithsonianmag.com/history/making-sense-of-robert-e-lee-85017563/.

38. James M. McPherson, *This Mighty Scourge: Perspectives on the Civil War* (New York: Oxford University Press, 2007), p. 13.

39. Comments on the Lee-Grant exhibition are from Charles McGrath, "Two Generals Still Maneuvering," *New York Times*, October 16, 2008, http://www.nytimes.com/2008/10/17/arts/design/17hist.html.

40. Dowdey, *Wartime Papers*, p. 939.

41. Grant, *Personal Memoirs*, pp. 629–30.

SELECT BIBLIOGRAPHY

Agood many books, papers, articles, and reports were consulted during the preparation of this book: everything from medical journal reports on General Lee's heart condition to recent biographies of Lee and Grant to diaries and letters from those who were present during the events described to the invaluable *Official Records*, which was first published in 1900.

This "Select Bibliography" is just that—a listing of selected sources that were referred to most often. It is not a complete bibliography, and is not meant to be. A complete listing would go on for many more pages, and would be much too long to be included here.

Abraham Lincoln Papers. Library of Congress. Transcribed and Annotated by the Lincoln Studies Center, Knox College. Galesburg, Illinois.

Allen, Stanton P. *Down in Dixie: Life in a Cavalry Regiment in the War Days, From the Wilderness to Appomattox.* Boston: D. Lothrop, 1893.

Badeau, Adam. *Military History of Ulysses S. Grant.* 3 vols. New York: D. Appleton, 1895.

Ballard, Brigadier General Colin R. *The Military Genius of Abraham Lincoln.* Cleveland: World, 1926.

Bartlett, A. W. *History of the Twelfth Regiment New Hampshire Volunteers in the War of the Rebellion.* Concord, NH: Ira C. Evans, 1897.

Bicknell, Reverend George W. *History of the 5th Regiment Maine Volunteers.* Portland, ME: Hall L. Davis, 1871.

Blackford, Lieutenant Colonel W. W. *War Years With Jeb Stuart.* New York: Charles Scribner's Sons, 1945.

Blount, Roy, Jr. "Making Sense of Robert E. Lee." *Smithsonian Magazine.* July 2003. http://www.smithsonianmag.com/history/making-sense-of-robert-e-lee-85017563/.

———. *Robert E. Lee.* New York: Viking/Penguin, 2003.

Bonekemper, Edward. *A Victor Not a Butcher.* Washington, DC: Regnery, 2004.

Boyd, Thomas. *Light-Horse Harry Lee.* New York: Charles Scribner's Sons, 1931.

Brinton, John H. *Personal Memoirs of John H. Brinton.* New York: Neale, 1914.

Carelson, Oliver. *The Man Who Made News: James Gordon Bennett.* New York: Duell, Sloan and Pierce, 1942.

Catton, Bruce. *Glory Road.* Garden City, NY: Doubleday, 1952.

———. *Grant Takes Command.* Boston: Little, Brown, 1969.

———. *A Stillness at Appomattox.* Garden City, NY: Doubleday, 1953.

———. *This Hallowed Ground.* Edison, NJ: Castle Books, 2002.

———. *U. S. Grant and the American Military Tradition.* Boston: Little, Brown, 1954.

Chamberlain, Joshua Lawrence. *The Passing of the Armies.* Gettysburg, PA: Stan Clark Military Books, 1994.

Churchill, Winston S. *A History of the English Speaking Peoples.* Vol. 4, *The Great Democracies.* New York: Dodd, Meade, 1958.

Cramer, Jesse Grant. *Letters of Ulysses S. Grant to His Father and His Youngest Sister, 1857–78.* New York: G. P. Putnam's Sons, 1912.

Davis, Charles E., Jr. *Three Years in the Army: The Story of the Thirteenth Massachusetts Volunteers.* Boston: Estes and Lauriat, 1894.

Davis, Jefferson. *The Rise and Fall of the Confederate Government.* 2 vols. Richmond, VA: Garrett and Massie, 1938.

Donald, David Herbert. *Lincoln.* New York: Simon & Schuster, 1995.

Dowdey, Clifford, ed. *The Wartime Papers of Robert E. Lee.* Boston: Little, Brown, 1961.

Dowdey, Clifford. *Lee's Last Campaign.* New York: Bonanza Books, 1960.

Dugard, Martin. *The Training Ground: Grant, Lee, Sherman, and Davis in the Mexican War, 1846–1848.* New York: Little, Brown, 2008.

Elson's New History. Springfield, MA: Patriot, 1912.

Flood, Charles Bracelen. *Grant and Sherman: The Friendship That Won the Civil War.* New York: Farrar, Straus, Giroux, 2005.

Fox, William L. *Regimental Losses in the American Civil War, 1861–1865.* Albany, NY: Albany, 1889.

Freeman, Douglas Southall, ed. *Lee's Dispatches: Unpublished Letters of General Robert E. Lee.* Baton Rouge, LA: Louisiana State University Press, 1994.

Freeman, Douglas Southall. *Robert E. Lee.* 4 vols. New York: Scribner's, 1934.

Fritz, Jean. *Stonewall.* New York: G. P. Putnam, 1979.

Fuller, J. F. C. *Grant and Lee: A Study in Personality and Generalship.* Bloomington, IN: University of Indiana Press, 1957.

Gallagher, Gary W., ed. *The Wilderness Campaign*. Chapel Hill, NC: University of North Carolina Press, 1997.

Galloway, G. Norton. "Hand-to-Hand Fighting at Spotsylvania." In *Battles and Leaders of the Civil War*, edited by Robert Underwood Johnson and Clarence Clough Buel, pp. 170–74. New York: Century, 1887.

Gordon, General John B. *Reminiscences of the Civil War*. New York: Charles Scribner's Sons, 1903.

Grant, Frederick Dent. "Reminiscences of General U. S. Grant, Read Before Illinois Commandery Loyal Legion of the United States, January 27, 1910." *Journal of the Illinois State Historical Society* 7, no. 1 (April 1914): 72–76.

Grant, Ulysses S. *The Personal Memoirs of Ulysses S. Grant*. Old Saybrook, CT: Konecky & Konecky, 1992.

Hyde, Brevet Brigadier General Thomas W. *Following the Greek Cross*. Boston: Houghton, Mifflin, 1894.

Johnson, Robert Underwood, and Clarence Clough Buel, eds. *Battles and Leaders of the Civil War*. 4 vols. New York: Thomas Yoseloff, 1956.

Jones, J. B. *A Rebel War Clerk's Diary at the Confederate States Capital*. Philadelphia: J. B. Lippincott, 1866.

Jones, J. William. *Personal Reminiscences, Anecdotes, and Letters of General Robert E. Lee*. New York: D. Appleton, 1875.

Lee, Robert E., Jr., comp. *Recollections and Letters of Robert E. Lee*. New York: Barnes and Noble, 2004.

Long, A. L. *Memoirs of Robert E. Lee*. Secaucus, NJ: Blue and Grey, 1983.

Longacre, Edward G. *General Ulysses S. Grant: The Soldier and the Man*. Cambridge, MA: Perseus Books, 2006.

Longstreet, James. *From Manassas to Appomattox: Memoirs of the Civil War in America*. New York: Konecky & Konecky, 1992.

Lyman, Theodore *Meade's Headquarters, 1863–1865: Letters of Colonel Theodore Lyman from the Wilderness to Appomattox*. Boston: Atlantic Monthly Press, 1922.

Maihafer, Harry J. *War of Words: Abraham Lincoln and the Civil War Press*. Washington, DC: Brassey's, 2001.

Marshall, Charles. *An Aide de Camp of Lee*. Boston: Little, Brown, 1920.

Marvel, William. *A Place Called Appomattox*. Carbondale, IL: Southern Illinois University Press, 2008.

Maurice, Major General Sir Frederick. *Robert E. Lee: The Soldier*. London: Constable, 1930.

McNeil, Keith, and Rusty McNeil. *Civil War Songbook*. Moreno Valley, CA: Wem Records, 1999.

McPherson, James M. *This Mighty Scourge: Perspectives on the Civil War.* New York: Oxford University Press, 2007.

Miers, Earl Schenck. *The Last Campaign: Grant Saves the Union.* Philadelphia: Lippincott, 1972.

Official Proceedings of the Democratic National Convention, Held in 1864 at Chicago. Chicago, IL: Times Steam Book and Job Printing House, 1864.

Olsen, Bernard A., ed. *Upon the Tented Field.* Red Bank, NJ: Historic Projects, 1993.

Perret, Geoffrey. *Ulysses S. Grant: Soldier and President.* New York: Random House, 1997.

Pleasants, Henry Jr. *The Tragedy of the Crater.* Boston: Christopher Publishing House, 1938.

Porter, Horace. *Campaigning with Grant.* Secaucus, NJ: Blue and Grey, 1984.

Reeder, Colonel Red. *The Story of the Mexican War.* New York: Meredith, 1967.

Rhea, Gordon C. *The Battles for Spotsylvania Court House and the Road to Yellow Tavern, May 7–12, 1864.* Baton Rouge, LA: Louisiana State University Press, 1997.

Rhodes, Elisha Hunt. *All for the Union: The Civil War Diary and Letters of Elisha Hunt Rhodes.* New York: Vintage Civil War Library, 1985.

Royster, Charles. *Light-Horse Harry Lee and the Legacy of the American Revolution.* New York: Alfred A. Knopf, 1981.

Schaft, Morris. *The Sunset of the Confederacy.* Boston: John W. Luce, 1912.

Scott, Winfield. *Memoirs of Lieut.-General Scott, LL. D.* 2 vols. Freeport, NY: Books for Libraries, 1970.

Sheridan, Philip H. *Personal Memoirs.* New York: Charles L. Webster, 1888.

Sherman, William Tecumseh. *The Capture of Atlanta and the March to the Sea.* Mineola, NY: Dover, 2007.

———. *The Memoirs of William T. Sherman.* Bloomington, IN: University of Indiana Press, 1977.

Simon, John Y., ed. *The Papers of Ulysses S. Grant.* Vol. 20, *February 21–April 30, 1865.* Carbondale, IL: Southern Illinois University Press, 1985.

Stiles, Robert. *Four Years under Marse Robert.* New York: Neale, 1904.

Tarbell, Ida M. *Life of Abraham Lincoln.* 2 vols. New York: Doubleday & McClure, 1900.

Taylor, Walter H. *Four Years with General Lee.* Bloomington, IN: Indiana University Press, 1962.

Thomas, Emory M. *Robert E. Lee.* New York: W. W. Norton, 1995.

Tower, R. Lockwood, ed. *Lee's Adjutant: The Wartime Letters of Colonel Walter Herron Taylor, 1862–1865*. Columbia, SC: University of South Carolina Press, 1995.

Trudeau, Noah Andre. *The Last Citadel: Petersburg, Virginia, June 1864–April 1865*. Baton Rouge, LA: Louisiana State University Press, 1991.

Venable, Colonel C. S. *The Campaign from the Wilderness to Petersburg*. Richmond, VA: Geo. W. Gary, Printer, 1879.

War of the Rebellion: A Compilation of the Official Records of the Union and Confederate Armies. Washington, DC: Government Printing Office, 1891.

Ward, Geoffrey. *The Civil War*. New York: Vintage Books, 1990.

Weems, John Edward. *To Conquer A Peace: The War Between the United States and Mexico*. Garden City, NY: Doubleday, 1974.

Wilkeson, Frank. *Recollections of a Private Soldier in the Army of the Potomac*. New York: G. P. Putnam's Sons, 1886.

Wilson, James Harrison. *The Life of John A. Rawlins: Lawyer, Assistant Adjutant-General, Chief of Staff, Major General of Volunteers, and Secretary of War*. New York: Neale, 1916.

Wing, Harry. *When Lincoln Kissed Me: A Story of the Wilderness Campaign*. New York: Eaton & Mains, 1913.

Winik, Jay. *April 1865: The Month That Saved America*. New York: Harper Perennial, 2001.

Wise, John S. *The End of an Era*. Boston: Houghton, Mifflin, 1899.

Woodward, W. E. *Meet General Grant*. New York: Liveright, 1928.

Young, John Russell. *Around the World with General Grant*. 2 vols. New York: American News, 1879.

INDEX